Harness Lessons
with Doc Hammill & Friends

By Jenifer Morrissey

I am grateful to Torrin, Mya, Midnight, Lily, Rose, and all the other ponies who have helped me learn the teamster's art. Without them, this book wouldn't have been possible.

First published in the United States in 2017
Copyright © 2017 Jenifer Morrissey

All rights reserved. No part of this publication may be reproduced, stored in a retrieval system, or transmitted in any form or by any means without the prior permission of the copyright holder.

ISBN-13: 978-0692962800 (Willowtrail Farm)
ISBN-10: 0692962808

Published by Willowtrail Farm in conjunction with createspace.com and available worldwide on amazon.com

Acknowledgements

Doc Hammill and John Erskine discussing some fine point of working horses

Even in a self-published book, there are many people to thank, for without them the stories included here wouldn't have been possible.

We are grateful to Joe Mischka of *Rural Heritage* magazine and Mischka Press for asking for articles on harness several years ago and encouraging the articles to be put in book form more recently. The author is also grateful for the *Rural Heritage* Front Porch where master teamsters are given the opportunity to share their wisdom with the broader teamster community. Joe Mischka's support continues in the form of allowing use of the Allen photos to illustrate the articles and assist in teaching.

We are grateful for the words, wisdom, and illustrations shared by teamsters and harness makers John Erskine and Bernie Samson. Encouragement and photographs from Cathy Greatorex have greatly facilitated many articles. Contributions from teamster Rob Johnson and harness makers Mari Leedy and Abner Esh have also been invaluable.

Contributors to the *Rural Heritage* Front Porch enrich the teamster community. We appreciate: Mac, aherzog, Neal in Iowa, NoraWI, Jason Rutledge, Dale Wagner, Bob E., Marshall, Mark, Stitch-n-Hitch Harness Shop, TLR, KM, Chris F., Peter, Mooney Ranch, Vince Mautino, Buggy, Klaus

Karbaumer, Grey, wally b, Jerry Hicks, Dave W., stuck in the past albert Canada, Will Beattie, Ken, Bret4207, Don McAvoy, Tim Central IL, Dennis Decker, Dave, Brabant Owner in SC, and Sharon.

The late Tom Triplett, Doc's step-father and one of Doc's mentors.

The author is grateful to her Fell Pony friend and mentor Joe Langcake who has always generously shared from his many decades of knowledge that began with training pit ponies. In addition, the author is grateful to Patricia Burge who helped her put her first pony in harness and who introduced her to master teamster Steve Bowers.

Doc Hammill's mentors – Tom Triplett, Adam (Addie) Funk, Glenn Phanco, Doris Ganton, and Dr. Robert Miller – enrich every story through what they taught Doc, especially with how they approached working with equines.

Table of Contents

Preface by Doc Hammill	1
Foreword	5
Introduction	6
About Doc Hammill	13
Choosing the Right Harness	16
About Synthetic Harness Materials	29
Harness Variety and Function	36
Why Understand Harness?	58
Draft Geometry: Point, Angle, and Line	67
The Elusive Ideal Point of Draft	79
Measuring for a Collar	98
To Pad or Not to Pad (a Collar)	112
Adjustable Collar Considerations	124
Too Much Harness?	140
Variations on Harness	149
On the Lines	155
The Privilege of Harness Care	159
Parting Thoughts	170
Doc Hammill Horsemanship	172
Books by Jenifer Morrissey	176

Table of Important Illustrations and Topics

Team Harness Parts	12
Used Harness Checklist – Part 1	19
Used Harness Checklist – Part 2	20
Comparative Styles of Breeching Bands	24
Four Components of Harness	37
Field or Plow Harness	38
Box Breeching or Western Style Harness	40
Butt Chain or Short Trace Harness	41
Yankee/Hip Breeching Harness	48
Y Back Harness	50
Sidebacker Harness	51
New England/D-Ring Harness	53
Norwegian Harness	55
US Military Harness	60
Stagecoach Harness	62
Cart Harness	63
Point of Draft	70
Angle of Draft	73
Line of Draft	74
Three Bony Landmarks	84
Draft Area of Equine Shoulder	85
Draft Area of Collars	86
Collar Bed	87
Hames Ideal Point of Draft	91
Collar Styles	99
Critical Collar Dimensions	101
Two Additional Collar Dimensions	102
Collar Measuring Tool	105
Types of Collar Pads	116
Collar Top Pads	117
Adjustable Collar Definition	125
Adjustables and the Point of Draft	129
Adjustables and Body Condition	130
Effect of Collar Re-shaping	132
Adjustables and Hames	135
Half Harness	147
Steps in Harness Care	160

Preface by Doc Hammill

When I teach students, I constantly stress safety, comfort, and function in all aspects of horsemanship, but particularly when it comes to harness. Using harness to achieve these aims is using harness wisely. You would think, given that harness is fundamental to the work we do with horses, that using harness wisely would also be a given. But I regularly see - in novice students and experienced teamsters, in photographs, at shows, on internet videos, at work horse events – harness being used in ways that compromises safety, comfort and function.

My lifelong passion has been to learn everything I can about driving, working and training horses, mules, and donkeys. Because I had no help when I got started, my passion has grown to include sharing what I've learned with others. Pursuing this passion has defined and fulfilled my life for most of my seventy plus years. Along the way, I've been fortunate to learn from some truly great teamsters. And I was fortunate to meet Jenifer, a teamster in her own right, whose magic with words on the printed page has allowed lessons that I've learned to be shared in ways they never would have been otherwise. Thank you Jenifer for being the skilled and productive wordsmith that you are, and for your willingness and patience to collaborate with me and others to help good learning happen.

The chapters in this book began as articles for *Rural Heritage* magazine. As we worked on the articles, Jenifer and I called upon respected friends and acquaintances because some of the topics required experience, perspectives, and expertise that were different than ours. They patiently answered questions and generously shared their wisdom, technical information, opinions, suggestions and stories. We learned a lot from them and know you will too. This book is richer, more comprehensive and better because of them. Thank you Friends for your contributions.

In reality, the creation of this book was not accomplished by only those of us whose words are found on its pages. There would have been little to share had it not been for our teachers and mentors, and theirs, and theirs, and on and on - generations of horsemen, horsewomen, teamsters, harness makers, writers, illustrators, photographers, and others who have spent lifetimes gaining understanding, wisdom and skill about their crafts bit by bit, and at some point starting to pass it on to others who sought it. It is an honor to be able to pass on to you what others so willingly and generously helped us learn, and perhaps to have added some small measure of our own observations, insights, creativity, discoveries, and improvements.

Long ago I read somewhere, "It takes four generations to make a horseman." At the time it pretty much dashed my hopes and dreams of ever becoming one. Although there had been a continuum of teamsters on both sides of my family - draymen, horse and mule farmers, and builders of roads and railroad beds – they were all gone by the time my parents came along. There was no one left in our family who could teach me about horses. In spite of that, I can track my passion for horses, and even more specifically for driving and working them in harness, back to when I was only four or five years old. Which leads me to believe that I must have inherited a teamster gene after all!

Workhorses were on their way out by that time in my life, and it happened amazingly fast. Nonetheless, I was fortunate to grow up where workhorses were still in use. You can't imagine my delight sitting on the curb gazing at the brown horse in harness that pulled a wagon full of garden produce along our street and stood patiently while her owners sold it door to door. Or when my family occasionally traveled through nearby Amish communities where I delighted in seeing buggy horses on the roads and tied in town, and teams working the fields. When I was almost six we moved from town to five acres and unbelievably an old man next door cultivated his market garden with an old white horse. I would sit on the edge of our lawn and watch the horse coming towards me between the rows. Then I would move back to allow them to turn around into position for the next row, and pause to rest. I was fascinated by the horse, the harness, the lines from the horse's mouth to the old man's shoulders, and the cultivator. I never tired of moving over a row to watch them either go away or come back towards me. The days they cultivated were my most exciting days of summer. Back then I had no idea that in a few years I would be cultivating a sweet corn patch of my own with a pony named Little Joe.

Starting in 1969 my life in Montana was enriched by a group of old time horse and mule men who were master teamsters, riders, packers, farriers, etc. The best of them did it all, did it all their lives, and did it all extremely well.

While they were all comparable in experience and skill and masterful with horses and mules, I noticed early on that they could be divided into two groups. Group A rarely, if ever, experienced close calls, mishaps, runaways, wrecks or injuries. However, with Group B those types of things were not so rare, and sometimes people and horses or mules did get hurt. After I noticed the difference between the groups, I decided that I wanted to be in Group A, and I set out to discover what they did differently than Group B and why.

What it came down to included:
- Constant attention to details.
- Having good rules and not breaking them.
- Not taking shortcuts.
- Absolute attention to the mental/emotional/physical state of the animals at all times, and
- Ongoing observation and evaluation of the harness and other equipment.

They always had good reasons for the way they did things, and good reasons for not doing them some other way. They gave the comfort and wellbeing of their animals top priority at all times and often at the expense of their own comfort and wellbeing. With respect to harness, harness considerations, and harness accessories, much of what I learned from group A has been included in this book along with their reasons. We offer it as an invitation for you to seek membership in "Group A".

My pony Little Joe must have come into my life when I was about nine. Riding him was great but my biggest dream was to drive him. That teamster gene was still alive and well in me. I had absolutely no one to help me figure out how to drive him and no books or anything else to help either. It was all done by trial and error and probably some memories from occasional sightings of buggy horses or workhorses. Trial and error is typically a slow, uncertain, very limited, and often unsuccessful way to learn. I still remember what it was like to have a burning desire to learn to drive horses without someone to teach me. Because I had no help or teachers as a boy, I have been highly motivated to dedicate much of my life to providing opportunities for others with an interest/passion/dream to get the help and resources they need.

Harness as seen in Nicaragua. Courtesy Laura Meadows

In order to pull any kind of a load with an animal you need a way to attach the load to it. There have been infinite creative designs for accomplishing this all around the world over the centuries. Our focus in this book is primarily with several variations of harness and harness accessories in common use in this country for use on horses, mules and donkeys. The subject of harness lends itself very well to being presented in print, especially compared to other aspects of horsemanship and the teamster craft which require nuances of such things as tactile feel, reading and speaking equine body language, timing, and much more.

There is certainly much more to be said on this subject of harness, but it's time now to share more broadly what we have been fortunate to share with the *Rural Heritage* community so far. I sincerely appreciate your interest in learning to use harness wisely and well. You and your horses will work more safely, comfortably, and effectively as a result, contributing positively to the long tradition of the teamster's art.

Throughout this book you will find photos by Cathy Greatorex though not necessarily with credit to her. Cathy has her own long history with horses and driving and working them in harness. She is a serious and accomplished student of gentle horsemanship and the teamster art. Both as a couple and in our business, Doc Hammill Horsemanship, Cathy and I are blessed to share a common passion for learning and then sharing what we learn with others, for figuring out how to gently and effectively accomplish training and real work with equines, and for putting the physical and emotional wellbeing of these amazing creatures as our highest priority. Cathy's contributions to our life and work are essential, and appreciated – thank you Cathy.

October 2017

Foreword

By Jenifer Morrissey

In 2011, Joe Mischka, publisher of *Rural Heritage* magazine, asked me to write an article on the horse overpopulation problem. In return, I asked Joe who I might speak to in the draft horse community on the topic, and he electronically introduced me to Doc Hammill. I of course knew of Doc through his many contributions to *Small Farmers Journal*; he had even once answered a question I submitted to his "Ask a Teamster" column. I felt it a rare privilege to have the opportunity to speak to Doc in person.

At the time, I had been working my ponies in harness for more than a decade, and I had studied the teamster's art enough to know that it is indeed an art. Equines don't have to work with us if they aren't inclined; early in my career I had my share of catch-me games, wrong turns, and refusals. When I was given the opportunity to collaborate with Doc on articles exploring the teamster's art, I gladly accepted.

The author skidding brush on a defensible space project with her pony Mya.

After working with Doc on a number of articles for *Rural Heritage*, Joe Mischka asked us to do an article on harness. I wasn't interested in doing a 'how-to-harness' article or a harness-parts-and-pieces article, and fortunately Doc wasn't either. What resulted instead was a series of articles, as yet incomplete, about harness and the teamsters' art. The articles we've completed so far make up this book.

Doc is the first master teamster I've worked closely with; previously I'd read books and articles by others and seen demonstrations at expos. Through Doc and also with thanks to Joe Mischka and the *Rural Heritage* community, I've met several other master teamsters. Making explicit what is implicit for a master horseman – sharing in written and visual form what a master teamster intuitively understands - is a privilege and a pleasure. I look forward to future opportunities that present themselves.

Introduction

If we have worked an equine in harness, then we already know that every time we go to work, it is a different experience than the previous time. Even if it's the same equine we worked the day before, the work we're doing, the location we're doing it in, the day's weather, and even the mindset of that particular equine are new and different at the time. It is for these reasons that the work of a teamster is art and not science.

Because no two working situations with equines are ever the same, it's important that a teamster have a broad understanding of the teamster's art rather than rely on specific how-to's. No list of how-to's will ever apply to every working equine situation. Relying on such a list can be dangerous because it gives a false sense of security. Instead, as teamsters, we must be ever attentive in our work to ensure the safety of horse and human alike.

Because no two working equine situations are alike, harness for working equines varies to suit the needs of the teamster and their working situation. This book about harness then, does not pretend to rely on or recommend a specific type of harness. Instead it discusses what is common to the use of harness from multiple perspectives. Doc Hammill's decades of experience working equines in harness, coupled with his never-ending quest to ensure his equines work more comfortably and safely and then his desire to share what he learns with others, gives him an unequaled perspective on the teamster's art. Supplementing Doc's perspective is the wisdom of numerous teamsters in the *Rural Heritage* community, usually shared on the *Rural Heritage* Front Porch.

The chapters in this book originally appeared as articles in *Rural Heritage* magazine. As one master teamster expressed to the author, capturing Doc's wisdom in written form is a gift to the teamster community. Evidence for the importance of the topics included here is the number of times the original articles have been reprinted in other publications.

The first chapter discusses considerations in the choice of harness. While the choice to be made is often thought to be between leather and synthetic material, wisdom from master teamsters reveals that it's not about the material. Fit is key, and if we're somewhat new to working equines, getting good help in making a decision is also important. Unfortunately, as with most everything in life, the adage 'buyer beware' applies to shopping for harness. And then there's the fact that the needs of the equine must be considered. In the end, as one teamster said, "If you make the right decision for the horse, the people will be taken care of, too."

Harness made from synthetic materials is increasingly popular. Synthetic materials can result in harness that's lighter in weight, easier to clean, and less expensive. However, there are many different synthetic materials with different properties. The knowledge of the harness maker and the care they take ultimately determines whether a harness made from synthetic materials is safe to use and comfortable for the equine at work. As teamsters we need to understand harness materials well enough to know whether our harness is safe and comfortable.

Many books about harness name the different types. Doc enhances the discussion of variety by talking about how the same functions – Stopping & Backing, Communication, Support, etc. - are achieved differently in the different varieties of harness and why. Valuable illustrations enhance the discussion, with captions on many historic photographs that ask questions to encourage you to assess your understanding. In the end, no single variety is better than any other; the teamster's art involves using the right harness safely and effectively in any given work situation.

One of the things that's most interesting about the coverage of Horse Progress Days each year is seeing the advances made in utilizing horsepower. One might think that since the Industrial Revolution, things have stayed static in the horse powered world, that they haven't progressed. But things have progressed, allowing us to do new and different things with our horses than we ever have before. And the same is true for harness. Because the styles of harness that are available today are all so similar, it's easy to believe that they are all adequate for the job. Yet history tells us that for functional, safety, and comfort-of-the-horse reasons, harness has changed and evolved and continues to do so. It's up to us as teamsters to understand our harness and make changes to it as our functional needs change, as our understanding of safety improves, and as we become more aware of how comfortable our horses are when working. The chapter "Why Understand Harness" explores alternative approaches to harness from these perspectives.

To make the most and best use of real horsepower in getting our work done, we need to maximize the transfer of power from the horse or horses to movement of the load, whether the load is a log, a plow, a wagon, or anything else. Three common problems with harness adjustment cause this

transfer of power to be less efficient than it could be: incorrect point of draft, incorrect angle of draft, and broken line of draft. "You'd be surprised," says Doc Hammill, "how often these problems happen. Sometimes they're pretty obvious, and sometimes they're more subtle. On some level they always affect the comfort of horses and the efficiency of the work they do for us." The chapter on draft geometry discusses the point, angle, and line of draft with numerous historic photos with which to test your understanding.

The ideal point of draft is the most challenging of the three geometric considerations when it comes to harness because it requires the effective marrying of the ideal points on the horse, the collar, and the hames. In addition, each of the three points of draft – horse, collar, hames - has numerous influences that must be considered in order to get them right. The consequences of marrying these three points of draft poorly are inefficient conversion of horsepower to movement of a load as well as discomfort for our horses at the least and potential injury, permanent disability and/or psychological problems at the worst. The great benefit of marrying the three points of draft well, on the other hand, is the privilege of working our equines in harness. The chapter on the elusive ideal point of draft has numerous illustrations custom-crafted to enhance understanding.

One of the most important topics when it comes to harness is the fit of the collar. Collar fit is often compared to fitting human boots. You wouldn't attempt to climb a mountain in a pair of boots that were too big or too small, just as you shouldn't expect your horse to work with a collar that's improperly fit. The starting point on fitting a collar is knowing how to measure for one. Doc shares, "Like all other aspects of driving and working horses in harness, doing a good job of sizing and fitting collars is an art -part science, part numbers, and a lot of tinkering and fussing to get it right and keep it right." The chapter "Measuring for a Collar" collects wisdom on the topic from many master teamsters.

Collar pads of course impact collar fit as well as the size of collar needed so are part and parcel of selecting this most important piece of harness. As you will read in the chapter about collar pads, teamsters in the *Rural Heritage* community have a variety of experience with and opinions about collar pads. There is not a single right answer because we all work different equines in different places in different situations. We each, then, have a unique responsibility. It is up to us to ensure our equines are working as comfortably as possible, for their safety and for ours. Collar pads have the potential to help with that goal if used properly.

An option if we are in need of a collar for our working equine is an adjustable collar. Since our goal is to ensure a comfortable and effective working situation for our equine partner, we need to understand adjustable collars enough to determine if they might be an appropriate option before we either adopt them or cast them aside completely. Even if adjustable collars aren't of interest, the chapter discussing them will be of interest because it also covers how the draft area of a collar moves when a collar is reshaped. It isn't just about shorter or longer. Doc concludes the chapter by saying, "For me, adjustables play an important role for hard-to-fit horses."

The chapter "Too Much Harness" presents opportunities to assess whether you know which pieces of harness are fundamentally necessary for the work you're doing with your equines. Doc's mentors advocated the use of half-harness in certain situations for reasons of time, comfort for the horse, and economy. With fewer pieces on the harness, it takes less time to put the harness on and take it off. It also weighs less for the teamster and weighs less and is cooler for the equine. A teamster practices their art in part by how they use harness to accomplish the work that they do.

Rural Heritage readers generously responded to a request for unusual collar and harness pictures. The chapter "Variations on Harness" discusses reader submissions. The submissions illustrated that, just like other parts of life, human ingenuity and creativity have been applied to getting work done safely and efficiently with animals. Given that the harness we have today is a product of the past, it's interesting to think about how the harness of the future might differ from the harness of today.

When a *Rural Heritage* reader asked a general question about bits, we responded with the equally general chapter "On the Lines." A bit's use as an instrument of control is illusory. If bits were truly effective as instruments of control, then there wouldn't be runaways. Instead, bits must be looked at as instruments of communication. When we are on the lines, we are not controlling our horses, we are communicating with them. We 'speak' down the lines, and they 'speak' back to us with movement (or lack thereof) of certain or several parts of their bodies. It is the quality of our communication on the lines that controls our horses.

The final chapter of this book is about harness care. Caring for harness can be viewed as a chore, or it can be viewed as a privilege, an extension of the privilege of working equines in harness. Harness care becomes easier when we understand how our harness works. Harness care becomes easier when we understand how we use it to get our work done. Harness care is an integral part of this rewarding work we do with horses. In a day and age when we have alternatives to working horses, harness care is one way that we express our belief in the rightness of the work.

Undoubtedly you've thought of topics about harness that aren't addressed here, just as we have. We look forward to addressing those topics in the future. In the meantime, what Doc and the other teamsters have had to say about the teamster's art is important to share. We hope you enjoy what you find here.

Team Harness Parts

Courtesy Samson Harness Shop, Inc.

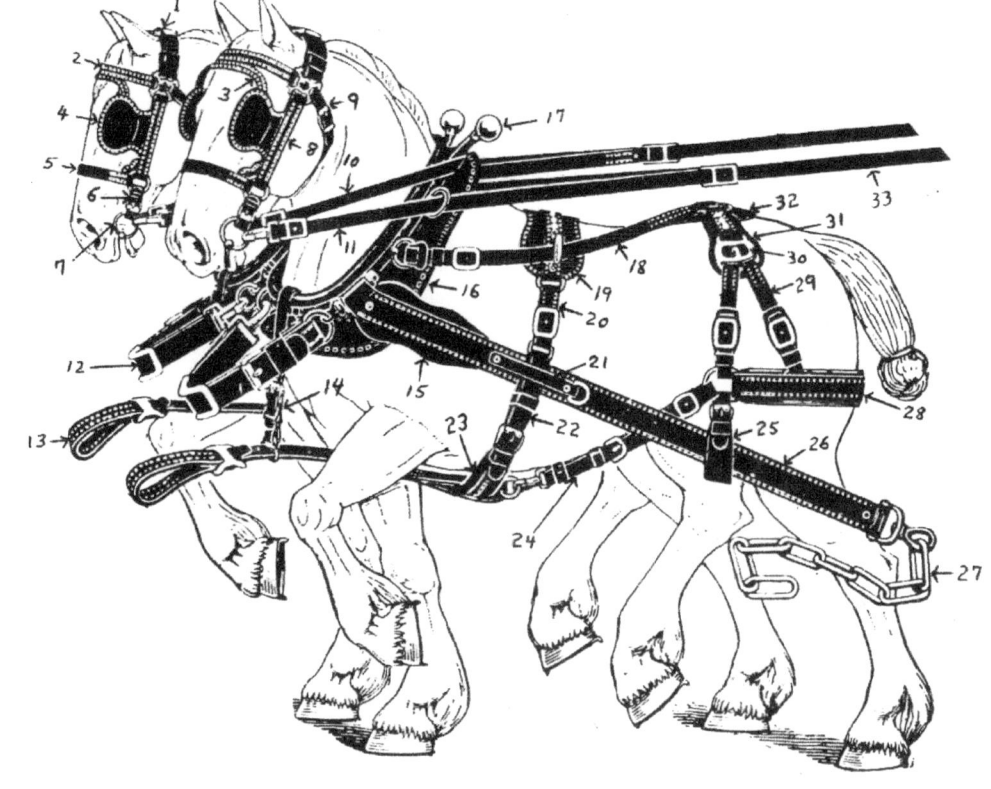

1. Bridle Crown
2. Brow Band
3. Winker Brace
4. Blind or Winker
5. Nose Band
6. Bit Strap
7. Bit
8. Bridle Cheek
9. Throat Latch
10. Flat Check Strap
11. Line – Front Part
12. Breast Strap
13. Pole Strap
14. Collar Strap
15. Safe on Trace
16. Collar
17. Hame
18. Back Strap
19. Back Pad
20. Back Pad Billet or Market Strap
21. Loop on Trace
22. Belly Band Billet
23. Belly Band
24. Side Strap
25. Lazy Strap
26. Trace or Tug
27. Heel Chain
28. Breeching
29. Hip Strap
30. Trace Carrier
31. Hip Pad
32. Rump Safe or Rump Pad
33. Line – Hand Part

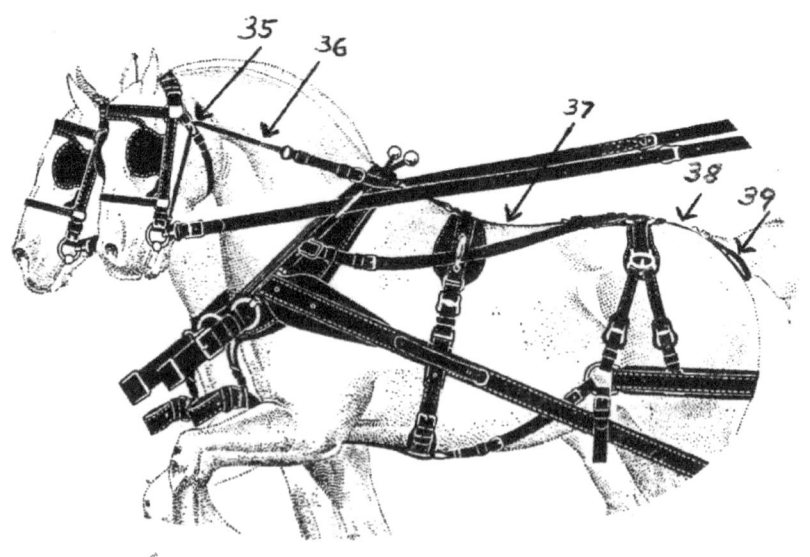

34. 1616 Combination Snap
35. Gag swivel
36. Round Side Cheek
37. Check-up strap or turnback
38. Crupper fork
39. Crupper

About Doc Hammill

Doc's Beginnings

Doc helps a horse learn that a trace against his leg is not something to be frightened of. Photo courtesy Theresa Burns

Several years ago, Doc Hammill set up a TV in his booth at Horse Progress Days and played for passersby his instructional videos on driving and working horses. Various groups of young Amish boys were frequent members of the audience, watching raptly and asking for the videos to be paused or changed as one topic was finished for another to be started. Doc was fascinated that these youngsters would not be distracted from topics that he felt they had been immersed in since birth. What did they find so fascinating?

Doc got an answer to his question when one of his colleagues did an impromptu survey of one of the groups of young boys. "We've always been told to do this or to do that," they said, "but he's a good teacher: he tells us why."

Doc's fascination with horses in harness began as a child growing up in Iowa. There were Amish communities nearby, and while he occasionally got to see horses working in fields at a distance, more often he saw women delivering vegetables door-to-door with a horse and wagon. "When I saw that horse and that vehicle, up close from where I was sitting on the curb, and I saw them driving it up and down the street, I decided that's what I wanted to do. I wanted to drive horses. Of course I grew up with Roy Rogers, Gene Autry, and The Lone Ranger. Every time a wagon or a stagecoach came on the television, it excited me more than the saddle horses. The saddle horses interested me, but it was driving horses that became my passion."

By the time Doc was eight or nine he got a Welsh Pony. Then he talked the neighbors out of a garden cart. "I took some pine 2x2s and I nailed them on. I stuck them through my stirrups, and tied them down solid to the cinch rings with baler twine. Then I punched holes in the end of my riding reins, extended them with baler twine and connected them to my riding bridle. I had no idea whether the pony had ever been driven or not in his life and not enough knowledge to even ask the question. I jumped up on that cart, standing up as if it was a chariot, and off we went. And believe it or not, it worked for quite awhile. Eventually we did have a runaway and trashed the cart, but that led to getting a real harness and a cutter and eventually a little wagon. I took my younger brothers camping, I cultivated a sweet corn patch and took the corn to the farmer's market, but it was all purely trial and error, no books, no video. My passion includes sharing what I've learned because when I was learning I had no one around who knew anything about horses, no mentor, and no formal training available."

Doc as Veterinarian

Doc was inspired to become a veterinarian when, at the age of nine, he watched a vet treat a foal that had tangled with a barb wire fence. "When I saw what the vet did – going around and taking care of people's animals all day - I never varied from that; that's what I wanted to be."

Early in his veterinary career, Doc had the opportunity to see a demonstration by Dr. Robert Miller, the well-known animal behaviorist and veterinarian, perhaps best known for his work with foal imprinting.

Doc describes the life-changing event this way: "Dr. Miller first talked about the nature of horses in general, how their minds work, how they learn, and what's logical to them. He then talked about their silent body language and how we can mimic that to better communicate with them. The idea was that as veterinarians, if we came from this perspective, we could better talk our patients into things and work with them in a cooperative way rather than have to drug them or physically restrain them so much. I was primed for a kinder, gentler way of working with horses. The learning that I'd had had been pretty conventional, pretty traditional: where you're good to horses and you like horses but if you're not getting what you want from a horse, then mechanics and force, and in the case of a veterinarian, drugs, come into the picture."

Doc continues, "I went home and started using what I got from Bob Miller, and I practiced it on every horse I worked on in that veterinary practice. The practice was heavily equine, so I had

Doc driving with well-known author and trainer Doris Ganton in British Columbia in the late 1970s.

opportunities every day, many times every day usually, to practice on client horses. It was the greatest practice builder there was. For instance, I worked with client's horses that were head-shy. We tube-wormed in those days – ran a tube down the nostril into the stomach -and every horse you worked on hated to be tube wormed. But if I took five minutes and worked with the horse's head before I got the tube out, if I got a little bit of trust and a little bit of respect and compliance and then introduced the tube right, it was amazing. They got better and better instead of worse and worse. And it was the same with all kinds of other things. I began to see that improving the everyday things translated into improvements when my client's horses and my horses were in harness."

Choosing the Right Harness

Harness for horses used to be so common that there were harness makers in every major city. Harness then was like tires now: a necessary part of our transportation solution. Harness now, though, is of course quite a specialty topic compared to car tires. How many tire ads have you seen on television recently? How many harness ads? How many tire stores do you pass on the way to the grocery store and how many harness shops? It's no wonder then that when it comes to choosing the right harness for horses, it takes a bit more study than it used to. There just aren't as many knowledgeable people out there.

Percherons drinking on the farm of C. Orr of Forest, Indiana from *America's Rural Yesterday Volume II: Barn & Farmyard*, courtesy Mischka Press Publishing.

In 2012, a roundtable discussion of long-time teamsters was asked about the best harness for horses. Leather was the unanimous answer. A brief review of recent *Rural Heritage* Front Porch visitors found synthetic harness to be preferred. An informal survey of harness retailers revealed a similar customer preference for harness made of synthetic materials instead of leather. Reasons given for preferring synthetic harness include the lighter weight of synthetic harness, ease of cleaning and maintenance, and somewhat lower price. Reasons given for preferring leather include the feel of the material and the comfort of the horse. Harness choice is obviously not a well-marked road. Not only are there not many people who understand the topic but there are also a lot of different options available that we didn't used to have.

One teamster summarized, "There's a good amount of little things that are really important that are getting missed when it comes to horse harness these days." This chapter attempts to capture those 'little things' known by experienced teamsters about choosing harness.

Function and Safety of Course

When considering what harness to buy for a horse, there are two obvious topics to be evaluated. First, the harness should be appropriate for the job to be done; you wouldn't want to use a breast strap type (driving) harness for logging. And a harness that is safe is important; no broken, worn, or cracked straps, for instance.

The Comfort of the Horse

What about the more subtle topic of the comfort of the horse? If the horse is comfortable in the harness, then there is less likelihood that the horse will get upset and cause accident or injury to either horse or human. "If you've got a horse that is not comfortable because of his harness, you're jeopardizing safety," says Doc. On several occasions, Doc has been told by respected equine professionals that they believe up to 80% of the behavior problems in horses are related to physical discomfort.

It's Not About the Material

Any harness material, if it's good quality and assembled with care and good workmanship, can be used to create a good quality harness. On a leather harness for instance, it's nice if all the straps are edged (rounded). The harness lasts longer and sharp edges don't have a tendency to scrape the horse. Some synthetic material has quite sharp edges, so it's nice if the pieces that are against the horse are trimmed in soft leather to improve comfort for the horse.

On the other hand, any harness material, if not used with care, can cause the horse serious discomfort. Because leather and synthetic have different properties, they require different approaches to harness construction to ensure the comfort of the horse. For many teamsters, harness made from synthetic material requires special attention because edges often aren't tapered and there are plenty of stories about synthetic harness causing injury to horses. "I know of a situation where three days in a synthetic crupper wore completely through the skin on the underside of the horse's tail," says Doc. "Even a leather crupper with rough edges or bad seams could cause problems."

Doc continues, "I've seen a lot of synthetic harness that has sharp edges, seams, and splices. One example is where a strap goes around a piece of hardware and is sewn back to

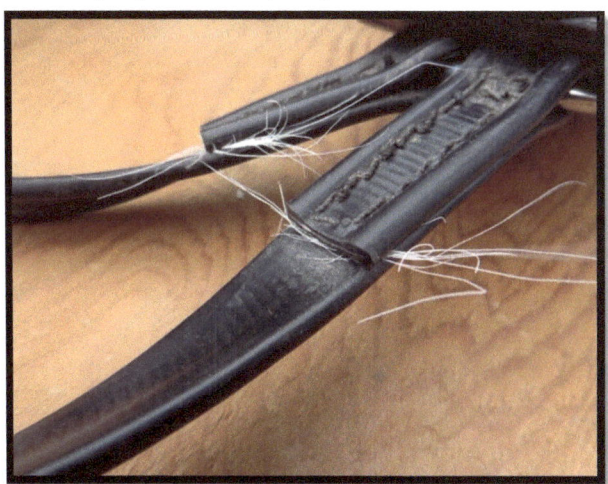

Synthetic straps often have abrupt terminations that can be irritating to the horse. Note how hair has gotten caught here, likely causing some irritation to the horse.
Photo courtesy Doc Hammill.

itself without being tapered in thickness and gradually blended in. If I run my hand under there, it's rough, irritating, where the strap stops and forms a ledge. With leather the harness makers will often taper the end. I haven't seen that done with synthetics so they have a sharp edge there. Low quality workmanship on leather may not be tapered, but leather is still more forgiving and less abrasive to the horse.

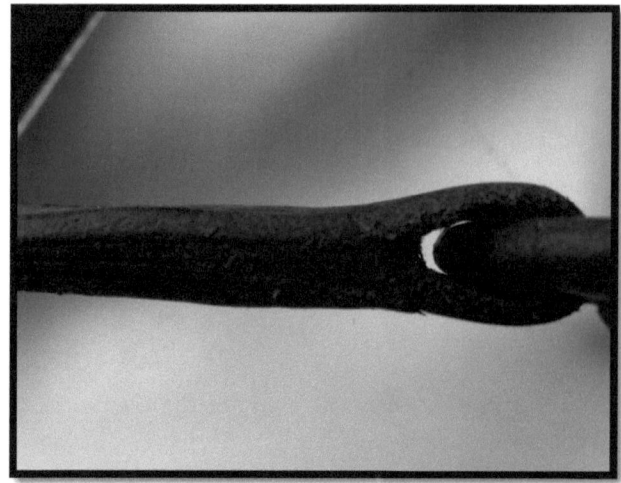

Harness makers working with leather have the ability to taper strap terminations, making them more comfortable for the horse. Photo courtesy Doc Hammill.

"Whether or not I feel synthetic harness is acceptable from the perspective of the horse depends first upon the type of synthetic material and then the workmanship on that specific set of harness. For the sake of the horse, please be extra attentive when examining any harness, and particularly a synthetic harness. In the end, I'd rather have a synthetic harness that was tops in quality and workmanship than a leather harness that was poor in terms of quality and workmanship."

Fit is Key

"Once we have a harness that is built so that it will not irritate or wear holes in the horse's skin, then fit becomes the next very important consideration," says Doc. "No amount of proper adjustment and fit will work if the harness has places or pieces that will cause damage."

While some people may think if it's a work harness and we have a work horse, we can just throw the harness on and go, in Doc's experience most people do care about fit but don't know how to accomplish proper fit. "They also don't know where to go to find out or very often have taken the advice of others who don't 'really' know how or why it should be a certain way."

Especially when dealing with unusual sized equines – ponies, cobs, draft crosses – harness off the shelf is unlikely to fit and will require adjustment. "I know someone who bought a 14.2hh pony and a 'pony' harness. The harness was sized for a Shetland and had no chance of fitting the pony it was purchased for," said one teamster.

A common technique used by harness retailers to ensure their customers are satisfied with the harness they purchase is to provide prospective customers with worksheets for measuring their horse. While this isn't a failsafe mechanism for assuring good fit, it is quite important in those instances when dealing with equines with uncommon dimensions: smaller than a draft but bigger than a pony, for instance, or bigger than a Welsh but smaller than a Quarter Horse.

Go With What You Know

When considering what type of harness to use on a horse, it's important to consider what you will be comfortable with. Many older teamsters are comfortable with leather, and so that material is their preference. They know how to repair it if they need to, and they know how to adjust it and maintain it. For others who know that their time for cleaning and maintaining is limited, synthetic harness might be a better answer.

One important consideration regarding synthetic harness is repair. It isn't possible to splice synthetic material as easily as it is leather if a quick repair is needed. Therefore, easy access to a harness shop capable of repairing synthetic harness might be an important consideration in the choice of harness for a horse. Many shops sell harness but do not repair harness, so buyers should have a repair strategy in place. Saddle shops and shoe repair shops may or may not have the knowledge, skills, and equipment to repair harness properly.

Horse Before Harness

"Sometimes I hear of people who get the harness before they get the horse," says Doc. "They were anxious to get started on their draft horse dream, and they had some money to spend, but not enough to buy horses, so they get some harness."

While it's admirable that they are so motivated to pursue their draft horse dream, getting the harness before the horse really isn't the right first step. "It's so important to get the horses first," says Doc. "One size harness does not fit all. Yes, there are lots of ways to adjust harness, but not all harness is constructed exactly the same, so having the horse first so you can actually try the harness on the horse or at least take measurements before purchasing the harness really is the best approach."

For example, Fjord horses typically have very wide foreheads. "So you can buy harness advertised as a QH/Haflinger/Fjord-sized harness that might fit the body, but the chances are the bridles are going to be too narrow in the brow band. A lot of browbands are not adjustable," says Doc. "Also, there is a lot of difference in neck size and shape in horses that are about the same size otherwise. Consequently, it is common for people to buy harness that can be adjusted to fit the horse only to find out that the hames are either too long or too short for the collar that fits the horse."

**Used Harness Check List
Courtesy Samson Harness Shop, Inc.
and Doc Hammill**

In looking over a used harness for either purchase or repair, the following points should be considered:

1. Look for cracks in the leather, stretched holes, and bent buckle tongues.
2. If the harness has either iron or steel hardware, check for 'rust rot' on the leather which frequently occurs under steel buckles or near rings or dees. This is very important on bridles and lines.
3. Particular attention must be paid to the following parts; they should be replaced if they show any signs of excessive wear or deterioration:
   a. Bit straps
   b. Hame straps
   c. Throat latches
   d. Bridle crowns
   e. Lines
   f. Breast straps
   g. Pole straps
   h. Holdback straps
   i. Snaps
4. Check the hardware for wear, especially the bottom clips on hames and the links attaching breast strap rings to the hames.

The Importance of Give

One concern that experienced horsemen have with harness made from synthetic material is that the material doesn't give. "What gives isn't the harness," says one teamster. "Hopefully it's not the horse."

An unfortunate story further illustrates the point. A well-broke driving pony was put to a cart wearing synthetic harness. The drive into the woods went well. Once in the woods, the party dismounted the cart, not noticing that the whip in the whip holder had caught in the tree branches above. Suddenly the whip gave way and smacked the pony on the rear, and the pony took off. When the pony finally stopped, the cart was completely wrecked, and the pony was severely cut up, especially on the inner rear legs where the traces had tangled. If leather harness had been used, it's

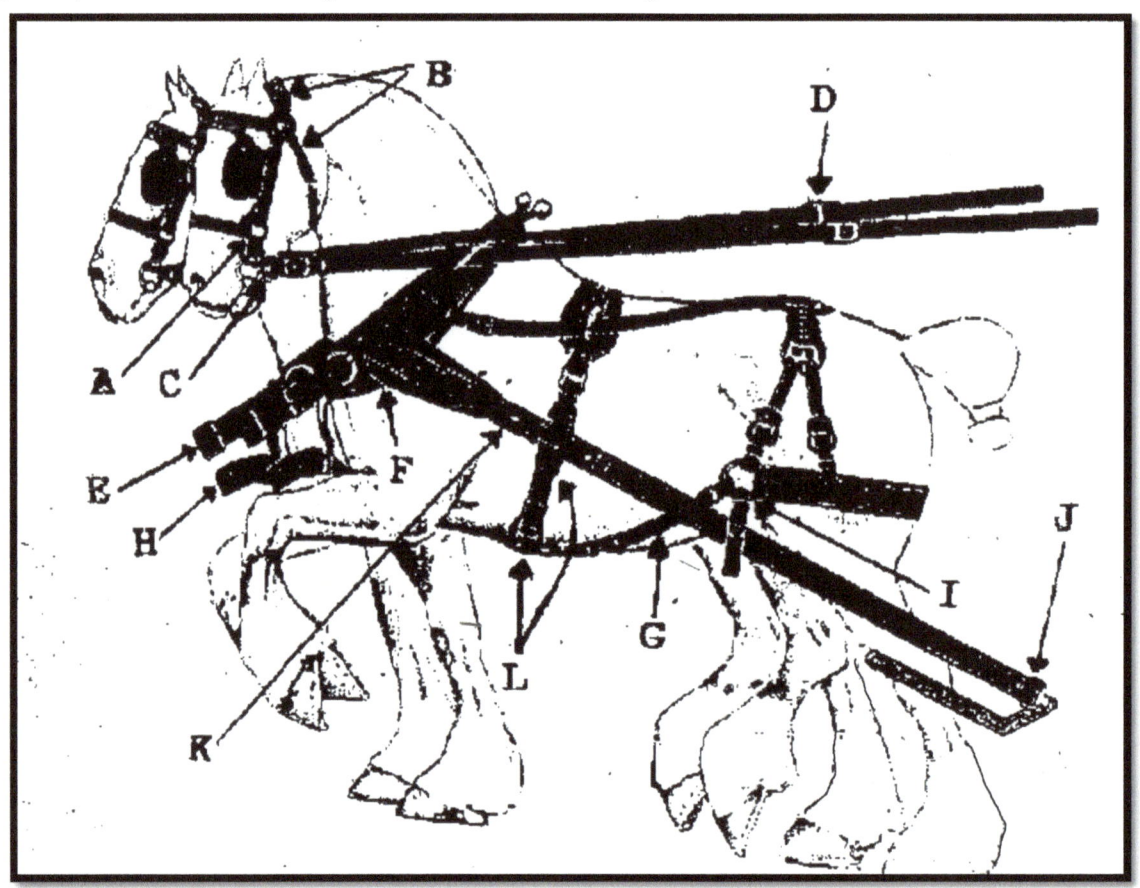

USED HARNESS CHECKLIST
courtesy Samson Harness Shop, Inc.

- A. Bit strap & lower cheek piece
- B. Bridle crown, throat latch & billet
- C. End of lines
- D. Point of crossline attachment
- E. Breast strap – entire length
- F. Trace: hame end
- G. Holdback strap – both ends
- H. Pole strap – both ends
- I. Breeching dees
- J. Trace: heel end
- K. Trace at center where billet layer rivets on
- L. Belly band and belly band billets

possible it would have broken, possibly saving the cart and inflicting less injury on the pony. "I know of two ponies that were so badly injured in a wreck due to wearing synthetic harness that they were never able to be driven again," said one teamster.

Doc adds, "Leather may not break either, especially traces, and I don't want harness to break in situations where extreme forces come into play such as a wreck, but leather is generally more forgiving and less damaging than many of the synthetics. Because synthetics are very strong, thinner synthetic material can have strength that exceeds that of thicker leather. Use of thinner and sometimes narrower material is part of the reason synthetic harness is lightweight. However, when synthetic harness parts are thin, have rough edges and strap ends, and are not as flexible and forgiving as leather, not only is the potential for harness sores increased, but there is more danger of cutting up a horse in the event of a mishap or wreck."

Getting Good Help

If you aren't sure about what harness is best for your situation and your horses, several teamsters advised asking for help. Experienced teamsters often know about different types of harness and can recommend an appropriate style for your situation. They also often can look at how a harness hangs on a hook and know whether it's any good or not. It's difficult, they say, to teach the details they can see instantly.

One harness retailer compared buying harness to buying a computer. It's important to learn about the features before purchasing so that the investment is worth it in the long run. For him, computers are a mystery, so he would want advice and he'd want to take someone knowledgeable with him to make sure he made the right choice for his situation. He advocates that novices buying harness should use a similar strategy.

Doc adds, "Keep in mind that advice varies in quality just as much as harness does. You will find a lot of different types of advice available out there in the horse industry. It's very important that you make sure the advice you get is good and sound."

Buyer Beware

Several harness makers expressed regret about some of the harness on the market. Some of it is being made overseas by people who have no horse experience, so harness makers can't take the horse into account as they build harness. Other harness is being made from poor quality materials; it can crack soon after purchase, and significant pieces of the harness must be replaced before it can even be put to use the first time.

Some harness is available for sale on the internet for very cheap prices. Buyer beware; there's a reason the prices are low. "The horse is kind of the victim in the middle," said one retailer. Another says, "Everything you see in full color doesn't necessarily mean it's good quality." And another: "Low end harness makers are doing just enough workmanship to fool the novices. I know of a lot of harness that got bought and then never put on a horse."

And remember that breakage in a harness can mean an accident with more adverse consequences than most of us want to deal with. It makes sense to spend time either examining a prospective harness yourself or having someone knowledgeable do the examination for you. It's a bit like a pre-purchase exam on a horse or a having a mechanic check out a used car before buying it.

New versus Used

One teamster says, "There's no sense buying used leather harness because very little of it has been properly taken care of. You're better off buying new." On the other hand, Doc Hammill regularly uses a set of harness that was probably at least forty years old when he bought it more than thirty years ago. At one point he sold a horsedrawn wagon/sleigh business including the horses and harness. But instead of selling his well-cared-for old harness, he bought new harness and sold that. "I bought new harness, and I let it go with the business, so I could keep my old harness. Because the break-in period would have been long; my harness was old, old, old, practically looked like the horse was in it when hanging on the wall. It was really sweet on the edges and all of that. Plus the difference in leather quality and workmanship compared to the new harness was plain to see. The new harness was very good harness but in my opinion not as good as my old harness."

Whether new or used, it's important to evaluate the 'health' of the leather. If you twist it tightly, does it crack or show rot? Regarding used harness, old leather in traces is most likely to break at a rivet. On the entire harness, are there any missing or loose stitches? It's also important to look at the entire length of the lines for slices, cracks, thin spots, or other damage. One teamster cautioned about other problems with used harness. "Sometimes not all the pieces are there; sometimes the pieces are mismatched in size – part for a draft, part for a quarter horse."

Examining Harness

Whenever Doc Hammill encounters a horse and harness he's not familiar with, he first examines the harness. "I know that I've examined harness and felt parts on the harness that definitely had potential to harm a horse. There may be sharp edges to the straps, rivets coming out, or seams that are not smooth and flat. Anything like that is uncomfortable to the horse, can irritate them, and potentially cause an accident." Another teamster adds, "I don't like synthetics because it's hard to find any that doesn't have rough stuff on the horse's side of the harness. You've got to really pay attention, find really good stuff – edges, strap ends."

Harness makers make decisions constantly about how to make a harness, and those decisions have the potential to impact a horse. Where is the lock in the seam? Many times the lock is not properly set in the leather, so it is visible. That means it may be next to the horse and could be irritating. Another example is the edges of the straps: are they rounded? Are the stitches recessed into the leather or riding on the surface?

On the left, an example of flat breeching. Note that this common breeching construction does not have tapered (edged) edges. On the right, an example of folded breeching.

Perhaps the easiest way to assess the concern a harness maker had regarding the comfort of the horse is by examining the construction of the breeching (some of the same considerations apply to the belly band). The simplest and least expensive construction is a single wide strap from breeching ring to breeching ring around the backside of the horse. The hardware is affixed with short straps riveted or sewn to the breeching.

A more common construction is for the strap that holds the hardware and connects to the rings to be stitched onto a wider strap that functions against the horse (the long layer type). Sometimes the edges of the wider strap (the breeching base) are edged. An even better breeching construction from the perspective of the comfort of the horse is for the breeching to be folded and/or padded. Folded breeching consists of a wide piece of leather with edges folded in and filled with another piece of leather. Then the thick strap that holds hardware is laid over that. Folded breeching makes the breeching thicker so it isn't as likely to work under the hair.

Two types of breeching shown on edge: flat breeching with little to no edging on the left and rolled and padded breeching on the right. Which do you think is more comfortable?
Photo courtesy Doc Hammill.

Comparative Styles of Breeching Bands.

Six samples of breeching bands are shown. Their variations include their bases – single versus folded; whether the top layer is raised or flat; and how the top layer is shaped and stitched. They are all made of full grain harness leather. Numbers 3. 5 and 6 show the roll away from the horse and the set of the layer into the fold. The harness maker shares, "All of these styles are used on harness from mini to draft and on both work and show harness, just to give people something a little special on their harness."

Six different approaches to constructing breeching:
#1 Single base, flat layer
#2 Single base, raised layer
#3 Folded base, scalloped layer
#4 Single base, raised and waved layer
#5 Folded base, raised layer
#6 Folded base, raised and waved layer

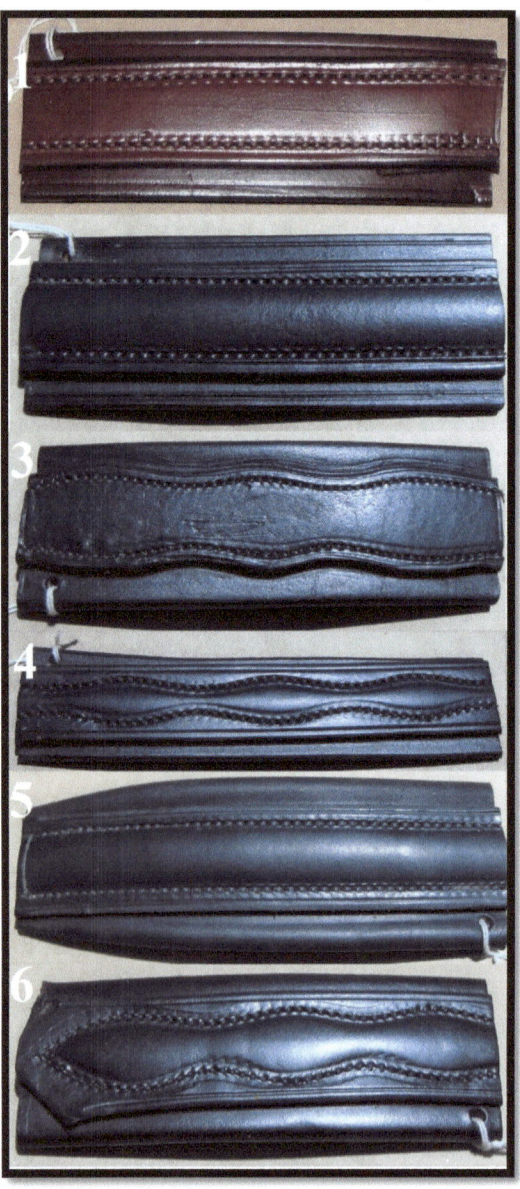

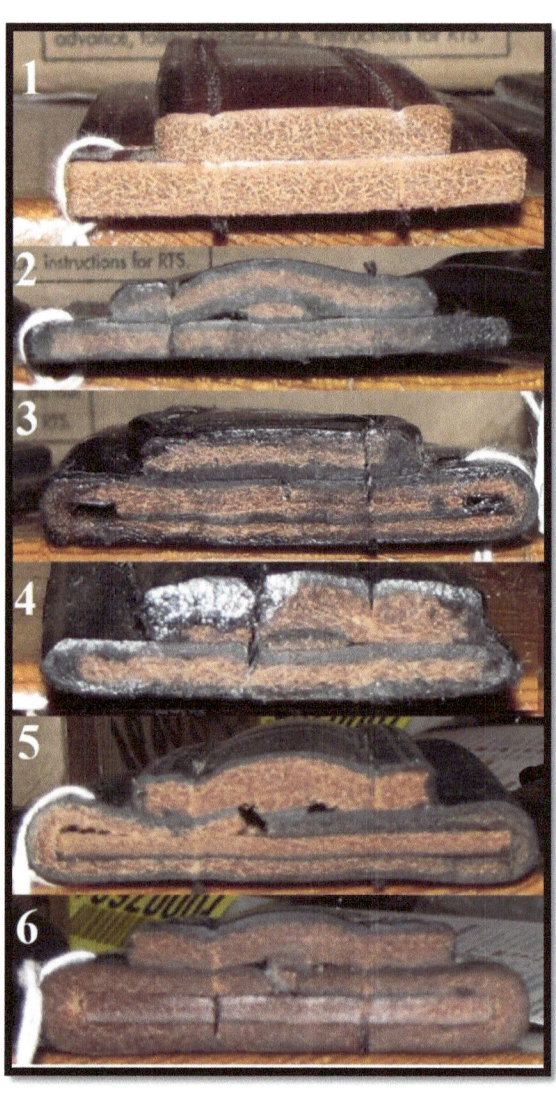

Samples courtesy Samson Harness Shop, Inc.

Doc Hammill observes, "If the harness maker just takes the strap and doesn't fold it, if they just edge the edges and get it as nice and with rounded edges as they can, you can still wear off hair and dig into the skin, particularly if you don't know how to adjust the hip straps to angle the breeching so it lays flat on the contour of the rump. If you hang a breeching level to the eye, you're going to be digging into the rump with the top edge of it."

Doc continues, "Once when I ordered a set of Yankee breeching (hip breeching), I told the harness maker to put the smooth side of the leather toward the horse. Padding wasn't as necessary as on a conventional breeching. The harness maker replied that the breeching won't look good with the rough side out. I said I didn't care – I wanted the smooth side toward the horse's body for the comfort of the horse. He was very reluctant, so I told him I wouldn't tell anyone who made it, so he went ahead."

Synthetic Harness Advantages

Synthetic harness's advantages have been very effectively marketed. For instance, regarding ease of cleaning and maintenance: just leave it on the horse and hose both of them down. For many, the lighter weight of synthetic harness is a really big draw. Many people, as they age, develop physical limitations that make lifting heavy objects above their shoulders difficult or painful. As one Front Porch visitor shared, "My wagon harness is leather. It's older but still good. If I ever buy a new set, you can rest assured it'll be bio, for no other reason than weight. I'm too old to throw a full set up that high now." (1) Finally, for many, the lower price of harness made from synthetic materials is an important consideration.

Synthetic harness also has advantages in extreme wet or muddy conditions because of its ease of clean up. People in damp and wet climates also often do better with synthetic harness because it's less likely to mold.

Doc Hammill leaves holdback straps attached to the shafts of some pieces of equipment that are outside year-round. He uses beta straps in that case because they can stand the constant exposure to weather.

While some people prefer synthetic harness in moist climates, many still make leather work.

Don't Rule Out Leather

Leather harness makers exclaim that people shouldn't rule out leather. They make convincing counter-arguments to the positive points about synthetic harness. Regarding price, for instance, according to one catalog, the difference between leather and synthetic can be as little as $170 for team harness ($1465 leather versus $1295 synthetic).

25

Regarding weight, one harness maker weighed boxes containing team harnesses of different materials without hames. The nylon harness weighed 55 pounds, the bioplastic harness weighed 68 pounds, and the leather harness weighed 74 pounds. One could argue that the weight difference of six pounds between the bioplastic harness and the leather harness was almost negligible given that one would only be lifting a single harness at a time, so the real weight difference would be just three pounds per horse harnessed.

These horses are wearing beta harness including beta bridles; note how the nosebands on the bridles are stiff and stand away from the horses' heads (there's a shadow on the face of the horse on the left in the picture).
Photo courtesy Harley Weyer

Leather harness makers also stress that there are ways to build harness to make it less heavy and/or easier to put on the horse.

For some, leather is the natural choice for ecological reasons. Leather biodegrades, unlike synthetics. In either case, harness hardware can be recycled.

The Best of Both Worlds

A great number of the best harnesses out there actually use both synthetic and leather materials. Many traces on leather harness have a nylon core to reduce the weight and increase strength. And many of the best synthetic harnesses incorporate leather where there is significant contact with the horse's body. As one Front Porch visitor shared, "I have a heavy built nylon d ring harness. There is leather stitched on anywhere it might rub. Hardly ruffles the hair." (2)

Some teamsters prefer the feel of leather lines so will splice leather ends onto their synthetic lines. And some teamsters have found that it's difficult to get synthetic lines to connect to bits cleanly so they use leather line adapters from the synthetic lines to the bits. In addition, they may use leather hame straps because the synthetic material won't lay flat.

These beta lines are terminated with a buckle connection to the bit which is safer than the more common but failure-prone snap termination.
Photo courtesy Harley Weyer

Many teamsters like beta lines rather than leather; they don't get as slippery when driving in the rain, and you don't have to worry about the ends touching the ground because they're easy to clean. Furthermore, there are no splices in beta lines to end up in your hands when driving. However, it's important to remember that just because they're synthetic doesn't mean they shouldn't be examined regularly for tears or other damage that impacts their function.

And again, many teamsters use leather bridles with their synthetic harness because there are so many wear points and it's so much easier to get them to fit and comfortably conform to the head. Doc explains the importance of well-fit bridles: "If the bridle doesn't conform well to the horse's head, the chances of it coming off are significantly greater. Many times we see people not wanting to tighten the throatlatch on a synthetic bridle up as tight as they should. It leaves a springy looseness that is a danger as well as not being comfortable for the horse." A Front Porch visitor confirms these cautions about synthetic bridles, "I have a bio team harness, complete with bio bridles. While I like the harness, I wish that I had not purchased the bio bridles, and instead paid more to have leather bridles made." (3)

The Memory of Leather

Many long-time teamsters won't consider anything but leather harness for their horses. "If I had a horse I really liked, it would be leather," says one. Leather conforms to the horse's body, it molds itself, creating a better fit. Synthetic materials often won't conform, so you can't get the fit. One teamster and harness maker asks, "If you had to hike to the top of that mountain, would you choose synthetic shoes or good quality leather hiking boots? The same considerations are true for the harness on a horse."

Leather also has a memory. Doc Hammill recalls, "My mentor Addie, when he would take the team lines off the harness for some reason, he could always tell by looking which line had been on the left and right hand horses, because the leather had a memory and had molded to the shape of the respective horse's body. He insisted that each line go back on the horse on the side it was conformed to."

A Personal Choice

According to many harness retailers, older people and experienced teamsters tend to prefer leather over synthetics. The retailers, though, are often dealing with people who work their horses only occasionally and don't feel they have a lot of time. The retailers tend to steer these folks to synthetic harness because of the ease of care, though they admit that a well-cared-for leather harness will outlast a synthetic one. Some retailers weren't as likely to recommend nylon harness because that material tends to fray and its pores fill with dirt, inflicting damage to the harness over time. One retailer said that he'd found granite, a type of synthetic harness material, to be easier to adjust around buckles than bioplastic.

Nylon harness material can have a tendency to fray, so while the material may have a long life, the harness's functional life may be much shorter.
Photo courtesy Harley Weyer

As one Front Porch visitor aptly summarized, "As to what the harness should be made of, of course, it's your decision."(4) Harness choice is and should be particular to a person's situation. Taking into account the horse must also be part of the decision-making process, since safety ultimately depends on the comfort of the horse. As one teamster said, "If you make the right decision for the horse, the people will be taken care of, too."

1) http://ruralheritage.com/messageboard/frontporch/17007.htm
    Response by Mac at 2013-02-02 22:12:25
2) http://ruralheritage.com/messageboard/frontporch/16940.htm
    Response by aherzog at 2013-01-14 20:39:42
3) http://ruralheritage.com/messageboard/frontporch/17007.htm
    Response by Neal in Iowa at 2013-02-02 10:34:48
4) http://ruralheritage.com/messageboard/frontporch/17007.htm
    Response by NoraWI at 2013-02-02 07:27:3

About Synthetic Harness Materials

Polypropylene. Bioplastic. Biothane. Granite. Nylon. Beta. Betathane. Coated Webbing.

Perhaps you've seen these terms in reference to synthetic harness. Perhaps you own a harness made from synthetic materials or perhaps these terms cause your eyes to glaze over. Understanding the difference between these terms will help you understand the tradeoffs regarding synthetic harness, especially when purchasing a new one or repairing one you already have. Even leather harness loyalists sometimes see synthetic harness materials in use that they would consider using because of their lighter weight and quality of workmanship. A better understanding of synthetic harness materials will ensure the best choice for your horse and for your working situation.

Synthetic harness materials have grown in popularity because they are strong and require one less step in the harness care process (see the chapter "The Privilege of Harness Care). As one harnessmaker suggests, many of our grandfathers who used leather harness would likely have embraced synthetic harness if it had been available because of its strength and easier care: "what do you mean it's just as strong but I don't have to oil it?"

Harness made from synthetic materials is growing in popularity due to the lighter weight and durability of the material.
Photo courtesy Chuck Cox

Regardless of the material that a harness is made from, harness is, at its most basic, a combination of straps and pads and hardware. Some of the straps experience more strain than others. Reputable harnessmakers select materials and hardware for each of the straps that will stand up to the strain they are likely to experience while also being comfortable for the horse.

Not all synthetic harness materials are the same, and not all hardware is the same. The expertise of the harnessmaker determines how the end-result harness turns out based on both the choice of materials and hardware and the way in which they are assembled. The expertise of the harnessmaker determines how functional the end-result harness is, how safe it is, and how comfortable for the horse it is. It's our job as teamsters to understand harness materials well enough to judge all of these harness characteristics so we make the best choice for our horse and our situation.

Raw Webbing Materials

Synthetic harness materials begin with some sort of webbing made from polypropylene, polyester, nylon, Kevlar® or cotton that provides strength. Then the webbing is either left exposed, as in nylon harness, or coated in some sort of plastic. Plastics typically used are polyurethane or vinyl. Many of us have seen webbing used in places other than harness. It is used in tow straps for instance. Other examples of webbing include seat belts, halters, and dog leashes.

Raw webbing materials, including polypropylene, nylon, and polyester, vary in their UV resistance, water resistance, strength, time to dry, and the degree to which they stretch or shrink. (1) We are fortunate when harnessmakers sort through these characteristics of synthetic materials to choose appropriately for the harness they create for us to use.

As teamsters we need to confirm that critical wear points of synthetic harness are lined for the comfort of our equines.
Photo courtesy Abner Esh

Coated Webbings

Coated webbing is the umbrella term for webbing that is covered in plastic. Polyurethane-coated polyester is the coated webbing typically used to make synthetic harness. The plastic coating makes the webbing easier to clean and makes it more durable.

It turns out that the terms bioplastic, biothane, granite, and beta all refer to products by a particular company - Biothane Coated Webbing in Ohio - and are in fact registered trademarks. One reason these names dominate synthetic harness conversations is that the company has been manufacturing coated webbing since 1977 and began when four engineers saw a need in the harness racing industry for a flexible high performance product. The company is now in its second generation of family ownership.

Bioplastic® is the umbrella term for the plastic-coated webbings made by the Biothane Coated Webbing Company. Biothane® is a coated webbing with a glossy finish, often considered an alternative to patent leather. Granite® is a semi-gloss coated webbing intended to look like dressed leather. Beta® is a softer coated webbing with a semi-gloss finish that is often used for lines. The term betathane was invented by the market to be more descriptive than Beta®.

Coated webbings are made by other companies both in this country and overseas with varying degrees of involvement in and attention to the equine market.

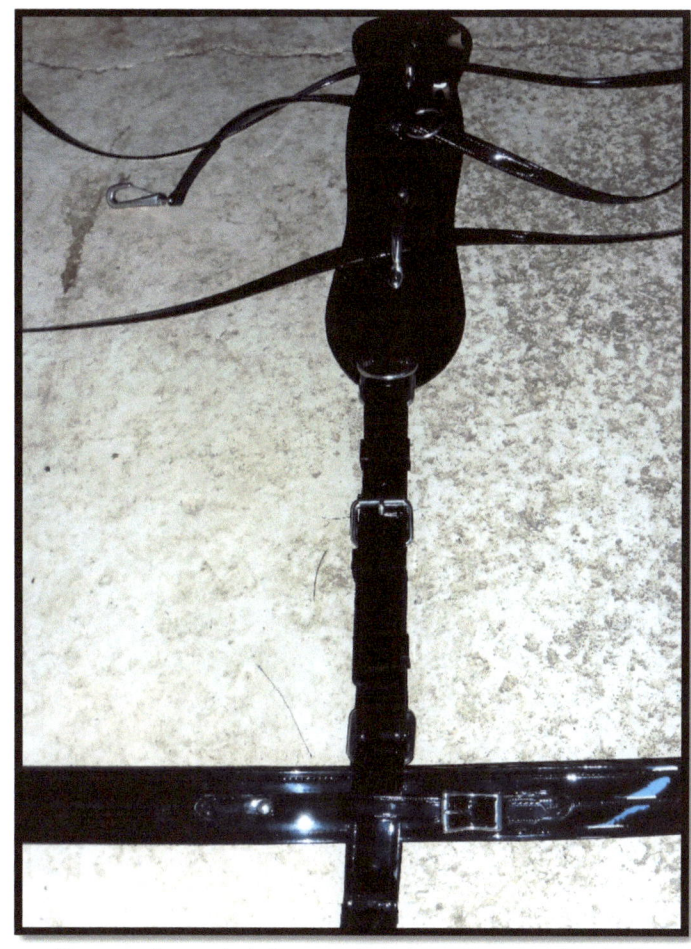

Harnessmakers make judgments about the performance of synthetic materials and then make choices such as a roller buckle to connect the market and billet straps rather than a Conway for safety and performance reasons.
Photo courtesy Abner Esh

Combinations

Rarely is a harness made from a single type of material, synthetic or otherwise. Reputable harnessmakers choose a specific material for a specific location in the harness for a specific reason. Many traces in leather harness, for instance, have some sort of synthetic material sandwiched between the leather to increase strength and durability.

Sometimes a combination of polypropylene web, nylon web, and coated webbing as well as leather are used to achieve a harnessmaker's desired strength, durability, comfort, and cost. Jason Rutledge commented on the *Rural Heritage* Front Porch in 2007 about the multi-material harness he uses: "I [call] it integrated harness, because it has leather where it needs a memory and nylon where it needs strength. They have worked for us for a long time with little to no upkeep. We do take them to the high pressure car wash and knock some dust, dirt and mud off them occasionally. This harness may be somewhat more expensive than some cheaper nylon harness, but given the years of regular serious work they have done for us, I am delighted to get what I paid for." (2)

This photo shows how coated and raw webbing stand up to abrasion. You can see that the raw webbing has begun to fray.
Photo courtesy Biothane Coated Webbing Company

Polypropylene harness material

Polypropylene is used for harness by some harnessmakers because it is a lighter weight webbing that is lower in cost. It is usually sewn into multiple layers to increase its strength. When used on its own, its primary use is in medium-duty harness. In heavier-duty harness it is used in combination with nylon and/or coated webbing to achieve the harnessmaker's goals for lightweight but strong, affordable, and comfortable harness.

Nylon harness material

Nylon harness is made predominantly from nylon webbing. Nylon is often the harness material of choice when cost is an issue and appearance is less important since this uncoated webbing can pick up and hold dust and dirt over time. Harness maker Abner Esh advises people interested in nylon harness to pay close attention to the edges of the webbing: "When you look at webbing material, look for tight weave on the edges. Some are not as tight on the edge. Tight weave on the edges is important because it is less likely to suffer from abrasion. You have to use a good quality webbing to make a serviceable harness."

Compared to most coated webbing harness, Abner has observed that nylon harness tends to show wear sooner. He has also noticed that nylon harness seems to get stiffer with time, likely due to accumulated dust in the webbing. Another factor that people consider when choosing nylon harness is weight. While only slightly lighter at 5-10 pounds per harness, some people prefer nylon over coating webbing harness because it weighs a bit less. Finally, nylon harness is typically quite a bit cheaper than comparable coated webbing harness, making up for some of the disadvantages of the uncoated material.

Lining Harness Pieces

While cheaper harness is often what people find attractive about synthetic materials, it's important to remember that in harness as in most things in life you get what you pay for. One place where corners are sometimes cut to reduce the cost of the harness is lining of the wear points. For the comfort of the horse, the breeching, back pad, and belly band at a minimum should be lined, especially in nylon harness. Some harnessmakers line the head crown and spiders and other harness parts as well. As teamsters we should confirm that at a minimum the most important wear points of our synthetic harness are lined for the benefit of our equine workmates.

Two examples of synthetic harness with different degrees of care taken regarding the comfort of the horse. On the left, the strap ends have been stitched and skived to create a smooth transition on the horse-side of the harness. On the right, the strap ends are not well finished, so they catch and pull out the hair of the equine.
Photo on left courtesy Abner Esh

Coated Webbing Harness Material

There are two finishes of coated webbing that are made into harness: glossy and semi-gloss. Semi-gloss is becoming the most popular because it looks most like leather. The appearance of the materials, though, is the least important factor in terms of having a serviceable synthetic harness. Other factors such as how the coated webbing is made and then how the harness is made contribute more to a safe and effective end product than a glossy or semi-gloss finish.

Abner Esh shares, "I've used coated webbing materials from several companies. I keep coming back to the one that is consistent in performance because my clients end up with a better harness which means I get fewer complaints. People think coated webbing can't rip and tear; that's not true. Poor quality coated webbing can have this problem. When you have a good product, the thread tears first, not the coated webbing."

Another example of different degrees of care in synthetic harness. On the left, the strap end on the horse side has an abrupt ending. On the right the strap end on the horse side has been skived to provide a smooth transition.

In coated webbing, how well the web and the plastic coating are married is called adhesion. Adhesion is one of the most important characteristics of coated webbings because it determines the durability of the material. Related to adhesion is coating tear strength – the tendency for the plastic coating to pull away from itself. Obviously this characteristic also contributes to the durability of the material. Different coated webbings have different adhesion and tear strength characteristics. Harnessmakers make tradeoffs between price and durability of the material they use in the harness they make. Some are attracted to cheap materials available at auction or on sale to keep the price of their harness low, while others prefer materials that have performed consistently for them over time.

Coated webbing harness materials also vary in terms of hardness and flexibility. Abner Esh says, "I use the hard type when I need stiffer, stronger material. Some use it for the whole harness, but I don't because it makes the harness not as flexible. I do use the hard where strength is really important, like the hame strap, for instance." Many teamsters have found that glossy coated webbing is too stiff to work well as lines, so they prefer lines made from a softer material such as Beta®. Beta® has the added advantage that it doesn't become stiff in cold weather. Some harnessmakers only provide Beta® lines just for these reasons. Some teamsters who have experience with both Beta® and leather lines find that Beta® lines stretch more than leather and therefore change their communication with the equine on the other end of their lines.

Regarding lines, Abner states, "Do not buy lines with a Conway at the snap. They can come undone and cause a very dangerous situation." And of course many teamsters feel lines shouldn't have snaps at all, only a roller buckle at the bit. Several teamsters concur that some coated webbing is so stiff that it can jump off a Conway in places other than lines when it is jiggled due to the motion of the horse. Examining the hardware used in a synthetic harness is an important exercise when evaluating a harness.

Workmanship

In addition to their choice of materials, harnessmakers make choices about how to assemble the harness, too. Those choices can impact the comfort of the harness and therefore our safety and that of our equines.

It is our responsibility as teamsters to choose harness for our equines that ensures they can do their work safely which includes being comfortable. Knowing that different synthetic harness materials have different properties helps us to ask questions about harness we are considering using. And knowing that different harnessmakers have different degrees of care when it comes to assembling functional harness helps us ask questions as well.

1) http://www.qualitylogoproducts.com/blog/polypropylene-polyester-nylon-guide-to-materials/
2) Response by Jason Rutledge at 2007-09-16 08:40:29 at http://www.ruralheritage.com/messageboard/frontporch/9597.htm

Abner Esh has been making harness at Peach Lane Harness for more than twenty years and can be reached at (717) 687-5122. The author is grateful to Mari Leedy of Stitch 'N Hitch Harness Shop, www.stitchnhitch.com

Harness Variety and Function

J.C. Allen Picture #1: What is wrong with this harness?

J.C. Allen Picture #1

What is wrong with the harness in Allen Picture #1?

In Steve Bowers' book *Farming with Horses*, Bowers states, "According to my research, about 80 percent of the draft-type harness used are [the Box Breeching or Western] style." (1) The Box Breeching or Western Style harness is also sometimes called a Bellybacker harness. This style of harness is illustrated in the diagrams below. If Steve Bowers found that 80% of harness is the Box Breeching style, then most of us, when we think about harness, probably have a mental image of this sort of harness in our minds. The harness in Allen Picture #1 doesn't even come close to matching this image. Yet the harness shown in Allen Picture #1 is perfectly suitable for the job it's doing. There's nothing wrong with it.

The Four Components of Harness

We can think of harness as having four distinct components, highlighted in different colors in the drawing below:

1) The Communication Component: to communicate with and direct the draft animal. The Communication Component is highlighted in yellow in the drawing. It consists of the bridle, bit and lines.

2) The Draft Component: to accomplish the drawing or pulling of the load. The Draft Component is highlighted in green in the drawing. It consists of the collar, hames and hame straps, traces, and trace chains.

3) The Stopping and Backing Component: to stop a load, slow down a load, or back up. The Stopping and Backing Component is highlighted in red in the drawing. It consists of the breeching band (sometimes called a britchen), quarter straps (sometimes called side straps or hold back straps), pole straps (sometimes called martingales), and breast straps.

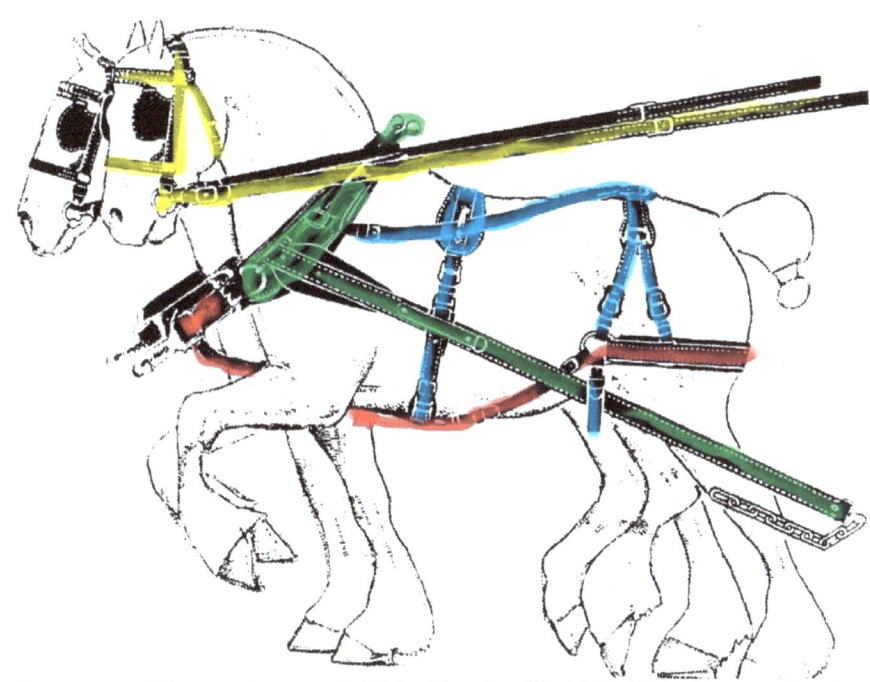

Components of Harness: Control is highlighted in yellow; Draft is highlighted in green; Stopping and Backing is highlighted in red, and Support is highlighted in blue.

4) The Support Component: the portions of the harness necessary to keep the pieces of the other Components in their proper positions. The Support Component is highlighted in blue on the diagram. It includes the back pad (sometimes called a saddle) and back pad billets, the belly band and belly band billets, the spider (back straps, rump pad, hip pads and hip straps), lazy straps (sometimes called trace carriers), and crupper, if present.

All four of the components are found in the common Box Breeching/Western style of harness, but there are many examples of perfectly functional harness that have only one or two of the components. In Allen Picture #1, for instance, the harness does not have a Stopping and Backing Component, and the Support Component is very simple: just the backpad for holding the traces up.

Simple Harness

The simplest harness is one with just the Control and Draft Components. Doc Hammill recalls, "Old timers that were my mentors told me about half-harness: collar, hames, traces. That's all you really need to pull a load as long as the load won't roll forward to hit the animal. It's a really basic pulling system. A lot of people don't understand that that's all you need to pull a load. When people are concerned about the weight of harness, depending on what they're doing, they can have this sort of harness and do a lot of this type of work. It's cooler, it's lighter, there's less things rubbing on the horse. If you look at stuff from third world countries, you'll see an incredible amount of this sort of harness. It's economical and it works."

In rare circumstances, the Control Component can even be optional. Where there is an exceptional teamster working with an exceptional equine, the equine can be worked loose-headed, without bridle and lines, maybe with just a lead rope tied up to the hames. Skidding logs is an example of a job that is occasionally performed loose-headed. Equines pulling ore carts in mines were also sometimes worked loose-headed.

Dale Wagner shared the following on the Rural Heritage Front Porch:
"Keep your harness as simple as possible. All that is really needed is a collar, hames and tugs. I have a picture of my grandpa taken about 1900. He has a four-up hooked to his freight wagon. Bridles, lines, collars, hames and tugs was all he had. No belly bands, back pads or britching. No dropper from neck yoke to the lead chain. He had to cross several coulees to go get groceries 80 miles away. He did have brakes on his wagon." (2)

Dale's grandfather was obviously an exceptional teamster who knew how to use brakes to help his horses do their job safely and comfortably. Doc emphasizes, "I certainly wouldn't recommend making the choice to put a wheel team on a wagon without breeching, unless there was no other choice. It certainly can and has been done but there are potential safety issues. Also, with a four-up, only the back two (wheel) horses would be able to utilize breeching anyway, since the leaders aren't connected to the tongue in a way that lets them hold the load back unless a false tongue is used."

Field or Plow Harness

The Field-style or plow harness also does not include the Stopping and Backing Component. Yet it differs significantly from the harness in Allen Picture #1 and from the half-harness that Doc describes. What are the functional differences?

The most obvious difference is the Support Component for the traces over the hips of the horse, which includes back straps, rump pad, hip pads, trace carriers, and crupper.

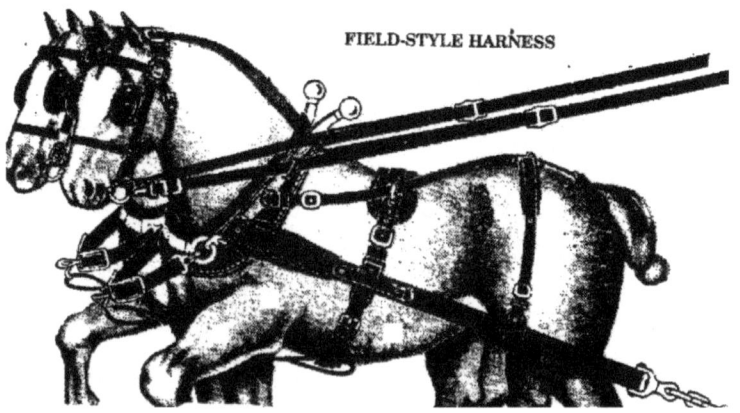

Field or Plow Harness
How does this harness differ from the one in Allen Picture #1?
courtesy Samson Harness Shop, Inc.

What function do these additional pieces of harness serve? They keep the traces from getting tangled with the horse's legs by keeping the traces up off the ground.

What part of this harness most needs adjustment?
Photo courtesy Heather Havens

A disadvantage of trace carriers is that if they are adjusted too short, they can break the line of draft, which interferes with the efficient transfer of power from the horse to moving the load. The same problem can occur with a lazy strap on any style of harness that has them if they are adjusted too short. The photo of the single horse skidding a tire illustrates this problem. You can see that the trace is deflected upward where it passes through the lazy strap. To correct the problem, the lazy strap needs to be lengthened so that the line of the trace from hame to load is a continuous straight line, not broken as it is in the photo.

Doc shares, "When trace carriers are too short, the horse feels a downward pull on the rear quarters when under draft. Many horses will pull light loads in such cases but become balky with heavier loads. It's common for trace carrier straps or lazy straps to not have enough adjustment available in them to pull loads on the ground properly. They typically end up being too short, as in the photo, so the horse feels a pull down on the hips. If the chain between the single tree and the tire was lengthened enough, the trace could theoretically be straightened out (the singletree would be lifted into the air in draft), making the line of draft straight, but for draft advantage and maneuverability, we want the load we are skidding close to the horse."

Another obvious functional difference between the harness in Allen Picture #1 and the plow harness is that the plow harness is set up to be a team harness that can be hitched to and steer a tongue, so there is a breast strap. Though not all plow harnesses have a pole strap, the plow harness in the illustration does have one; it acts as a choke strap, buckling around the bottom of the collar and with a loop at the other end to allow the belly band to pass through it. It acts to prevent the collar from being pulled up. Yet this plow harness still differs from the Box Breeching/Western Style that is so common.

Box Breeching or Western Style Harness

What the box breeching/Western style harness has that the plow harness doesn't have is – surprise - the breeching. The breeching is part of the Stopping and Backing Component, which also includes quarter straps. The Support Component for the Box Breeching Harness includes the back straps, hip straps, rump pads and hip pads. In the case of a team harness of this style, the Stopping and Backing Component also includes the breast strap and pole strap.

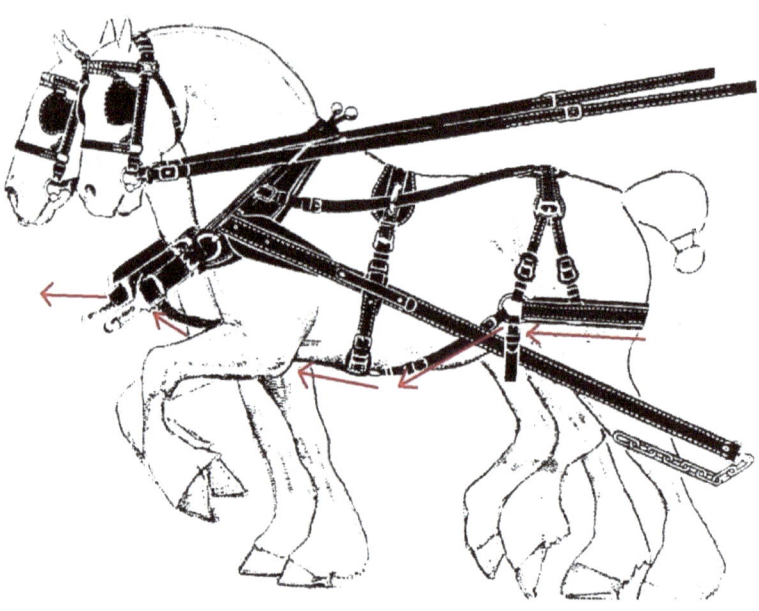

Box Breeching or Western Style Harness
Red arrows indicate stopping forces
reverse the arrows for backing forces

The red arrows in the drawing of the Box Breeching or Western Style Harness indicate the forces exerted during stopping. If a team of horses on a tongue is asked to slow down or stop a load, when the horses decelerate, the tongue and its load have forward momentum, so the tongue pushes forward on the neck yoke which pulls forward on the breast strap, which pulls forward on the pole strap, which pulls forward on the quarter straps, which pull forward on the breeching, against which the slowing horses hold steady or exert more pressure until their speed and their load's speed is equalized.

For backing, the red arrows in the drawing would be reversed. From a standing position, if a team of horses on a tongue is asked to back, they push into the breeching band, which pulls on the quarter straps, which pulls back on the pole strap, which pulls on the breast strap which pulls on the neck yoke attached to the tongue. In the case of a single horse in shafts, the backward pressure on the breeching band pulls back on the two hold back straps which are attached to each of the shafts of the load.

Looking back at the plow harness and the harness in Allen Picture #1, you can see that indeed they do not have a fully functioning Stopping and Backing Component because they lack the breeching and associated Support Components. Doc notes, "The plow harness does have a semblance of a Stopping and Backing Component that I think a lot of people rely on. The pole strap hooked to the neckyoke and belly band is expected to serve the function of a stopping and backing system. There's some capability there, but it's not very good."

We know that people use harnesses without effective stopping and backing capabilities on wheeled loads, as Dale Wagner's grandfather did, but using them in that way requires a brake or some other mechanism to hold back the load. Even some plows that have wheels and are used in hilly country must be operated skillfully if harness without breeching is used; teamsters must be prepared to drop the plow in the ground to slow it down for instance. Doc shares, "If you don't have breeching, you will need some kind of solution to keep the load from running up into the horses, and you'd better know how to operate it and be 'up in your riggin' at all times."

Butt chain or Short-Trace harness

A slight variation on the Western Style or Box Breeching Harness is the Butt Chain or Short-Trace harness. The name 'butt chain' comes from the fact that the chain on the trace disconnects from the trace at the butt rather than at the heel, as in heel chain traces. Where the chain meets the trace, there is a hook on the trace to accept the butt chain. A Western Style/Box Breeching Harness can be converted to a Butt Chain Harness by swapping out the traces and modifying the trace carriers.

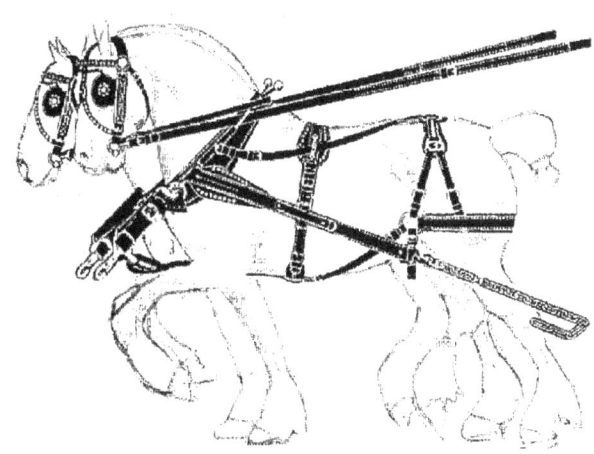

Butt Chain or Short-Trace harness
Courtesy Samson Harness Shop, Inc.

Doc shares how helpful he finds this sort of harness in logging applications. "My butt chains have a ring at one end, and I have singletrees specifically for butt chains that have rings instead of hooks. I thread the chain link end of the butt chains through the singletree rings and when the rings on the butt chains come up against the singletree rings, they won't go through, and they cannot come unhooked. To hitch the horses to the singletrees, the ends of the butt chains are hooked to the hooks on the end of the traces. When the horse or team walks off without a load, the singletree or team rigging drags behind with the chains full length where they won't hit the horse's heels. When hitching to a load (for maximum draft advantage and lift) I shorten the butt chains by simply pulling the butt chain rings forward and hooking them onto the trace hooks. This quickly and easily doubles and shortens the butt chains by half for pulling the load. No counting links or extra chain dangling or dragging. When dropping the load, I don't have to go clear to the ground to lengthen the chains to drag the rigging back on the ground empty. I simply pull the rings off the trace hooks at knee height and the chains lengthen as the horses walk away."

Doc continues, "If I'm hooking to singletrees with hooks instead of rings with this sort of harness, I hook the butt chain rings to the singletree hooks, and then hook to the trace hooks with whichever chain links give me the right adjustment."

This harness also allows the trace chains to be left attached to the singletree or vehicle. Leaving the trace chains elsewhere makes the harness lighter. Doc recalls, "One of reasons this type of harness was popular with the big hitches in wheat country and the big plow hitches was that the butt chains were separate from the harness. Say you had a combine hitch with as many as 33 horses on it. All the chains could be left on the singletrees. You could get everything set the way you liked it, then when you unhitch at end of the day, you unhook the chains from the trace, and leave them with the singletree. You don't have to take that weight on and off with the harness. When you hitch in the morning, all you had to do was hitch on the end link; you didn't have to count any links to drop and remember how many to drop for each horse."

Another advantage of this type of harness is that the traces are shorter and are less likely to be stepped on by the horses or to get soiled in muddy conditions. Doc adds, "Also, there's no hooking trace chains up on the hips when unhitching and taking them down to hitch up. I just pull the chains off the trace hooks and drop them."

In logging applications or other situations where horses are wearing calked shoes, the short traces being up out of the way keep the traces from being stepped on and damaged by the calks. In addition, when this type of harness is hung up for storage, the traces hang straight as opposed to with a long tug harness, the traces tend to bend in storage, especially if hung on a single hook.

A disadvantage of this type of harness is that if horses are moved between several pieces of equipment, it can be easy to lose track of the butt chains or lose them. Having multiple chains, one set for each piece of equipment, is one possible solution to the problem.

J.C. Allen Picture #2: Seeding oats with a team.
What is unusual about how this western/box breeching harness is being used?

J.C. Allen Picture #2

Allen Picture #2 shows a team hooked to an end-gate seeder; the team is wearing western/box breeching style harness. What is unusual about the way the near horse is harnessed?

It appears that the quarter strap on the near horse is hooked up to the backpad instead of down to the pole strap where it would normally be as part of the Stopping and Backing Component. Could it be that someone forgot to fasten this strap when they were harnessing? Or perhaps the horses were muddy, and the teamster didn't want to soil the strap? Since the ground appears to be extremely level, perhaps the teamster felt that the weight of the wagon and the roughness of the ground were sufficient slowing and stopping forces.

In extreme cases with using harness in this way, the belly band could come up behind the horses' elbows. The red arrows in the harness diagram at right illustrate the force of a slowing wagon on the harness via the tongue. Without the quarter straps attached to the pole straps, the horses are forced to take the strain of slowing, stopping, or backing the load on the collar and back pad/belly band system which could jeopardize the comfort of the horses and therefore jeopardize safety.

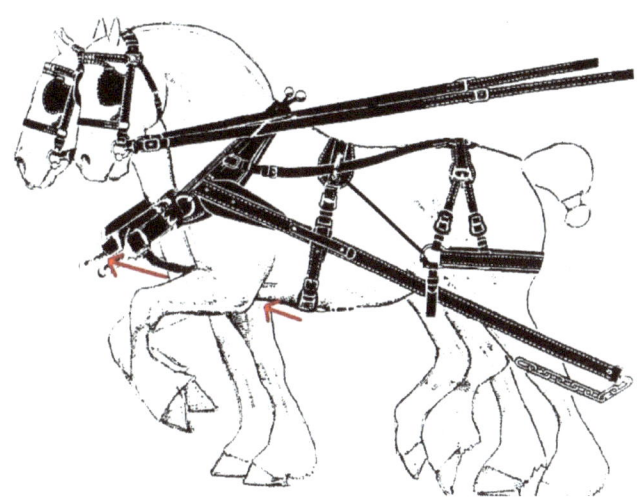

Western or box breeching with quarter strap attached to backpad instead of pole strap
Red arrows show force of slowing wagon on harness and horse

J.C. Allen Picture #3: Two wagon loads of cotton begin their journey to the mill.
What is unusual about how this harness is being used?

J.C. Allen Picture #3:

Allen Picture #3 shows a team hooked to a lead and a trail wagon. Is the team wearing western/box breeching harness or plow harness? The team is wearing plow harness, which means it doesn't have breeching, which is part of the Stopping and Backing Component. These wagons represent a pretty heavy load. The teamster may be compensating for the lack of Stopping and Backing Component in his harness by the levelness of the ground, feeling he can ease the wagons to a stop. He must also not need backing power.

Mac, a visitor to the *Rural Heritage* Front Porch, explains his reasoning for using plow harness in a similar situation:

"I've got two sets of harness: one wagon harness and one for plowing. I'd say I've pulled the wagon more with the plow gear than I have with the wagon harness. I don't like adjustments and I don't like heavy either. I use my plow harness for everything except going to town in the buggy or wagon. It's my experience when you get up at 5 and go to the field, you don't want to be making adjustments in the dark. Chuck the gear on and go." (3)

Doc observes, "Obviously Mac is capable of taking care of his horses and making sure he uses the brake so that he never lets the wagon run into the horses. I once heard Neil Dimmock say that brakes cause more problems than they solve because they make people think they can stop their horses if they run away. Neil said, 'You don't need brakes; the brakes are between a horse's ears.' While plow harness on wagons may work for experienced teamsters like Mac and Neil, I still advise my students that they need a fully functioning Stopping and Backing Component including breeching, if they're going to pull wheeled loads safely and comfortably. Brakes are meant to help hold back vehicles and equipment, not stop horses. On my harness, the Stopping and Backing Component can be quickly and easily removed by simply unsnapping the hip straps from the hip pads and unbuckling the collar straps to detach the pole straps. It's there when I need it and gone when I don't."

J.C. Allen Picture #4: Cultivating corn.
What added feature does this box breeching/western style harness have?

J.C. Allen Picture #4

Allen Picture #4 shows a three-abreast on a cultivator. The horses are wearing a type of box breeching/western style harness. However, on the near horse the harness has a feature that is not common on this style of harness. There is a hip drop with a lead line snapped from there to a hame ring. What function might this feature serve? In many towns during the horse era, there were laws requiring that horses that were driven into town must be able to be tied at a hitching rail. Harness makers provided the optional hip drop on harness for tying up a lead line to facilitate compliance with such laws.

You may also notice that this harness is fancier than it needs to be for farming. It has 'spots' in many places (metal ornamentation), has fancier hames than in the previous pictures, and has terrets on the backpad for the lines to pass through. Perhaps the farmer always wanted his horses to look nice when working, or perhaps he was a breeder and needed his breeding stock to be shown at their best.

One other difference between the harness in Allen Picture #4 and typical box breeching/western style harness is that back straps aren't visible running from the hames through loops on the back pad to the rump pad. The function of the back straps is to keep the collar from falling forward when the horse puts its head down. Perhaps there is a strap not visible here from the top of the collar to the rump pad that serves this function.

Doc adds, "Most western style harness has double back straps angling from the hames to the rump pad to keep the hip plate from sliding sideways off the hips. On single back strap style harness, you need a crupper to stabilize the hip plate. I would guess that these horses were most likely wearing cruppers."

J.C. Allen Picture #5: Planting corn in a dusty field
How does the adjustment of the breeching on these horses look to you?

J.C. Allen Picture #5

The function of the breeching is to give the horse something to push back against when asked to slow or stop a load or back a load. However, if the breeching is set too low, the horses are in danger of having their rear leg function interfered with or their rear legs pushed forward out from under them when slowing, holding back, or backing a significant load.

46

Doc says, "There seem to be a lot of misconceptions about how breeching should be adjusted. I feel there's only one way for it to be adjusted: the way that allows the horse to do its job safely and comfortably. What many folks don't realize is that when horses counteract the push of the load or back a load with breeching, their body length compresses which lets the rump pad slide rearwards and in turn the breeching moves several inches lower. Therefore, if the breeching when not engaged looks like it does in Allen Picture #5, then when the horse's body length compresses and engages the breeching, this breeching will even be lower and much more of a safety issue. Breeching set too low is one of the most common harness adjustment problems there is."

Breeching adjusted just right.
Photo courtesy Doc Hammill.

Doc continues, "The breeching should be adjusted so that it sits just below the point of the buttock. If you run your hand slowly from above the point of the buttock down the rump (near the tail) to the back of the thigh, you will feel a continuous curve until just below the point of the buttock where it flattens slightly for a few inches before the curve resumes. The breeching should be adjusted so it rides on that flattened portion of the buttock. Too high and it could ride up under the tail; too low and it will interfere with the horse's ability to use its rear legs, keep its balance, and control the load."

In Allen Picture #5, what do you think about the adjustment of the breeching? Doc comments, "The breeching on the bay is several inches too low and on the gray it is extremely low. While both these breechings should be adjusted higher, I've seen a lot worse."

Doc continues, "The quarter strap on the near horse is snapped into the trace instead of into the pole strap. Why might this be the case? Perhaps the horses were kicking at flies and the teamster didn't want them to hang a foot up. Perhaps it was just expediency; the teamster knew that he was working level ground and had quite a bit of drag from his load so he didn't feel the need for a fully functioning Stopping and Backing Component."

Yankee/Hip Breeching Style

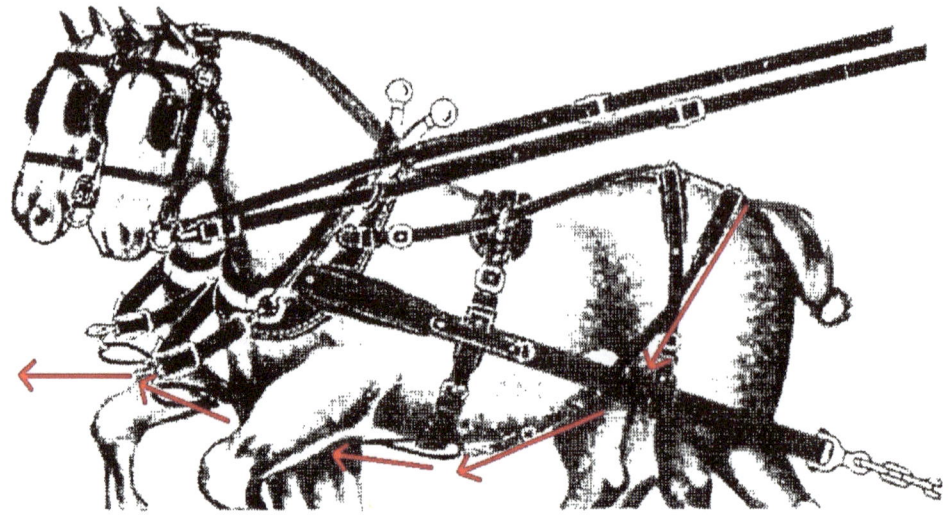

Yankee/hip breeching style harness.
This harness has a different Stopping and Backing Component.
The red arrows show the forces when the horses are asked to slow or stop a load.

A variation on the Stopping and Backing Component of the western style harness is called Yankee or Hip Breeching (sometimes also called Mormon harness.) "The advantage of the Yankee brichen is that the weight of the load when the horse is backing pushes down on the horse's rump. This provides better traction than the box-type brichen, which tends to push the horse forward." (4) Note that Yankee breeching works well for teams but not for a single horse in shafts.

The Yankee/ Hip Breeching Harness requires a variation in the Support Component as well. There is a crupper to which the Yankee Breeching is attached to keep the breeching in place just above the tail head.

In the diagram of the Yankee/Hip Breeching Harness, the red arrows indicate the forces when the team is asked to slow or stop a load. When the horses slow, the momentum of the load pushes the tongue and attached neck yoke forward which pulls the breast strap and the pole strap forward, which pulls down and forward on the quarter straps, which pulls down and forward on the breeching, against which the horse pushes.

Rural Heritage Front Porch visitors make these comments about Yankee or hip breeching harness:
- "The [breeching] crosses above the animals' tail on the croup rather than below across the hams. I like it because there is less movement closer to the joint so there is less chance for chafing. The line from the croup to the neck yoke passes through the center of gravity of the animal, and there is a little less leather involved." (5)
- "That is what I use and I like them. They seem to be lighter and you don't have any straps under their butt to get pooped on. Also, when stopping or backing, it pulls down on their rear end instead of pushing on the back of their legs." (6)
- "We use the Yankee breeching a lot. It is lighter and cooler, but we use it because mules seem to be able to back a heavy load and hold better. Works well in Tennessee hills." (7)

- "This design is excellent if you back or hold heavy loads as it uses the most muscular part of the butt and can never pull the legs out from under when the britchen is dropped too low. And yes, it does eliminate manure on the britchen although it does require a crupper so that needs to be kept clean." (8)

Similar to concerns about defecation on breeching, Doc bought Yankee breeching to replace the box breeching on one set of his harness because of issues with urination. "Every time my mare Misty urinated in harness, she hit the breeching and splattered urine all over her hind legs. Not so with Yankee breeching. It didn't matter how high or low I adjusted the box breeching, she would hit it. The final decision to invest in the Yankee breeching was out of consideration for Misty."

Doc continues, "On the steep mountain roads of the west, this sort of harness was common. It is also popular for bobsleds because the downward pressure on the hips provides better traction for horses holding back loads on snow and ice. I even had a man tell me that an old timer told him that a horse could back as much with a Yankee breeching as he could pull; not so with a box breeching."

A combination of box breeching and Yankee/Hip Breeching is called basket breeching. According to Dale Wagner, "The Kitteredge ranch used both hip and butt breeching together on buckrakes. This was because after being on a buckrake for a long time, when you ran a tooth in the ground, the horses had a tendency to fly back and break breeching especially when it had some age on it." (9)

Doc shares, "Jerry Lee from Oregon tells of his grandfather using basket breeching on his big lumber wagon for maximum hold back and backing capability for big heavy loads. Also, if one system failed the other would maintain function."

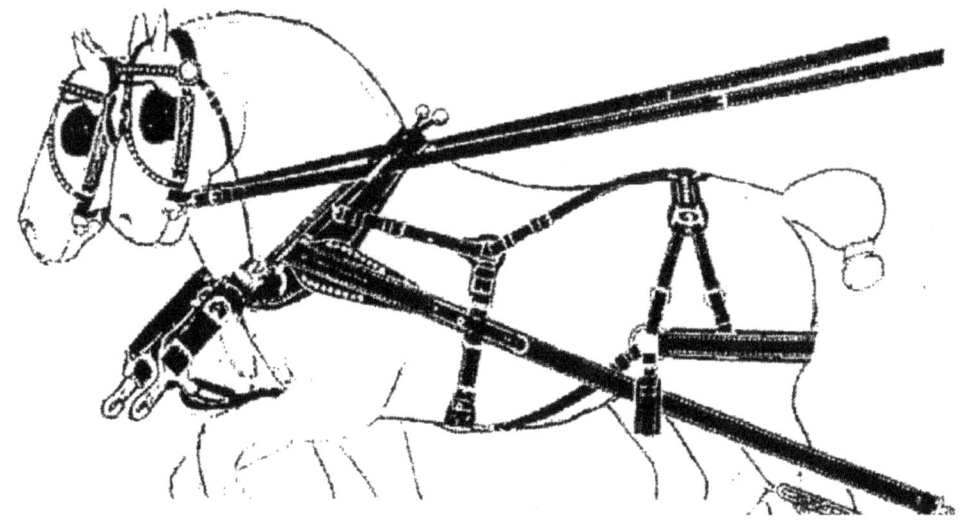

Y Back or Market Tug Harness
courtesy Samson Harness Shop, Inc.

Y-Back Style

A departure from the box breeching/western style harness is the Y-Back, Dakota, or Market Tug Harness. This harness type lacks a back pad/saddle, and the back strap is broken into two pieces, one from the rump pad to the top of the market strap and one from top of the market strap to the hames. The name 'market tug' for this harness may be confusing to some people because the terms tug and trace are often interchanged. In the name 'market tug harness,' tug refers to the harness pieces from the hame to the rump pad; there are two pieces, a shoulder strap and a back strap, instead of one, the back strap as in the Box Breeching harness.

In the Box Breeching/Western Style harness, when the horse lowers its head, it pulls the collar forward, which pulls the breeching up. In the Y-Back harness, when the horse lowers its head, the breeching stays in place. This harness was commonly used in the large grain-harvesting hitches of Oregon and Washington where hitches of 33 mules, horses, or combinations of both were common. These hitches typically had five tiers of six abreast with 3 abreast in the lead. The logistics of feeding and watering the equines during the work day were significant. Often the horses or mules were left hitched together in their rows for feeding and watering, so it was important for the efficiency of the work that their harnesses stay in place. The Y Back harness was a significant enabler of efficiency because it allowed the equines to be fed and watered in harness without harness adjustments needing to be made afterwards since the collars weren't pulling the breeching forward with the back straps.

When working, horses tend to sweat first under the backpad. The Y-back harness is often preferred in hot sunny locations because it lacks a backpad. The absence of the backpad also reduces the weight of the harness by a small amount.

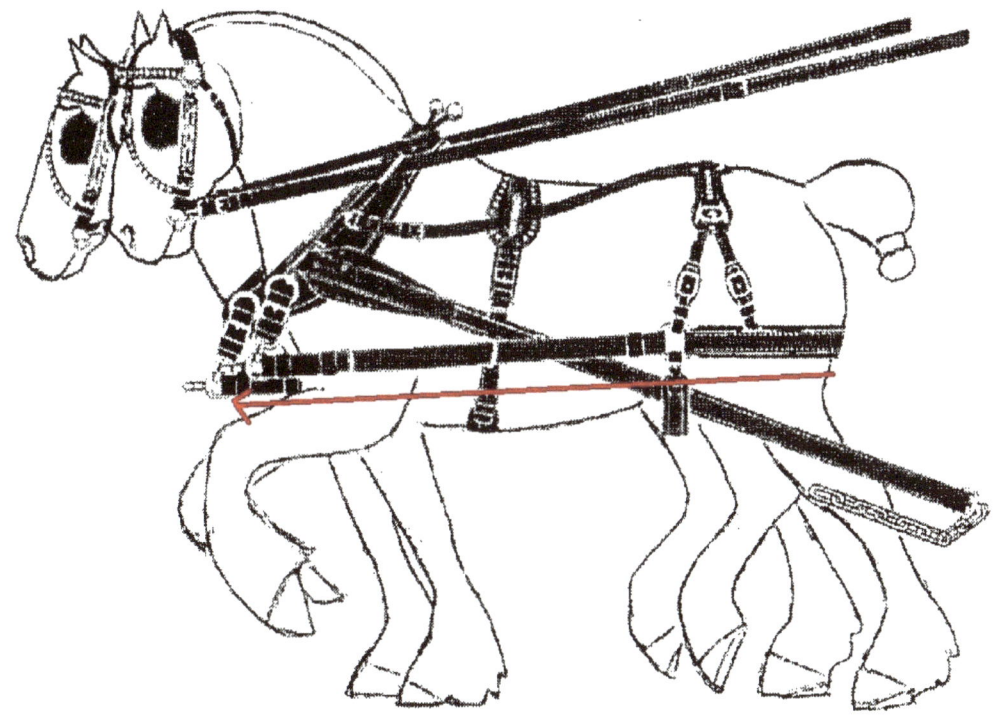

Sidebacker Harness.
This harness has a different Stopping and Backing Component.
The red arrows indicate the forces when slowing or stopping a load.

Sidebacker Style

Like the Yankee/Hip Breeching Harness, the Sidebacker Harness has a different Stopping and Backing Component from the Box Breeching/Western Style Harness. (The Sidebacker is also known as the Boston Backer Harness.) The breeching is connected straight forward to a jockey yoke that then connects to the neck yoke. Note how the forces, indicated by the red line in the drawing, are more direct when the horse is backing in this harness than in the Box Breeching/Western Style harness.

Doc observes, "It's very easy to convert conventional box breeching harness to this style; you don't have to buy all new. Note how the breeching and hip straps are the same here as they are in the Box Breeching harness. The difference is between the breeching ring and the neck yoke connection. Rather than the breeching connecting to a pole strap with quarter straps, we instead have side straps. We don't have a pole strap; the side straps replace both the quarter and pole straps. We don't have a breast strap either; it's replaced by a pair of jack straps or jockey straps. Jack straps suspend a jockey yoke (also called twin yoke or double yoke) from the hames, replacing the breast strap as the system that holds the neck yoke and tongue up. When my back was real bad, it was a lot easier to harness with this harness; the only thing I had to bend over to do was buckle the belly band; not quarter straps one on each side. When your back hurts, it's a big help to not bend over so often."

Rural Heritage Front Porch visitors make these comments about the Sidebacker Harness:
- I use the sidebacker harness and love it. I was using harness with the quarter straps and pole strap. One day while hooking up to a stiff tongue wagon one of my mules got his hind leg

caught in a quarter strap while stepping across the tongue. I live in the mountains. Use them a lot for holding back. Sometimes the pole strap would gall the inside of their front legs. Sidebackers don't do that. (10)

- Two advantages to the side backer are working pregnant mares without the up pressure of the belly backer's quarter straps and less chance of a wreck when horses are trying to knock insects off their bellies in fly season. (11)
- Never get a more complicated or heavier harness than you need. Buckrake, header, or push binder is about the only place you need a side backer style. If you have a tongue, the belly backer is all you need. (12)
- The disadvantage of a side backer is the tongue can raise up high as the horses back. I think it comes down to what you are used to. (13)
- [When] horses were commonly used for farm work around here (especially in steep hills) most used side backer harness and D-ring traces. They still used the pole straps and martingales hooked into the belly band to hold the neck yoke at the right height. The jockey yokes sat behind the neck yoke instead of on top of it and were only responsible for holding back the load and not holding up the pole. I'm assuming this was to stop the pole from lifting. In my opinion this is getting the best of both worlds. (14)

One feature of the sidebacker harness shown in the drawing above is a ring on the belly band billet through which the side strap passes. This ring serves two functions. First, it holds the side strap up in place. Second, it acts to prevent significant upward motion of the tongue above the belly band billet.

Doc adds, "They used the sidebacker with breast strap and pole strap on a lot of the logging sleds in western Montana in the old days. If a horse in the pole team fell down, it would tend to be pulled along rather than spill out of the harness and get run over by the sled. There was a basket of straps down the sides, under the belly, and between their front legs to drag them along until the sled stopped.

"One disadvantage of the sidebacker is that it can allow the tongue to swing side to side more than the bellybacker depending on the breast strap style. My first experience with this problem was raking hay with a dump rake on a rough field; the mower wasn't too bad, but on the dump rake, if one wheel hit an irregularity, it tended to swing the tongue sideways. The first morning the rake tongue was hitting the horses in the front legs, so I took the foam pad that I was sleeping on and wrapped it around the tongue. That night I went home and got quarter straps, breast straps, and pole straps and converted back to a bellybacker style. There was no problem whatsoever then."

New England/D-Ring Harness

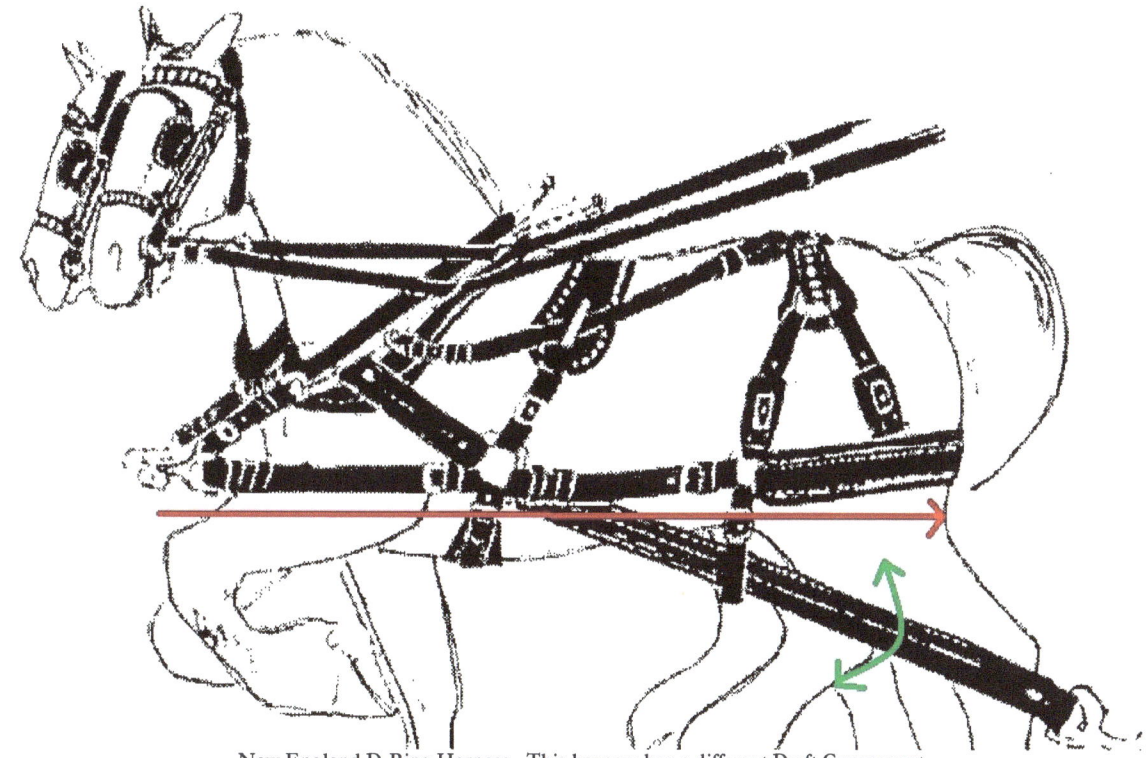

New England D-Ring Harness. This harness has a different Draft Component as well as a different Stopping and Backing Component. The red lines show the forces when slowing or stopping. The green line shows how the trace can move up and down without changing the angle of draft at the collar.

The New England D-Ring Harness has a different Draft Component compared to all the other harnesses discussed so far. It is designed to keep the angle of the trace at the collar fixed at the ideal angle of ninety degrees while the position of the trace attached to the load can change. The intent is to maximize the transfer of power from the horse to moving the load. Some D-ring harnesses have more range of motion than others, depending on the room on the ring for the leather to slide.

In addition, this harness is intended to transfer the weight of the tongue to the backpad rather than having it pull down on the collar as it does with the other harness designs. This feature is accomplished by adjusting the traces and neck yoke so that the tongue is suspended rather than a dead weight attached at only the neck yoke, as in the Box Breeching harness.

Disadvantages often cited about this harness include that it is heavy and it is hotter for the horses in warm weather. It also requires very specific adjustments to work correctly.

Rural Heritage Front Porch visitors have shared the following about D-Ring harness:
- I've used d-ring harness for 7 or 8 years now and would be hard-pressed to go back to standard harness. I agree … that they really do make a difference at the end of a long day in the field or woods. (15)
- The only problem that I have ever had with a D ring is that they are heavy. My Suffolks work on many different kinds of equipment and the point of draft can change without

adjusting the harness. Working a heavy load in the hills of Vermont, a D ring with jockey yokes keeps the horse square with the pole when being pushed down a steep hill.... To be set up right it needs to be tight from the jockey yoke to the evener to have the pole weight on the back pad. (16)

A 1917 harness catalog shows a New England Harness (shown in drawing at right). How does this harness differ from the New England/D-Ring harness previously shown? The 1917 version lacks a backpad. What is the implication of this harness not having a backpad? The function of the backpad in modern-day New England harness is to accept the weight of the pole. The 1917 version of this harness was apparently expected to be used in an application where there wasn't pole weight; perhaps with the types of poles/tongues that are self-supporting.

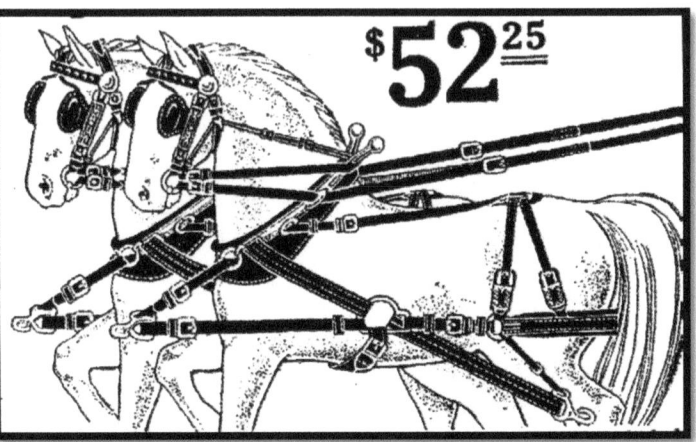

Charles William Stores catalog, New York City, circa 1917,
Richland Special New England Farm Harness
courtesy Samson Harness Shop, Inc.

Doc comments, "Even though the trace is free to change its angle up or down behind the ring on a D-Ring Harness, one should be careful to avoid extremes. A trace pulling at a more upward angle than ideal behind the ring can apply force upward on the belly band, and a trace pulling at a more downward angle (less common) can pull down on the backpad. Either of these can cause discomfort for the horse and therefore can potentially create safety issues. An important purpose of the belly band on any harness is to maintain a 90 degree angle of draft on the collar if the traces pull up too high. A straight line of draft from hames all the way to the hitch point, and the proper 90 degree angle of draft off of the hame, is always preferable."

Norwegian Harness

Norwegian Harness has a different Draft Component as well as different Stopping and Backing and Support Components.

Norwegian harness is considered by some to be the inspiration for New England/D-Ring harness. As with the New England harness, Norwegian harness incorporates a different Draft Component, and it also has a different Stopping and Backing Component as well as a different Support Component.

Like the New England harness, Norwegian harness is designed to keep the angle of the trace at the collar fixed at the ideal of ninety degrees. Unlike the New England harness, the trace in the Norwegian harness ends at the ring, and all loads are attached there, either via traces for skidding or via shafts (teams are worked in a double shaft set-up). Also unlike all the harnesses previously discussed, the Norwegian harness features an integrated collar and hames with adjustments top and bottom to accommodate changes in the shape of the neck over the course of the seasons.

The Stopping and Backing Component differs from the New England in that there is an extra padded strap (ring girth) under the belly designed to hit behind the elbows in case the breeching system for stopping isn't sufficient. The Support Component differs in the backpad. Because the backpad is intended to take significant strain from the load, it is a bow with two separate pads on either side of the backbone behind the withers. Another difference from the New England harness in the Support Component is that the belly band doesn't go to/through the ring, so that the ring is less congested and can be set farther forward to accommodate the ring girth.

Harness Variety

With the exception of the Norwegian Harness, the various harness types mentioned above are those commonly in use today. They are depicted in books about draft horses and included in harness catalogs. However, there are several harness types that do not show up in these places because the jobs they helped accomplish no longer exist. Special harnesses, for instance, were used for stagecoaches, for hauling freight, and for express deliveries, activities that are no longer provided with horsepower except in re-enactment circumstances. How did these harnesses differ in the various Components? See the next chapter to explore this question.

Doc always emphasizes safety, function, and comfort when talking to clients about harness. "Safety and comfort go together. Most of the behavior problems we see with horses are caused by some sort of physical discomfort. Some say it's as much as 80%, with the remaining 20% of the problems caused by something psychological."

One *Rural Heritage* Front Porch visitor aptly concluded: "[There] are as many styles of harness as there are harness makers and at least that many reasons one is better than the other." (17) It's up to us as teamsters to understand how the various Components of harness work together so that we can choose the right harness type for the jobs we have to do with our horses.

Extra credit questions

1) How would you rate the breeching adjustment in the harness drawings in this article? Doc observes, "In all cases except the Yankee/Hip Breeching, the breeching is set well below the point of the buttock. I'd like to have the artist raise those breechings up at least the width of the breeching band and in some cases even more."
2) How would you rate the trace angle in the harness drawings in this article? Doc notes, "In nearly all cases, the angle of the trace at the hames isn't ninety degrees, so it isn't optimal for converting the horse's push into the collar into forward movement. When the angle differs from ninety degrees, there is also the potential for draft activity to damage the shoulder. Even in the two D-ring drawings the angle isn't optimal. Regardless of the style of harness, it is extremely important that the traces leave the hames at a 90 degree angle from the line of the hame/collar/shoulder. Otherwise the forces of pulling a load can have potentially damaging consequences on the animal's shoulders."

Doc concludes, "Unfortunately, incorrect angles of draft, broken lines of draft, and breechings set way too low are very common in diagrams, harness catalogs, and photographs. They provide bad examples for folks who may not know better. I feel those of us with some depth of understanding have a responsibility to share what we have been fortunate to learn and experience to the benefit of our fellow teamsters and for the welfare of the animals."

1) Bowers, Steve and Marlen Steward. *Farming with Horses*, MBI Publishing Company, St. Paul, MN, 2006, p. 10.
2) Response by Dale Wagner, "Disadvantages to the D-ring Harness?" at http://ruralheritage.com/messageboard/frontporch/15722.htm, timestamp 2012-01-27 02:16:17

3) Response by Mac ,"Disadvantages to the D-ring Harness?" at http://ruralheritage.com/messageboard/frontporch/15722.htm, timestamp 2012-02-03 00:26:11
4) http://www.stitchnhitch.com/optattachm.htm
5) Response by Bob E , "Yankee Britchen" at http://ruralheritage.com/messageboard/frontporch/15000.htm, timestamp 2011-07-25 09:30:57
6) Response by Marshall, "Yankee Britchen" at http://ruralheritage.com/messageboard/frontporch/15000.htm, timestamp 2011-07-25 10:04:31
7) Response by Mark, "Yankee Britchen" at http://ruralheritage.com/messageboard/frontporch/15000.htm, timestamp 2011-07-25 13:25:48
8) Response by Stitch N Hitch Harness Shop (signed Mari Leedy), "Yankee Britchen" at http://ruralheritage.com/messageboard/frontporch/15000.htm, timestamp 2011-08-01 18:02:13
9) http://albrechtsanimals.typepad.com/understanding_harness/2013/03/breeching-basket.html
10) Response by TLR, "Sidebacker" at http://ruralheritage.com/messageboard/frontporch/9450.htm, timestamp 2007-07-27 14:06:54
11) Response by Neal in Iowa, "Difference between a belly-backer and side-backer harness" at http://ruralheritage.com/messageboard/frontporch/14016.htm, timestamp 2010-12-17 17:09:40
12) Response by Dale Wagner, "Difference between a belly-backer and side-backer harness" at http://ruralheritage.com/messageboard/frontporch/14016.htm, timestamp 2010-12-17 10:35:50
13) Response by KM, "Difference between a belly-backer and side-backer harness" at http://ruralheritage.com/messageboard/frontporch/14016.htm, timestamp 2010-12-18 08:52:59
14) Response by Chris F., "Difference between a belly-backer and side-backer harness" at http://ruralheritage.com/messageboard/frontporch/14016.htm, timestamp 2010-12-18 18:36:50
15) Response by aherzog, "Disadvantages to the D-ring Harness?" at http://ruralheritage.com/messageboard/frontporch/15722.htm, timestamp 2012-01-31 10:12:01
16) Response by Peter, "Disadvantages to the D-ring Harness?" at http://ruralheritage.com/messageboard/frontporch/15722.htm, timestamp 2012-02-02 15:46:18
17) Response by KM, "Disadvantages to the D-ring Harness?" at http://ruralheritage.com/messageboard/frontporch/15722.htm, timestamp 2012-01-25 22:25:18

The black and white photographs in this chapter are from America's Rural Yesterday, Volume I: Fieldwork *published by Mischka Press and are used with permission.*

Why Understand Harness?

Why is it important to understand harness? At a clinic, Doc Hammill helped a student with a beautiful team of Haflingers by suggesting some adjustments to their harness. Because their check reins were very tight and adjusted very short, Doc then lengthened the check reins by at least ten inches. On the next day of the clinic, the student was seen sitting on his wagon in the lane between the barns with his team standing quietly. When asked "How are you today?" he replied, with a big smile on his face, "Just great. I'm sitting here enjoying watching these horses finally be comfortable and willing to stand still. They've never stood quietly like this in the three years I've had them." What's different, he was asked. He replied, "Doc lengthened the check reins; I can't believe the difference."

The student had been around horses for years, but this was his first experience with horses in harness. He was using the harness that came with the team, adjusted the way the previous owners had adjusted it. The student knew his team wasn't comfortable because they would never stand still, but he didn't understand what needed to be done to help them. His relief from finally getting some help for his horses was evident after he understood his horses' harness better.

Doc explains, "Some of the things that are being done with harness these days - changes in design, changes in material - some are better and some are worse. A lot of people out there making harness don't have generations of knowledge or practical working horse experience. They don't have the firsthand experience for why one thing is an advantage or disadvantage. In some ways it feels like some new harness is taking us backward in terms of safety, function, and comfort. That's why it's so important that we as teamsters have some depth of understanding about our harness."

Virgil Weaver, West Point, Indiana, harrows with a hitch of white mules.
J.C. Allen photo from *America's Rural Yesterday, Volume I: Fieldwork* published by Mischka Press and used with permission.

One harness maker that has a lifetime of knowledge and practical working horse experience is Bernie Samson of Samson Harness Shop, Inc. in Gilbert, Minnesota. Bernie answers the "why understand harness" question this way: "Why does a person have to understand how a car or a truck or an internal combustion engine runs if they're going to drive it? Because they need to get the most efficient use of the vehicle. If you want to get the most efficient use out of your animal, you have to have a basic rudimentary understanding of what the various harness parts do and how they work. The harness and how it works affect the horse's willingness and ability to pull and the safety of the horse and the teamster. You don't have to know the depth and detail that a harness maker knows, but you have to know something or at some point something will happen that will stop you in your tracks."

Image of a neck strap harness from Trajan's column in Rome, circa 113AD. What are your thoughts about this harness?
Photo courtesy Wikipedia.com

Harness on Trajan's Column

The previous chapter explored the components of the equine harness system: Draft, Communication, Stopping and Backing, and Support. It also described common harness types in use today. With that background, it's interesting to look at images from history and compare them to how we work with horses now. For instance, there is an image of a horse in harness on Trajan's Column in Rome, dated from 113AD. The image shows a horse in a harness consisting of a loop around the horse's neck with a single "trace" from the top of the loop back to the load. What are your thoughts about this harness?

Several thoughts come to mind. First, horses are amazingly accommodating creatures, letting us put them to work, sometimes in difficult conditions. Second, from a safety standpoint, there is no Stopping and Backing Component on this harness (no breeching or even a belly band). From the effort that the person is shown putting into turning the cart's wheels, though, it's likely that stopping and backing were not the highest priority for this teamster and his team.

From a functional standpoint, the Draft Component of this harness does not allow for maximum conversion of horse power to movement of loads; the connection point (top of the neck) is too far above the center of gravity of the animal (midpoint of the chest). In addition, the conversion of horse power to movement of loads would be constrained by the pressure of the neck strap on the equine's neck muscles, nerves, windpipe, and carotid artery. Therefore, from both a functional and comfort-of-the horse standpoint, this harness is far from ideal. To improve conversion of power and improve comfort of the horse, then, it's no wonder that breast strap and then neck collar harness were developed, moving the point of draft closer to the center of gravity of the animal, off of the neck and onto the chest and shoulders.

"I have learned a tremendous amount," says Doc, "about how it feels for horses to pull a load by pulling loads myself. I've pulled loads under widely varying circumstances of terrain, grade, and footing. I've used garden carts forever, I've pulled a sled with hay on it, I've pulled a tire a really long way because I had a flat that I couldn't fix. Whenever I'm pulling a load or holding it back going downhill, I think about horses and how it feels for them both physically and psychologically.

"The most effective way for me to pull a load isn't with a strap around my neck. It's with a cinch around my waist near my center of gravity. Even a strap up around my shoulders puts forces on my spine and upper body that limit my ability to pull. If I put it around my waist, I can pull from my hips with much more power and efficiency. Pulling loads myself and figuring out how to pull them efficiently has helped me learn how to look at harness and see how it's helping or impeding the horse's ability to do its job. Then I can help people adjust their harness appropriately for safety, comfort, and function."

US Military Harness

The US military harness shown in the photograph incorporates a saddle into the harness system. The rider seated in the saddle drove the horses, often four or six up. Why might this be the case?

In some cases, there was no accommodation for the driver on the implement being pulled, such as a cannon. In some cases there was a desire to maximize space for cargo, in the case of wagons. And often these sorts of harness were put to use because it was what was approved by the government decision-makers and therefore

US Military Six Mule Wagon team harness (near wheel).
Why might there be a saddle integrated into the harness?
photo courtesy The National Archives

acceptable for purchase, even if a different harness system would have better suited the situation.

An uncommon implementation of the Communication Component: the teamster is driving from a mounted position.
Cultivating sudan grass, Plains Kansas, 1932
J.C. Allen photo from *America's Rural Yesterday, Volume I: Fieldwork* published by Mischka Press and used with permission.

A picture from *America's Rural Yesterday: Volume I Fieldwork* shows a similar implementation of the Communication Component, with a mounted teamster driving a team of four cultivating sudan grass in Plains, Kansas, 1932.

Doc Hammill observes that "On big, long string hitches on freight wagons, it was very common for the teamster to ride the near wheel horse. Of course that meant that horse was doing two jobs, so it was common to put a bigger stronger animal in that position to compensate to some degree."

In addition, Bernie Samson observes, "On some of the big circus wagons, when they needed extra power for soft ground for instance, they'd add hook rope teams that were driven from someone riding the near wheeler, usually with no saddle, just like in the Allen photo."

Stagecoach Harness

Harness catalogs dating from the 1880s still show coaching harness; catalogs from the 1920s do not. Trains began replacing stagecoaches starting in the 1860s. How would you expect stagecoach harness to differ from draft harness? The loads weren't insignificant, and speed was an important consideration. Stagecoach harness, then, was strong but light with just enough leather in the straps to achieve the desired function without unnecessary weight and just enough straps to accomplish the work without any extras.

How would you expect stagecoach harness to differ from draft harness?
Photo courtesy Hansen Wheel and Wagon Shop www.hansenwheel.com

Doc's student with the Haflingers was using harness that had come with the horses. When Doc adjusted the harness, it wasn't the harness adjustments that made the most difference for the horses, it was letting out the check rein. "The average person looking at them wouldn't have noticed," says Doc. "We often have an idea in our heads about what horses should look like in harness and we don't stop to think if that image is consistent with what's best for the horse." Bernie Samson adds, "Every horse's conformation is different. Just because we see one horse in harness going well with a certain head set doesn't mean our horse can do the same."

Bernie continues, "People often buy harness because of the way it looks rather than what they really need. Maybe they think wider straps look better on their big horse than are necessary for draft work, or maybe they come from a tradition that requires a certain look that doesn't necessarily conform to function. Maybe they think they need a full Western harness because that's what draft harness is supposed to look like when in reality a plow harness is good enough. Most people in the draft horse world would look at that stagecoach harness and think it's way too light for serious work. They'd be surprised."

Cart Harness

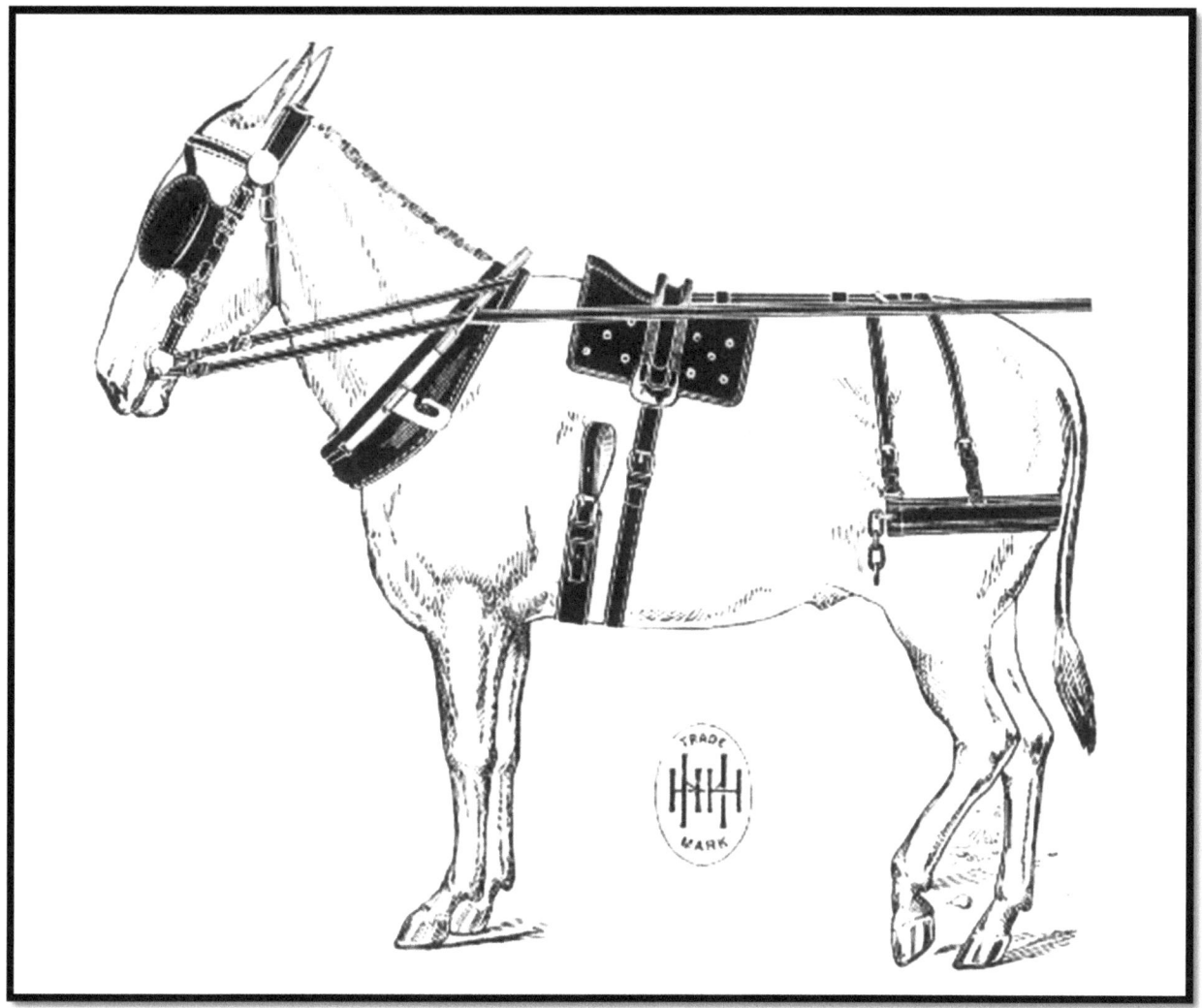

No. 499 Dump Cart Harness from Heiser catalog, courtesy www.cabincreekcds.com
How would you put this harness to use?

"It pays to hitch to the House of Heiser"

This slogan appears at the bottom of every page of Catalogue No. 21, circa 1920, of The Hermann H. Heiser Manufacturing and Selling Company based in Denver, Colorado. The Heiser catalog was published near the end of the horse-drawn era, after trains had replaced stagecoaches and cars had replaced buggies and light vehicles as people-moving modes. All of the harness depicted with one exception is draft harness since at that time tractors had not yet displaced horses on farms.

The Dump Cart Harness from the Heiser catalog lacks traces. How might that harness be put to use? An illustration from *Mosemans' Illustrated Guide for Purchasers of Horse Furnishing Goods* answers this question. The Moseman catalog was published around 1880 by C.M. Moseman and Brother in New York City (with branches in London, Paris, Berlin, and Moscow). One entire floor of their store in New York was devoted to harness. The catalog contains illustrations of a wide range of harness, from racing to driving to heavy hauling, indicating its publication before the horse-drawn era began to wane.

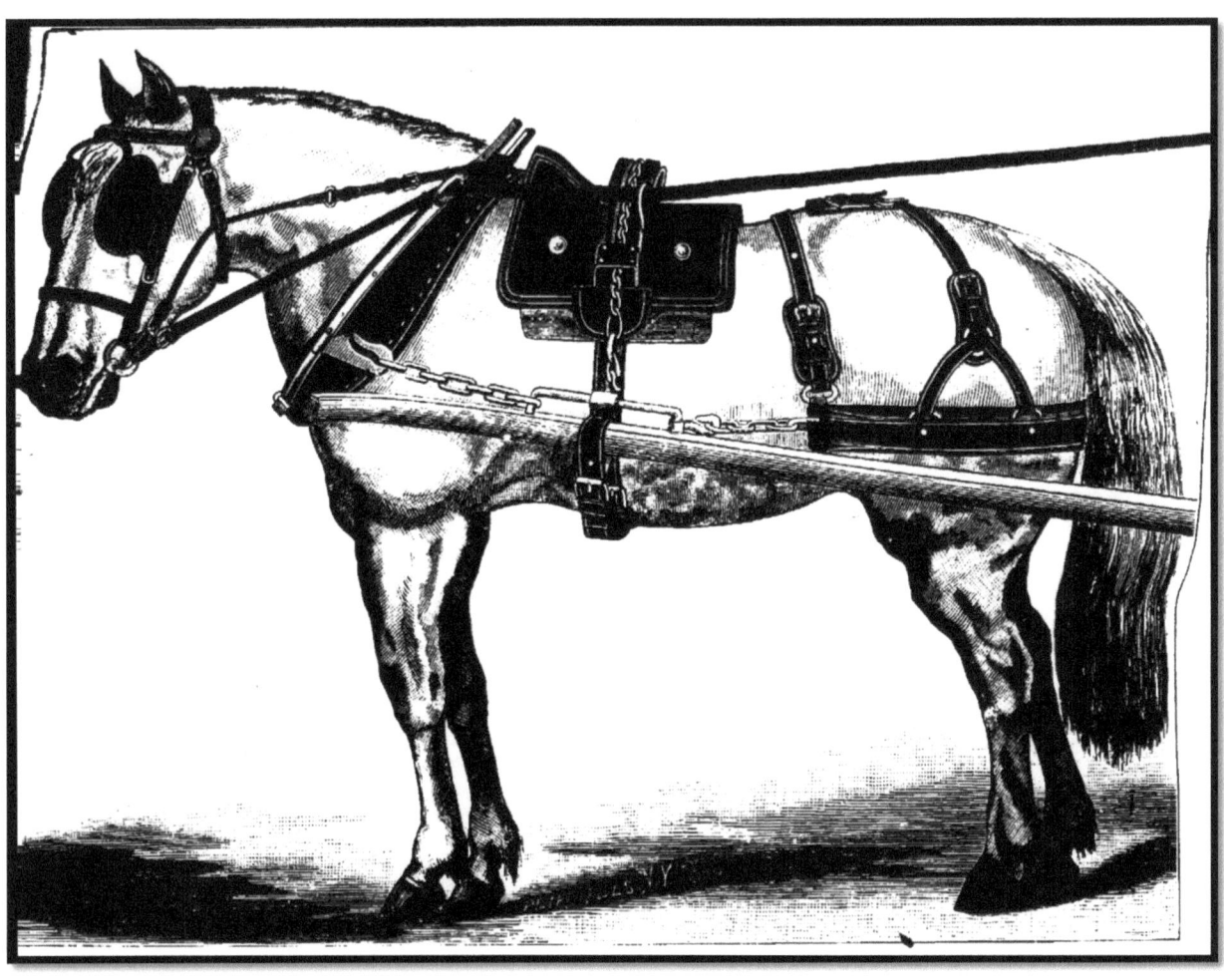

Moseman Cart harness 1755. Courtesy Samson Harness Shop, Inc.

Moseman cart harness #1755 illustrates how the Heiser Dump Cart Harness was put to use, showing that the harness is connected to the shaft at the belly band via three chains, one to the hame, one over the saddle, and one to the breeching.

Doc observes, "The Heiser image shows an unfortunately tight check rein; there's no room to put the head down or nose out to do a good job of pulling. We see that a lot in these drawings and diagrams and unfortunately everywhere we go in real life, too. It's no wonder that people like our student don't see the problem with their horses when these images are so common."

Bernie adds, "The Moseman cart harness is set up for heavy short hauls because of its design with no singletree; it's pretty primitive. The majority of the weight of the load will be placed on one shoulder and then the other; the only place for the horse's movement to be expressed in that hitch is inside the collar. Singletrees are a vast improvement because they absorb the natural side-to-side movement of the horse when they walk so there isn't rubbing and friction on the shoulders under the collar. It's impossible to consider the harness's role in the comfort of the horse without also considering the vehicle that you're hooking to."

Changes to Conventional Draft Harness

Changes in harness over time have been made for functional reasons, such as the breast strap and neck collar replacing the neck strap shown on Trajan's column. Changes continue to be made to the neck collar harness even today. Two examples here illustrate changes for safety and for the comfort of the horse; many more examples exist in the functional, safety, and comfort of the horse departments (see, for example, "Preventing Wrecks" in the April/May 2012 issue of *Rural Heritage*).

Left picture shows harness construction with tongue buckles that causes safety issue by catching line. Right picture shows a Conway buckle construction that doesn't catch the line.

The first example here concerns the construction of the harness spider (straps dropping from the hip pad to the breeching). Two pictures show alternate construction of a harness spider. In the left photo, the harness design using tongue buckles leaves the strap end dangling, making it possible for a line to be caught under it. If this occurs, communication through the line from teamster to horse is impaired and in the worst case all communication is lost. The right photo shows a harness design that puts the strap end underneath by using a Conway buckle construction, so the line can move freely up and down the hip of the horse without catching on a strap end. The second design is safer because it doesn't have the potential of interfering with communication between teamster and equine. Interestingly, the less-safe construction is on a newer harness than the safer construction, indicating that it's up to us as teamsters, no matter the age of the harness, to understand our harness and how it contributes to a safe working relationship with our equines.

Another harness adaptation focused on improved communication between equine and teamster addresses line arrangement. The conventional line arrangement in draft harness has the line going through the top hame ring. For most horses, it is too high, as in the photo on the left. Pressure on the bit through the lines at that much of an upward angle sends the wrong messages to the horse by pulling up too high. Drop rings or line holders can be used to resolve this issue, lowering the angle of contact and pressure on the bit from the lines, as shown in the photo on the right. Using drop rings also improves the comfort of the horse by letting the horse carry its head in its natural position because it's not trying to avoid uncomfortable contact from the bit.

The left photo shows a conventional line attachment that puts confusing upward pressure on the bit. The right photo shows use of a drop ring to straighten the line and improve comfort of the horse and communication with the teamster.
Photos courtesy Doc Hammill

Conclusion

One of the things that's most interesting about the coverage of Horse Progress Days each year is seeing the advances made in utilizing horsepower. One might think that since the Industrial Revolution, things have stayed static in the horse powered world, that they haven't progressed. But things have progressed, allowing us to do new and different things with our horses than we ever have before. And the same is true for harness. Because the styles of harness that are available today are all so similar, it's easy to believe that they are all adequate for the job. Yet history tells us that for functional, safety, and comfort-of-the-horse reasons, harness needs to change and evolve, too. It's up to us as teamsters to understand our harness and make changes to it as our functional needs change, as our understanding of safety improves, and as we become more aware of how comfortable our horses are when working.

Remember Doc's student who was so elated when his horses willing stood calmly and still? What better testament to working with horses is there than a team who will stand in a calm and relaxed manner? There are those that insist that putting horses in harness is inhumane and that horses shouldn't be used for work. For those of us who want to work with horses, one of the best things we can do is work our horses as comfortably as possible to give our critics something to think about.

Draft Geometry: Point, Angle, and Line

When we choose to do work using real horsepower rather than the fossil fuel variety, there are of course benefits beyond just getting our work done. Nonetheless, getting work done is an important part of why we work horses. To make the most and best use of real horsepower in getting our work done, we need to maximize the transfer of power from the horse or horses to movement of the load, whether the load is a log, a plow, a wagon, or anything else. Three common problems with harness adjustment cause this transfer of power to be less efficient than it could be:

- Incorrect point of draft
- Incorrect angle of draft, and
- Broken line of draft

"You'd be surprised," says Doc, "how often these problems happen. Sometimes they're pretty obvious, and sometimes they're more subtle. On some level they always affect the comfort of horses and the efficiency of the work they do for us."

"When I teach students, I constantly stress comfort, function, and safety. Safety depends on the comfort of the horse and the function of the equipment. A huge percentage of behavior problems in horses are comfort issues. Incorrect point, angle, and line of draft are functional problems with harness that can cause comfort issues. So behavior problems can stem from these functional problems, and of course both behavior and functional problems can lead to safety problems."

Getting it Just Right

Doc continues, "I remember watching my mentor Addie persist over a three-eighths inch adjustment in the point of draft. I couldn't believe he could even see that fine a detail much less think it made that much difference. But he was adamant about getting it just right. And for Addie, the point of draft was just the starting point. Next he moved to adjusting the angle of draft and then finally to the line of draft, getting them all just right. He knew that ensuring the comfort of the horses meant more work, better work, and safer work. He not only knew it; he lived it every minute he was with horses and mules."

The point of draft on the harness is the point where the trace is attached to the hame. This point of draft on the harness needs to be matched to the ideal point of draft on the horse's shoulder. Locating that ideal point of draft on the shoulder is the subject of the next chapter.

Locating the point of draft of the harness over the ideal point of draft on the horse's shoulder is a matter of proper collar size and fit and proper hame size and hame adjustment. It's not just as simple as getting a collar that fits the horse and then putting the hames on and expecting the point of draft to be right for the horse. Ideally, the point of draft on the hame should be adjustable; some hames are highly adjustable, while many allow for only minor adjustment.

The point of draft needs to be adjusted just right so that the pull on the collar is distributed across the collar face that lies on the "collar bed/collar shelf" of the horse's shoulder. Doc explains, "If the point of draft is too high, it's going to do a couple of things. First, we're going to be transferring too much of the draft to a smaller surface area of the shoulder that is not as anatomically well suited for the pull. Second there can be a tendency for the collar to be pulled upward against the windpipe."

"On the other hand," Doc continues, "the problem with the point of draft too low is that the forces are being concentrated too low on the shoulder. There they can interfere with the horse's stride and cause damage to anatomical structures of the horse's shoulder joint that don't have an adequate cushion of muscle to protect them from the forces of the load."

Allen Picture #1: What do you think about the point of draft, angle of draft, and line of draft in this picture, especially on the horse nearest the camera?"

Regarding Allen Picture #1, Doc calls attention to where the trace leaves the hames on the horse closest to the camera. "You can see that the trace leaves the hame above the point of the shoulder so the trace passes over the well-muscled part of the shoulder. While it's always impossible to tell for sure from pictures, the point of draft on this horse looks pretty good as it does on the other horses in the hitch where you can see it."

The angle of draft is the angle at which the trace leaves the hame. Visualize the long axis of the hame as a line and visualize the trace being another line; the angle between those two lines is the angle of draft. For the most efficient transfer of power from horse to load, the angle between those lines needs to be as close to a right angle (ninety degrees) as possible. If the angle is different from ninety degrees, Doc cautions that there is the potential for draft activity to cause discomfort to the horse and possibly damage the shoulders. Regarding Allen Picture #1, Doc comments, "The angle of draft on the horse nearest the camera appears close to ideal and the angle of draft on the horse behind him appears to be ideal. Collar sores are not only a result of ill-fitting collars; point of draft and angle of draft are important contributing factors as well."

The line of draft is how the trace runs from hame to load. The line of the trace should be straight and unbroken, as shown in Allen Picture #1. Often, though, when loads are closer to the ground, such as harrows, logs, stone boats (or tires during training,) the trace carriers or lazy straps on the harness aren't long enough and they cause the trace to bend as it passes through them. When in draft, the trace tries to straighten, pulling down on the trace carrier which in turn pulls down on the horse's hips.

Doc observes, "Few people know this causes problems for horses. They hitch to a load and don't realize that the trace carriers on most harness are made to pull vehicles where the hitch point is elevated rather than being near the ground. I see a lot of people pulling loads on the ground with trace carriers that are too short. They may or may not be having trouble with their horses, but the line of draft is broken and the potential for problems exists."

Point of Draft

Allen Picture #2: What do you think about the point of draft on these horses?

Allen Picture #2 shows a team of horses on a manure spreader. What do you think about the point of draft on the harnesses on these horses? Doc observes, "If you compare the distance between the point of the shoulder and the collar on the black horse and the point of the shoulder and the collar on the gray horse, you can see that the distance is much greater on the gray horse. This is because the point of draft on the gray horse is significantly higher than it should be. The high point of draft on the gray horse is creating disadvantages for her, as is the fit of her collar."

Doc continues, "Of course there's a relationship between collar fit and optimal point of draft. On the gray horse, the collar appears to be too small, especially too short in length. If these collars were fit when the horses weren't checked up, and then they were checked up, the collars are going to be a lot tighter and the point of draft is going to be higher. The opposite can be a problem, too. If you fit the collar with the horse's head up and then they work with it lower, then the collar will be too long and the point of draft will drop. It is extremely important to fit collars to horses when their heads are very close to the average height that they work in order to avoid these problems."

The close-up of the hames in the photograph at right shows that an adjustable draft point hame is being used, also called a lonestar hame. Using this sort of hame allows the teamster to adjust where the trace ties into the hame to ensure that the point of draft is correct. Doc notes, "Because the collar doesn't fit correctly, lowering the point of draft by dropping the traces to the lowest setting on the hames will not solve the problem. The point of draft would still be too high. You'd need a longer collar and longer hames. Then you could set the traces where the point of draft needs to be."

Doc adds, "The high quality collars we have for horses in this country are artfully designed to fit the anatomy of horses' shoulders. If we get them to fit properly to protect the shoulder, they give the horse the best advantages of comfort and draft. You need to get the collar fit right first, and then work on the point of draft."

Can you see how the hames in this photo have more adjustment than most?

Allen Picture #3: What do you think about the point of draft on these mules?

Allen Picture #3 above shows a team of mules. The collar on the mule farthest from the camera looks like it fits very well, and the point of draft looks good. On the mule closest to the camera, though, the point of draft is low because of a combination of the collar being too long and the hame being adjusted too low on the collar. Doc says, "Almost everywhere I go, I can show you collars that are too long. Like in Allen Picture #3, that puts the point of draft too low. Then the force of the load is being concentrated too low and can cause damage to skin, tendons, ligaments and bone associated with the shoulder joint."

Doc continues, "As if collar fit and point of draft aren't challenging enough, there are also considerations related to the conformation of the horse. The other day I was working with a team of Haflingers and dealing with the relationship between collar fit and point of draft. The owner had an adjustable collar. If I adjusted the collar to be the right length, the draft area of the collar where the point of draft needed to be was way too high relative to what the horse's shoulder needed. If I lengthened the collar to get the draft area of the collar down to where the point of draft should be on the horse, the collar was way too long. It was just this particular horse's anatomy. Even though I had an adjustable collar, it couldn't be made to fit the neck and shoulder conformation of that horse. With the other horse in the team, when I got the length of the same collar right, the draft area was just where it needed to be on the shoulder. It all went together easily by comparison. Due to his conformation, the first horse was a rather unusual situation."

Angle of Draft

The truck harness depicted in the drawing from the Heiser Harness catalog at right shows a non-optimal angle of draft. Doc observes, "The angle of the trace relative to the line of the hame from top to bottom in this drawing isn't ninety degrees, so it isn't optimal for converting the horse's push into the collar into forward movement of a load. When the angle of draft is like that shown in the picture, pulling the load would tend to pull the collar upward and against the windpipe. If the angle of draft is opposite, it tends to create pull downward on the top of the horse's neck and could potentially put the forces of draft down closer to the shoulder joint where important anatomical structures could be damaged. With this harness on these horses with their conformation, it would be tough to pull much of a load without problems because you can't even get close to an optimal angle of draft.

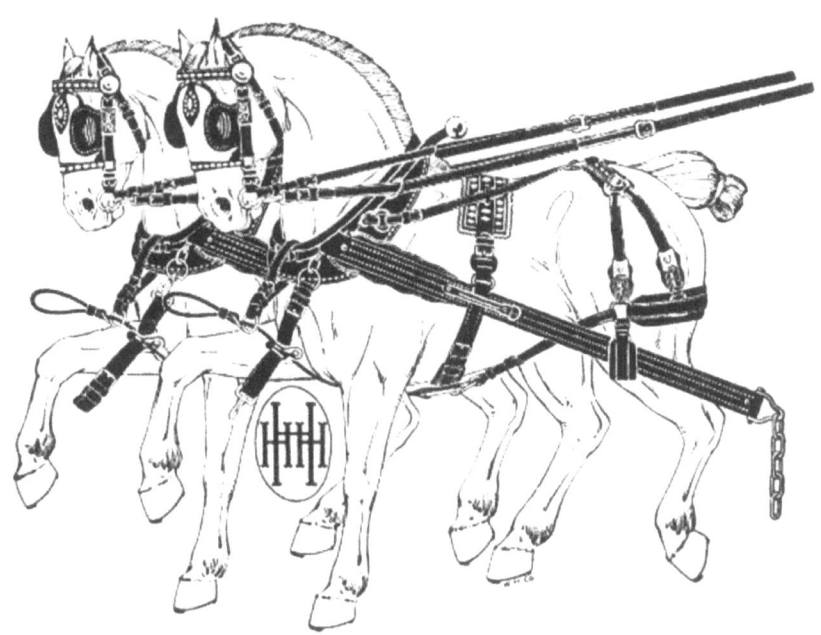

A truck harness from the Heiser Harness catalog, circa 1920.
What do you think of the angle of draft shown here?
courtesy www.cabincreekcds.com

"In most circumstances when we hitch, if the hitch point is a reasonable height, the optimal angle of draft will be easily acquired. If we have a hitch point and have 90 degrees naturally, we want to adjust the belly band and backpad billets to fit where that trace is running. Once it's set that way, if we hitch to a hitch point that is too high, and there's a force wanting to pull the back end of the trace up, it will break the line of draft at the belly band-back pad billet level, but 90 degrees will be maintained forward. In such cases, the line of draft will be broken which is less than ideal."

"Another thing I'm watching," says Doc, "is the hitches using rope-and-pulley systems. With every team that you put out in front of another, the angle of draft gets higher. With wheel teams, the angle of draft is close to correct depending on the height of the hitch point, then the next team in front is pulling on the same hitch point but they're further away so it brings the trace up higher on their legs above the hock. If you have a third team out front, then the trace is up closer to the stifle joint. Each team forward is losing draft efficiency, and the angle of draft is distorting the lay of the collar, rotating it and changing the balance of the load on the shoulders."

Line of Draft

Allen Picture #4 at right shows the most common manifestation of draft inefficiency. The trace carrier (or lazy strap in a Western type harness) isn't adjusted long enough, and it is deflecting the trace from being a straight line from hame to load. This horse, of course, isn't in draft, so the trace will be less deflected when the load is engaged. Nevertheless, the trace will still be deflected upward by the trace carrier, and there will still be an inefficient transfer of power. In addition, with the horse feeling downward pressure on its hips from the trace pulling down on the trace carrier, there may be a balking issue or safety issue if the horse becomes concerned with that feeling of downward pressure, especially in the case of heavier loads.

Allen Picture #4: Can you see the broken line of draft?

Doc shares, "I have seen many situations where problems have developed because the line of draft is broken by trace carriers that are too short. Many horses appear comfortable pulling light loads under these circumstances but become balky with heavier loads. I once had a client who had this problem with a mare who would willingly pull a pickup tire on the ground but when hooked to a semi tire and wheel, she got balky. The mare would go to the right and to the left trying to evade the downward pressure on her hips, then going forward she'd stop and rear up. I put in trace carrier extensions so that the line of draft wasn't broken, and again she was fine on the pickup tire to warm her up, then I switched to the semi tire and wheel. When she felt the additional weight she didn't want to go forward. I kept being patient and asking her to go forward; as soon as she found out that the load wasn't going to put downward pressure on her hips, she walked off with it. Within ten minutes I had her pulling me standing on the tire. That mare has been a solid puller ever since."

In Allen Picture #4, lengthening the heel chains to put the load back further would reduce the deflection of the trace, but it would also decrease the efficiency of draft. The better solution is to lengthen the trace carriers so the trace is free to ride in a straight line from hames to load.

Doc shares, "We worked with four horses over the course of a few days, three at one place, one at another. As is usual, every one of them had trace carriers that couldn't be adjusted long enough to pull a load on the ground. As a temporary fix, I carry baling twine, and I take the trace carriers off the breeching rings, make loops of bailing twine on the rings, then let the trace carrier hang at the proper height from the baling twine. Trace carriers/lazy straps are made just long enough for pulling equipment/vehicles where the hitch point is higher. All other aspects of the harness are capable of pulling loads on the ground, just not the lazy straps/trace carriers.

"Almost all of our clients want to pull things on the ground with their animals. Where they really gain their skill is ground driving and pulling something on the ground. When I'm training young horses, I spend a lot of time teaching them to pull things on the ground, so I am constantly aware of the need to make adjustments to the trace carriers/lazy straps. I wouldn't use baling twine to temporarily modify a harness just anywhere. The trace carrier isn't a piece of harness that if it fails is necessarily going to be a problem. The function of the trace carrier is simply to hold the trace up off the ground when the horse is not in draft. Since the trace carrier does not function when the horse is in draft, I feel comfortable using baling twine as a temporary fix."

Doc adds, "When we help clients order new harness, we make sure the trace carriers/lazy straps have enough adjustment. The only way I know to do that is to have them custom-made with longer straps. Either we have the trace carrier straps made extra long, or we have them extended with an additional strap that can be buckled on to the end of the trace carrier strap then the other end into the trace carrier."

Allen Picture #5

Allen Picture #5: What do you think of the point of draft on these horses? What about the angle of draft? And the line of draft?

"Before I can even start contemplating point of draft, angle of draft, and line of draft in Allen Picture #5," says Doc, "I have to comment on collar fit. These collars are too small for these horses. They aren't sitting down on the shoulders. They're up on the wedge of the neck rather than seated down on the shoulder beds. Those collars are causing compression on the tapered part of the neck, and they're going to just squeeze like the dickens all the way around the neck and put pressure on the windpipe. These horses are very attentive to what is behind them, but they're also telling me they're very uncomfortable. Seeing what I see with the harness, how could they possibly be comfortable?"

Doc continues, "This is a perfect picture to headline the high point of draft. The reason that the point of draft is so extremely high is that the collars and hames are much too small. You can't bring it down using those collars and hames. You'd need larger collars and longer hames to bring the point of draft down where it needs to be. Even if you lowered these hames down as far as you could on the collar, you still couldn't get the point of draft where it needs to be. These horses are also checked up uncomfortably high which brings the point of draft up even higher than it would otherwise be. While letting their heads down would lower the point of draft somewhat, it would still be much too high because of the collar fit issues."

Allen Picture #5 shows another broken line of draft scenario. Doc explains, "The traces are deflected steeply upward as they travel forward from the belly band billets to the hames. This is because the point of draft is extraordinarily high due to the undersized collars sitting so high up on the necks. The solution to this broken line of draft is to solve the high point of draft issue with well-fitting collars and appropriate, properly adjusted hames. Once that is done if the horses were to step forward into draft, the single trees, the trace chains, and traces behind the belly band billets would be pulled upward causing the line of draft to straighten all the way from the new point of draft to the single trees. Then it might be necessary to make adjustments to the back pad and belly band billets, especially on the off horse where the belly band is very loose."

Doc has some other comments about the harness in Allen Picture #5. "First, you see that there are chains connecting the tongue to the collar. A lot of times these chains were used on stiff-tongued vehicles, tongues that didn't hinge and drop down to the ground. So the tongue weight was supported by design; the horses weren't required to hold the weight of the tongue up with the chains. Still, this hitching system is pulling the bottom of the collars towards the tongue and into the outside of the shoulders. You can see how the breast strap is pulling inward, not straight forward as it would be with a neck yoke set up. This causes unequal forces on the inside and outside shoulders of both horses. It can potentially result in discomfort and shoulder soreness, or irritate the horses and cause behavior and safety problems.

"Next you'll notice that the bridles are different from one horse to the other. The off-horse has some sort of cavesson around his nose, perhaps to keep his mouth shut. It wouldn't surprise me if all the harness fit and draft efficiency issues weren't causing behavior problems that prompted the teamster to force his mouth shut. Both horses are also working on leverage bits, one on the most extreme setting and the other on the second. Perhaps the severe bits would be unnecessary if other issues affecting the horses' comfort were dealt with."

Dynamic Adjustments

Doc observes, "Although I repeatedly emphasize the importance of proper angle of draft and line of draft, please realize that while the proper angle of draft is critical, it is not always possible to maintain a proper and straight line of draft at every moment with certain types of work and loads. Let me explain. A well-designed and adjusted harness has provisions for maintaining the all-important angle of draft at the shoulder. In most collar-and-hames harness, this is accomplished by a properly adjusted belly band and its billets holding the traces from being pulled up too high, and the back pad and properly adjusted billets holding the traces from being pulled down too low. The proper 90 degree angle of draft of the trace coming off of the hames is then maintained back to where it passes through these billets. Then, if the point of hitch at the load is temporarily too high or too low, the harness will compensate and keep the angle of pull on the traces at the proper 90 degrees between the hames and the billets. In such situations the horse will experience either a temporary pull upward on the bellyband or a temporary pull downward on the back pad in which case the line of draft will be deflected from straight until the hitch point returns to a better height."

Making the Right Decisions

Doc concludes, "While I could argue that the correct point of draft, angle of draft and line of draft are important for the comfort and welfare of the horses, it's equally true that correct point of draft, angle of draft, and line of draft are important for the teamster, too. To get the best out of our horses, they need to be given every mechanical and comfort advantage. This is especially true in smaller or more sensitive equines and in animals working long hours or under heavy draft. And correct point of draft, angle of draft, and line of draft also contribute to our horses being as comfortable as possible in their harness so that safety issues are less likely to arise. As my good friend and master teamster John Erskine often says, 'If you make the right decision for the horse, the people will be taken care of, too.'"

The black and white photographs in this chapter are from America's Rural Yesterday, Volume I: Fieldwork *published by Mischka Press.*

The Elusive Ideal Point of Draft

We are indebted to Bethany Caskey for her illustrations in this chapter.

"Look, see those horses pulling a wagon?!"
"Wow, that's a lot of weight those mules are pulling."
"Oh, look at that horse pulling that carriage!"
"See the pony pulling the sleigh?!"

These mules aren't pulling this end-gate seeder; they're pushing into their collars to move it forward. This fact has enormous implications for how well our equines work. J.C. Allen photo.

These types of comments are often made by the general public when they see our equines working, but of course we know they're not accurate. Our horses don't pull; they push into their collar. When they push into their collar, their forward movement is translated back through the hames and traces to the load, drawing it forward, too.

That our horses push has enormous consequences for how well they work. If we have adjusted their harness and collars correctly for their conformation in the draft area of the front of their bodies, they will be comfortable and able to perform at their highest level. On the other hand, Doc observes, "I see a lot of horses that are being asked to work with improperly fit harness and collars. Because they're not fit correctly, they actually impede the horses' ability to move freely and efficiently and therefore interfere with working comfortably and with good attitudes."

Doc continues: "Horses can and do tell us if they are uncomfortable. The problem is that many people misinterpret the communication as a bad attitude, lack of respect, disobedience, laziness, or being stubborn. It really pays to get harness and collar fit just right and then keep it right. Whenever an animal is acting up it's extremely important that we find the real reason. They always have a reason, and in their mind it's always a good reason. Horses that are physically and psychologically comfortable being driven and worked seldom act up."

Finding That Elusive Point

Of course the reason that Doc sees so many horses with improperly fit harness and collars is that proper fit and adjustment is not easy and never has been. Consider the following from an article from the year 1900 entitled "To Properly Fit a Horse Collar":

"The necks and shoulders of no two horses are alike, and it is very seldom indeed that the shoulders of any one horse are exactly the same in size and form. The collar that will fit a horse in the early spring, when he is fat, will generally be found too large at harvest time, and the shoulder of the fat horse is different in form from when he is thin in flesh; consequently, the importance of watching the adaptation of the collar to the shoulders… (1)

The article goes on to say:
"There is just a proper place (according to the conformation of each and every horse) for the draught of the hame-tug, and the owner or handler should be observing enough to know where that is, as no rule can be given that will be sufficient for all horses; it must be left to the good judgment of those in authority."

The 'proper place' for 'the draught of the hame-tug' is what we refer to as the ideal point of draft. The reason that the ideal point of draft is elusive and 'no rule can be given that will be sufficient for all horses' is that to achieve the ideal point of draft requires coordinating the points of draft in three places: the horse's shoulder, the collar, and the hames. While the ideal point of draft on a particular equine will never move, the points of draft on collars vary, and hames are of course adjustable. Marrying these three properly is the goal of collar and harness fit. When we marry them properly, we enable our horses to work comfortably and at maximum efficiency. Marrying these three properly need not be elusive if we understand how to find the ideal point of draft in each place first.

Influences on the Three Points of Draft

Each of the three points of draft – horse, collar, hames - has numerous influences that must be considered in order to get them right. For instance, the ideal point of draft on the horse depends on the anatomy and specific conformation of his draft area. The ideal point of draft on the collar depends on the shape and proportions of the collar. The ideal point of draft on the hames, though, is a little more complicated. While you can determine the ideal point of draft on the horse standalone and the collar standalone, the ideal point of draft of the hames CANNOT be determined without putting the hames on the collar on the horse. It's where the rubber meets the road because it's where the load meets the horse.

The horse's draft area is a function of skeleton, musculature, and conformation as well as working condition. It is important to identify the horse's point of draft in the draft area first. Next comes the collar. We can fairly easily identify the ideal point of draft of a collar. The challenge is finding a collar that properly fits the draft area of the horse. Then comes the ideal point of draft on the hames; it is the last of the three points of draft to be located. Most hames have some ability to be adjusted to enable them to finish the job of marrying the three points of draft in an ideal position for work.

The consequences of marrying these three points of draft poorly are inefficient conversion of horsepower to movement of a load as well as discomfort for our horses at the least and potential injury, permanent disability and/or psychological problems at the worst. The great benefit of marrying the three points of draft well, on the other hand, is the privilege of working our equines in harness.

The collar rests on an elegant exterior that masks a complex assemblage underneath.
J.C. Allen photo.

The Draft Area

The draft area of the front of the horse's body is where the collar rests. Of course attached to the collar are the hames, and attached to the hames are the traces. The draft area, then, is where the weight of the load meets our horse's body in forward motion. To get work done, there is no more important place that we must pay attention to. What makes things challenging is that this draft area has an elegant exterior that masks a complex assemblage underneath. That assemblage works surprisingly well most of the time, but it also has vulnerable areas that we must be mindful of to ensure our horses are comfortable and able to work at their highest level.

The Skin

Obviously what we are most aware of in the draft area is the skin with its hair. Because the skin is quite thin, most ill effects of collar or harness problems usually show up on the skin before serious damage is caused to underlying tissues. If the hair is ruffled when we remove our harness, for instance, we will want to check for issues with fit. Doc adds, "There are several warning signs that people need to constantly be on the lookout for that indicate issues anywhere collars and harness touch horses:

1) areas that are tender to the touch;
2) patches of dandruff or exfoliating skin;
3) areas of skin with micro wrinkles – patches of tightly packed, tiny skin wrinkles - maybe the size of a nickel up to a half dollar or sometimes larger, where tiny muscles associated with the skin are inflamed and contracting;
4) an area that sweats and stays wet after the rest of the hair and skin is dry – this is an indication that the sweat glands have been abused, are inflamed, and are producing sweat excessively;
5) hair being rubbed off or shaved off;
6) patches of thickened or puffy skin – from very slight to quite obvious;
7) areas of heat of any size that remain after the rest of the shoulder has cooled off."

Doc continues, "Hair that is disturbed is often the earliest sign of a problem. Making changes at the first sign of abnormal hair is important in order to prevent skin and underlying tissues from being damaged – perhaps permanently."

If hairs are turning white, we need to find out what is causing distress to that area. Doc explains, "If hair turns white without having been preceded by an actual harness or collar sore, then it may have been caused by excessive heat affecting the hair follicles. Both heat from friction caused by a harness part or collar rubbing, or simply excess heat buildup under harness or a collar in hot weather, can cause it. White hair caused by heat is more apt to eventually be replaced by normal darker hair than is hair that turns white following an actual harness or collar sore. Either way, by the time hair turns white something has previously caused discomfort and damage has been done to the animal for far too long a time."

Muscles and Bones

While the skin provides us with visible feedback if anything is amiss with our harness and collar fit, its thinness also allows us to feel the muscles and bones underneath and locate areas that are vulnerable to damage from ill-fitting collars and harness.

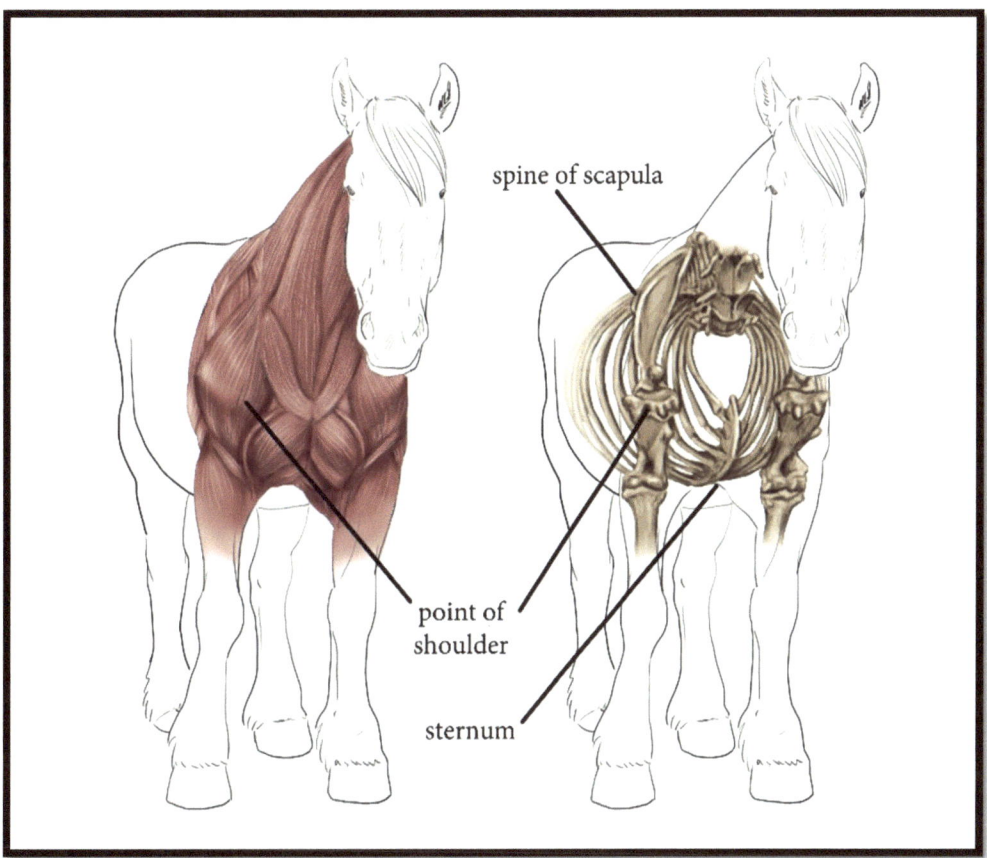

Illustration #3: The appearance of the draft area is a product of musculature, as shown on the left, and bone, as shown on the right, as well as working condition and conformation. Illustration © Bethany Caskey

The way the draft area appears to our naked eye is a product of musculature and the underlying skeleton. The left image of Illustration #3 shows a front view of a horse with the musculature of the draft area. A collar, when properly fit, rests on the muscles of the neck, the shoulder, and to a lesser extent the chest.

Of course the muscles are hung on the bones of the skeleton. The image on the right in Illustration #3 shows a frontal view of the skeleton of the draft area. The point of the shoulder is prominent through the musculature. The breast bone or sternum is less prominent but very important in the appearance of the chest. We'll discuss the spine of the scapula below.

Three Bony Landmarks

Illustration #4 shows a side view of the draft area of an equine skeleton. There are three important landmarks for determining the horse's ideal point of draft. The point of the shoulder is the portion of the skeleton in the draft area that is most towards the lower front and can easily be felt through the skin. In addition to the point of the shoulder, there are two other vulnerable places where the bones of the draft area come close to the surface and can be felt through the skin. They are the spine of the scapula (the scapula is also called the shoulder blade) and the tubercle of the humerus. The tubercle of the humerus is slightly above and behind the point of the shoulder on the side of the horse. The spine of the scapula is a ridge running up the center of the shoulder blade.

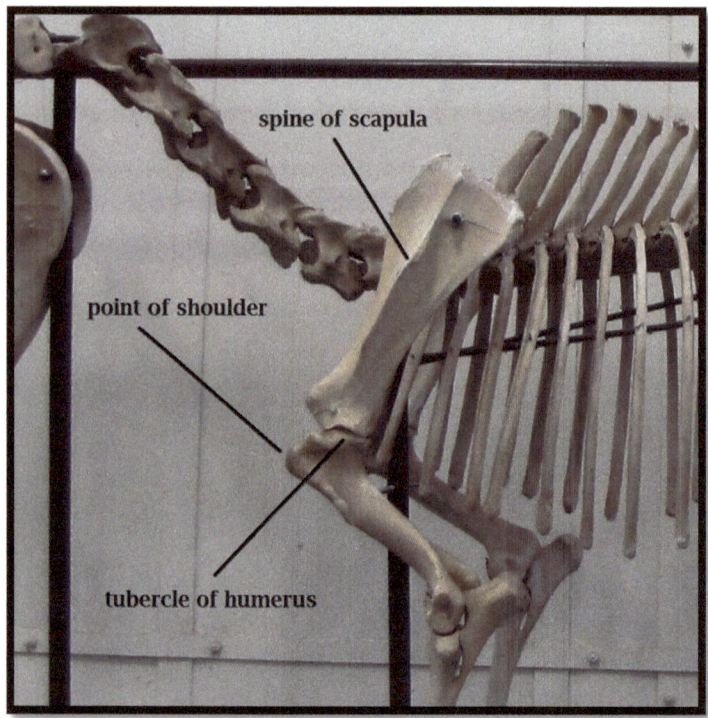

Illustration #4: These three places where the bones come close to the surface are easily felt through the skin on most horses. When harnessing our horses, we need to make sure that tissues aren't compressed between the collar and these bony landmarks.

If you look back at the skeleton view in Illustration #3, you can see the spine of the scapula sticking out like a fin away from the rest of the skeleton.

Doc suggests, "Go out and feel your horse in the draft area. You'll quickly realize how close these hard unyielding structures are to the surface; you can really feel them. If the collar even comes close to putting pressure on them, it can wear a hole in the skin and/or damage underlying tissues. What I have students do in workshops is to get them to feel for and find the spine of the scapula, then move their hand down the spine of the scapula and feel where it disappears into a softer cushion of muscles. Continuing down and forward over muscle, the hand comes to the bony structures of the point of the shoulder, including the tubercle of the humerus. Next I have them place one hand on soft muscle at the bottom-most end of the spine of the scapula and the other on the upper limit of the hard structures of the point of the shoulder. The line of draft needs to cross over the muscled area midway between their two hands, not near or over any of the bony structures."

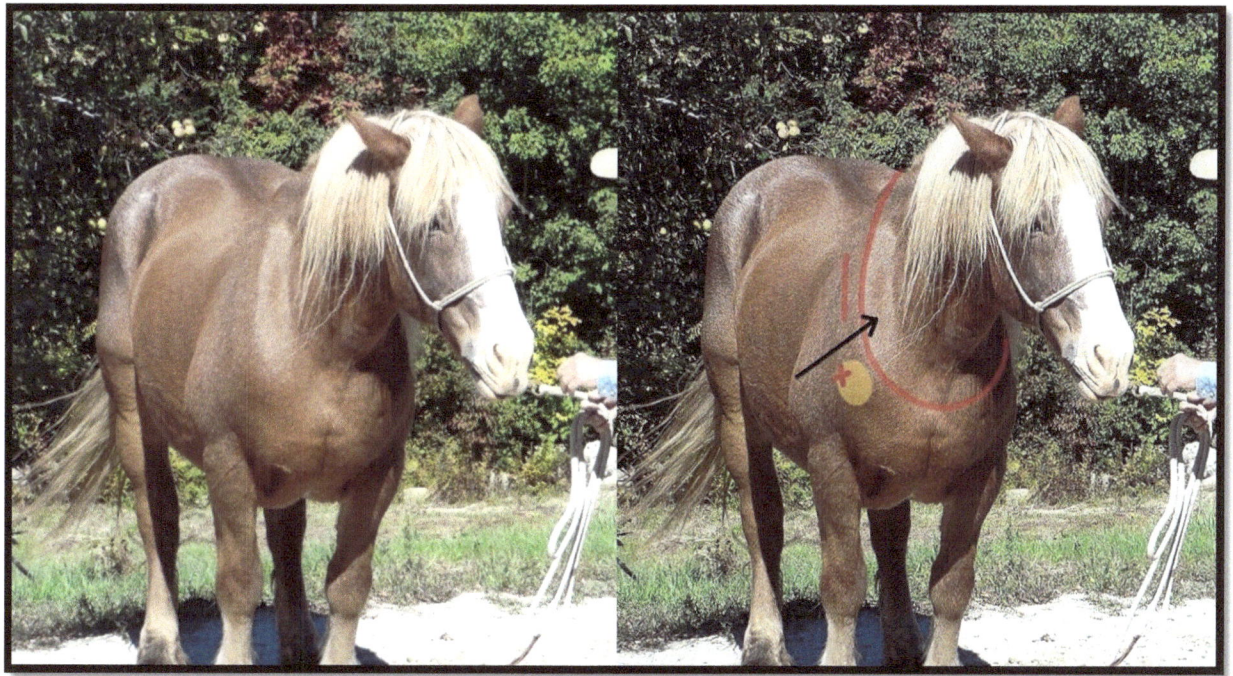

Illustration #5: Danny, a Belgian gelding, has a very well-defined draft area. The three bony landmarks have been roughly located; it's impossible to precisely locate them without putting your hands on the horse. The arrow points to Danny's ideal point of draft. Original photo courtesy Cathy Greatorex. With thanks to Bethany Caskey

The Horse's Ideal Point of Draft

Now let's meet Danny, a real horse. Danny is shown in Illustration #5. He has a large and very well-defined draft area outlined in red. Danny's draft area can help us use our understanding of muscles and bones to locate the ideal point of draft. The three bony landmarks– spine of scapula (line), point of shoulder (circle), and tubercle of humerus (X) – are identified on Danny's shoulder. Their location is the best that can be achieved on a photograph; you really need to feel your horse to precisely identify where the three bony landmarks are.

The ideal point of draft on a horse is in the draft area. It is centered such that the line of the trace will fall midway between the bottom of the spine of the scapula and the upper limits of the point of the shoulder. In Illustration #5, Danny's ideal point of draft is at the tip of the black arrow. It's very difficult to locate the ideal point of draft without actually putting your hands on your horse.

Doc comments, "In the herd of horses that Cathy and I have, there are Suffolks, Fjords, and a Welsh Pony. On the Suffolks, there is a three inch space where the trace coming off the hames should pass between the bottom of the spine of the scapula and the point of the shoulder. On the Fjords, the area is two-and-a-half inches average top to bottom. On the Welsh pony it's just two inches. I want the center line of the trace to pass through the middle of the space between these bony landmarks."

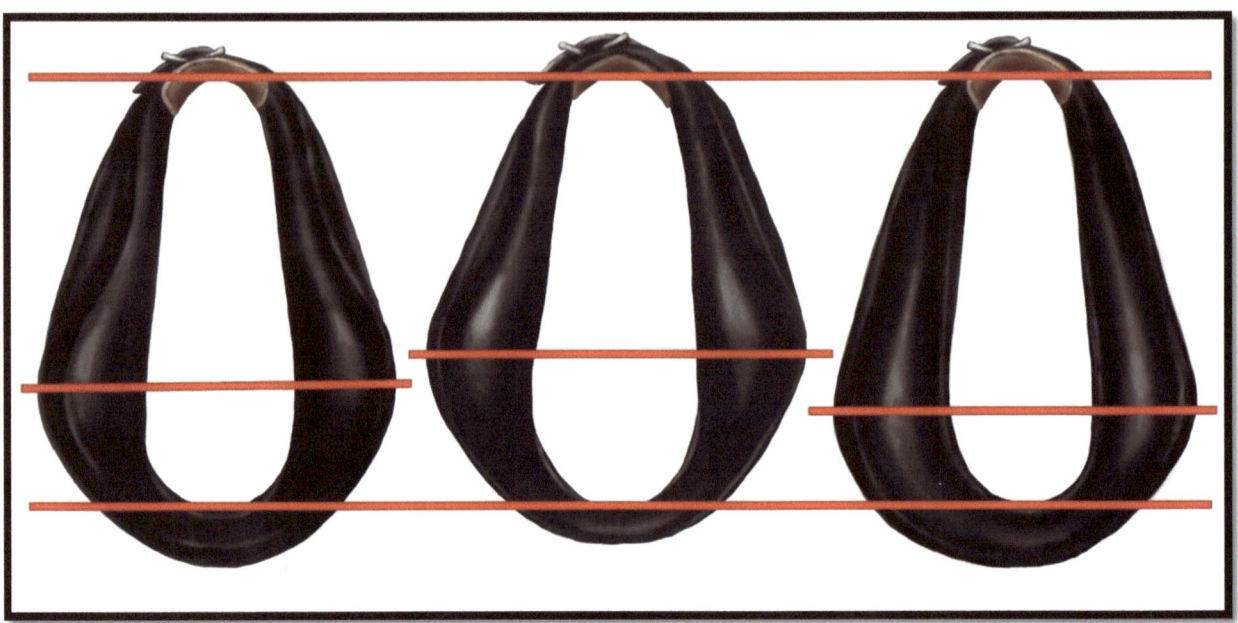

Illustration #6: Three different collars with three differently shaped and differently positioned draft areas with different ideal points of draft.
Illustration © Bethany Caskey

Collar Ideal Point of Draft

Now that we know how to find the ideal point of draft on the horse, we need to consider the ideal point of draft of the collar. The purpose of the collar of course is to distribute the force of the load in a comfortable fashion across the draft area of the horse. Collars have a major padded area or draft area that is wider than the areas above and below it. In an ideal world, the ideal point of draft on a collar is where the draft area has its largest diameter. But of course none of us live in an ideal world.

Illustration #6 shows three different collars with three differently shaped and differently positioned draft areas. Note that these collars are all the same length; however their ideal point of draft differs in location relative to the top and bottom of the collar. From this illustration we can see that not every collar of the correct length for our horse will have its draft area in the spot we need. We can also see from Illustration #6 that the draft areas of these collars differ in shape. Not every collar of the correct length will have a draft area that is shaped ideally to do its job of distributing the force of the load over our horse's draft area.

For a collar to do its job, then, either because of its design or because of the horse's anatomy, its ideal point of draft may not fall directly on top of the horse's ideal point of draft. Doc shares, "Maybe sixty to eight percent of the time, the largest diameter of the draft area of the collar ends up right over the horse's ideal point of draft. The rest of the time, we're having to do the best we can with the best collar we have. Fortunately, the size of the draft area of most collars gives us a little flexibility. When it comes to getting the overall ideal point of draft, the ideal points of draft on the horse and the hames are the most crucial."

Doc also cautions: "Collars often have wear leathers on the draft area. Sometimes, though, the wear leathers are not placed over the center of the draft area. I've even seen collars where the wear leather on one side of the collar was higher than the wear leather on the other side of the collar. Do not go by the wear leathers to determine the ideal point of draft of the collar."

Distributing the Load

So we now understand that the ideal point of draft on the equine is where the harness and collar avoid the bony landmarks. And we understand that the ideal point of draft on the collar is where the draft area of the collar is at its greatest diameter. Both of these first two points of draft can be determined stand alone. The third point of draft, the one on the hames, however, can't be determined without putting the hames on the collar on the horse. That is because the location of the point of draft on the hames ultimately determines how the forces of the load to which the horse is hitched are distributed over the draft area. The ideal point of draft on the hames concentrates and balances the forces of the load evenly across the collar bed.

Illustration #7: The collar bed is the portion of the draft area where the forces of the load should be concentrated and balanced. The location of Danny's collar bed is shown in this photograph; its shape is approximate.
Photo by Cathy Greatorex.
With thanks to Bethany Caskey

The Collar Bed

While the collar rests on the draft area of the front of the horse, the collar bed is the portion of the draft area where we want the forces of draft to be concentrated and balanced. (The collar bed is also known as the shoulder bed or the collar shelf.)

Illustration #7 shows the location and approximate shape of Danny's collar bed in his draft area. Note that the upper portion of Danny's collar bed and the draft area above are narrower than the main part of the collar bed lower down. We must ensure that the forces of draft are concentrated and balanced over the wide part of the collar bed.

Doc explains, "One reason the point of draft is so important is that you need to minimize getting a lot of pressure high on the neck or low on the chest and get it balanced across the collar bed. Finding the point of draft on the horse first enables us to get the points of draft on the collar and then the hames positioned correctly to put the forces on the collar bed where they're most comfortable for the horse."

Doc continues, "If the point of draft is too high, we're going to be transferring too much of the draft to a smaller surface area of the shoulder that is not as anatomically well suited for the pull. If the point of draft is too low, we potentially put pressure near the point of the shoulder where the bony landmarks aren't as well padded."

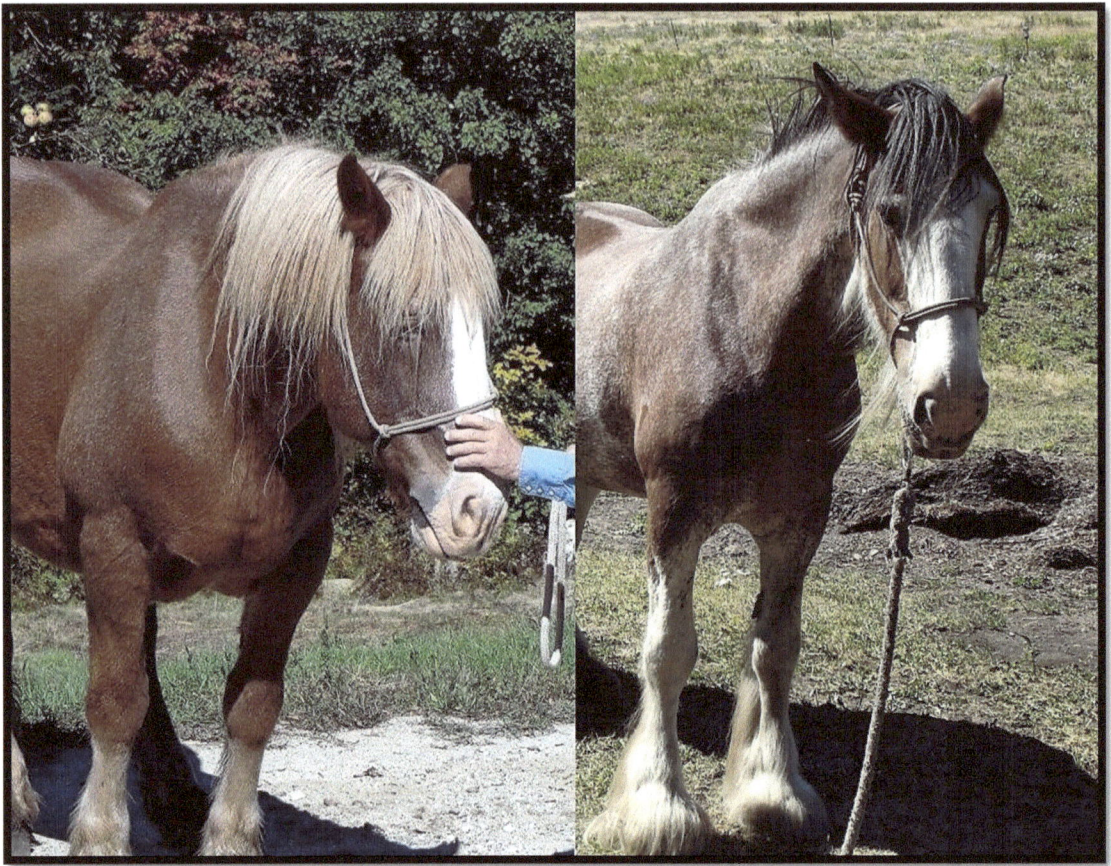

Illustration #8: Danny is shown on the left with his wide collar bed. On the right is Misty, a 26 year old Clydesdale mare with a narrower collar bed. Misty's age allows us to see her conformation more clearly. Misty worked consistently for more than two decades despite her narrower collar bed. Photos courtesy Cathy Greatorex and Doc Hammill

Note that many horses do not have as broad and as well-defined a collar bed as Danny. Illustration #8 shows Danny next to an aged Clydesdale mare. Her age allows us to see her narrower collar bed clearly. Doc shares, "Misty worked in harness at various jobs every year from age 4 to age 27 when we retired her from teaching students. The fact that she did not have an extraordinary collar bed did not keep her from staying sound and doing lots of work."

Doc continues, "The collar bed is the primary area of draft. There are also some forces on the chest below but ideally not as many as on the collar bed. There are also forces on the sides of the neck because it is usually tapered (think Misty rather than Danny.) I refer to these forces on the side of the neck as a wedge effect."

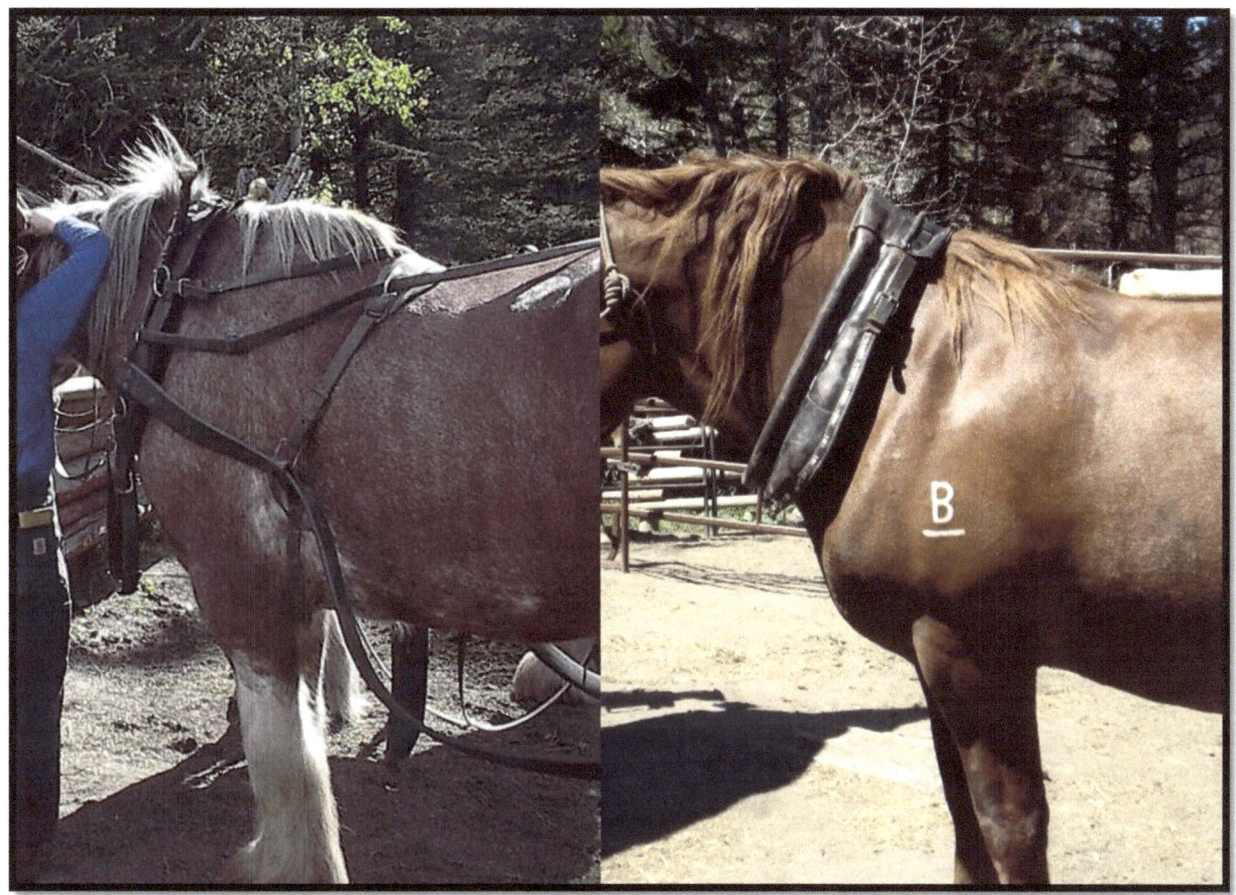

Illustration #9: 'Two examples of collars on the collar bed. On the left, a well-bedded collar. On the right, a collar that is too small that will put pressure on sensitive structures and tissues.

Illustration #9 shows a well-seated collar on the left. On the right, a too-small collar is shown. Doc says, "A collar that is too small is carried up on the wedge of the neck not down on the collar bed and will most likely cause discomfort and behavior problems, including balking."

Proper Collar Fit

Collar fit is involved in achieving the ideal point of draft in two ways. First, a collar must be appropriately sized to avoid the sensitive structures of the draft area. We don't want comfort issues distracting our horse from efficiently transferring their movement to movement of the load. Second, a collar must be well-seated on the collar bed so that the forces of the load can be distributed properly across the draft area, maximizing the work the horse can do. Collars that are too wide or too narrow prevent them from seating on the collar bed properly. Collars that are too long, too short, too wide, or too narrow can create comfort issues. Having a collar properly fit our horse is more important than having the collar's ideal point of draft exactly match the horse's ideal point of draft.

While in most places of the draft area there is adequate muscle for cushioning, the three bony landmarks don't have that cushion and merit our attention. Illustration #10 shows several collars overlaid on the skeleton of the draft area, with potential areas of discomfort shown in red. Image 10a shows a collar that is fit well.

Doc explains, "A properly fit collar concentrates and balances the force of the load evenly across the collar bed. The fit of the long collar in image 10b allows it to ride down near the point of the shoulder where it can put excessive forces of the load on the vulnerable structures and tissues there. Image 10c shows a collar that is both too long and too wide. A collar that is too wide up high can come back on the neck and shoulder and can compress the muscles onto the spine of the scapula and affect the nerves and blood vessels near the spine of the scapula. If a collar is too wide in the lower portion, it can allow the collar to come back onto the tubercle and/or point of shoulder, and wobble side to side, causing friction.

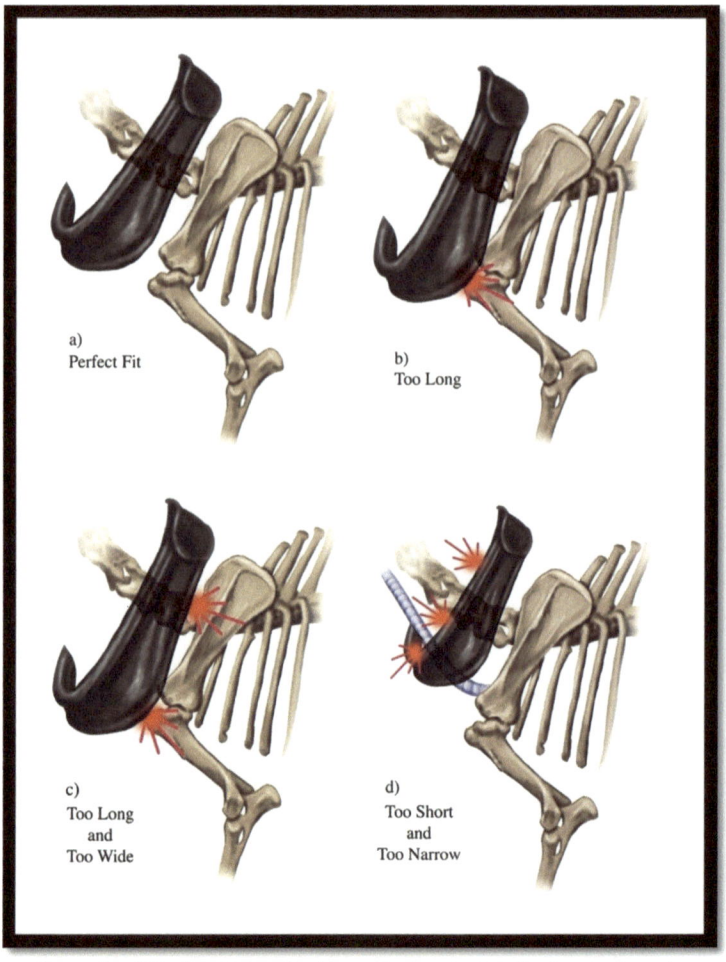

Illustration #10: A well-fit collar keeps the forces of the load away from the bony landmarks of the draft area. Collars that aren't well-fit cause discomfort at the least and permanent injury at the worst.
Illustration © Bethany Caskey

"Image 10d shows a collar that is too short and too narrow. A collar that is too short can put the point of draft too high and may put pressure on the trachea or windpipe, shown in blue in the image. If a collar is too narrow at any place up and down it's going to sit on the wedge shape of the neck instead on the collar bed where it should be. This will cause excessive compression of the neck muscles."

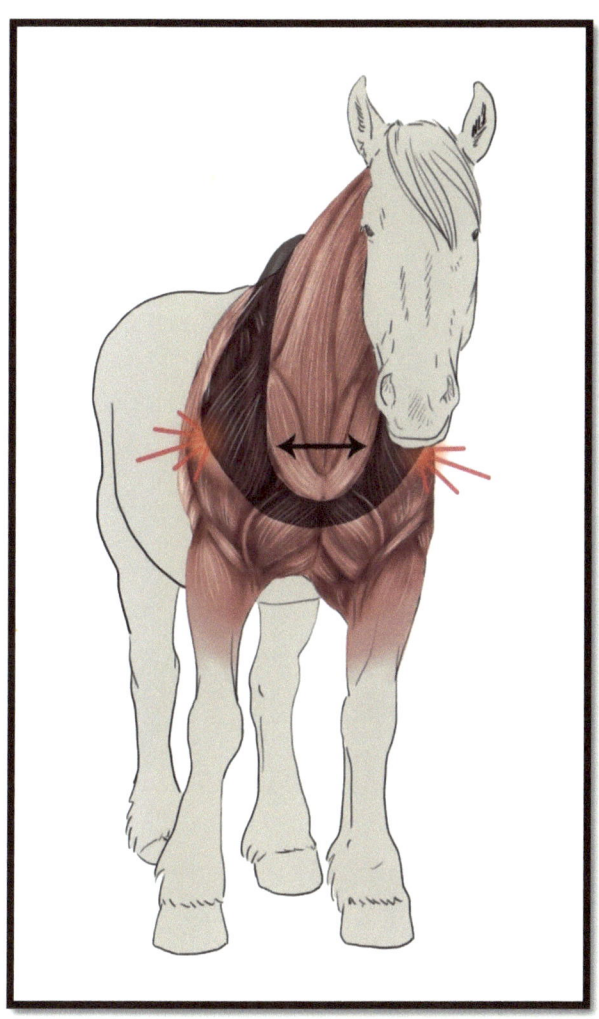

Illustration #11: This collar is both too wide and too long and can damage sensitive tissues in many places.
Image © Bethany Caskey

Illustration #11 shows a front view of a collar that is both too wide and too long. You can see how the draft area of the collar has swung out over the point of the shoulder where it can damage the sensitive tissues there. Doc says, "I see a lot of collars just like the one in illustration #11. I see a lot of horses wearing collars that are too long and too wide. I know horses are suffering because of this."

Doc continues, "Every step this horse takes is going to scrub this collar back and forth across the bony shoulder areas, and that movement will cause excessive friction and heat as well as excessive force of load on the bony structures of the point of the shoulder where there just isn't enough cushion to protect them."

Hames Ideal Point of Draft

Even if we locate the ideal point of draft of the horse's shoulder and we properly fit the collar to the horse's draft area, the overall ideal point of draft can still be elusive unless we find the ideal point of draft on the hames and marry it to the other two. We can't just assume that if we put the hames that we have on hand on the proper collar that they will have the right point of draft. We need to adjust them so that their natural point of draft sits over the ideal point of draft of the horse's shoulder and on a properly fit collar that then distributes the forces of the load appropriately across the collar bed.

Doc explains how this can be elusive. "You can take a collar that fits and a hame that is of a length that should fit that collar. You have a curve on the hame that has to be adjusted so that it will shape or reshape the collar for that particular horse. If I've got that curve down too low, a straight part of the hame might be pushing the collar in on the muscular area low on the neck. If I get the curved part where it's supposed to be so the curve is over the big muscle area of the lower part of the neck, if the attachment for the trace isn't on the right part of the curve, I'm not going to be able to get the point of draft that I need. This is why it's so important that you have at least some small amount of adjustability of the point of draft on the hame."

Illustration #12 shows a situation where the point of draft for the collar and hame are well married but they are not well married to the ideal point of draft on the horse because the collar is too short and too narrow. The collar is wedged on the neck and not seated on the collar bed. Even though the hame is a lonestar hame that has more adjustment than most, it's not possible to get the ideal point of draft because the collar isn't seated on the collar bed of the horse.

Hames of course vary in style and adjustability. Doc notes, "Lonestar hames give you the broadest range of adjustability because they let you move the point of attachment of the trace up and down several inches. On many other hames, you can of course make adjustments by moving where the top hame strap is seated in the ratchet. It's possible to then make more subtle adjustments with the hame straps."

Illustration #12: The ideal point of draft for the collar and hames are well married here but they are well above the ideal point of draft of the horse's shoulder because the collar is much too short in length, nor is it wide enough.
J.C. Allen photo

Doc continues, "A lot of hames have the potential for adjusting the point of draft in very small increments such as that shown in Illustration #13. A flanged spacer on the hame bolt allows for an adjustment of the point of draft up and down about ¼". The upper images in Illustration #13 show the spacer in a position to let the trace leave the hame at the lowest possible location. The lower two images in Illustration #13 show the spacer flipped over so the trace leaves the hame ¼" higher. It doesn't seem like much, but my mentor Addie Funk often made this adjustment because he felt it improved the horses' ability to work comfortably and at their highest potential. That we have the ability to make this ¼" adjustment shows just how critical the ideal point of draft is."

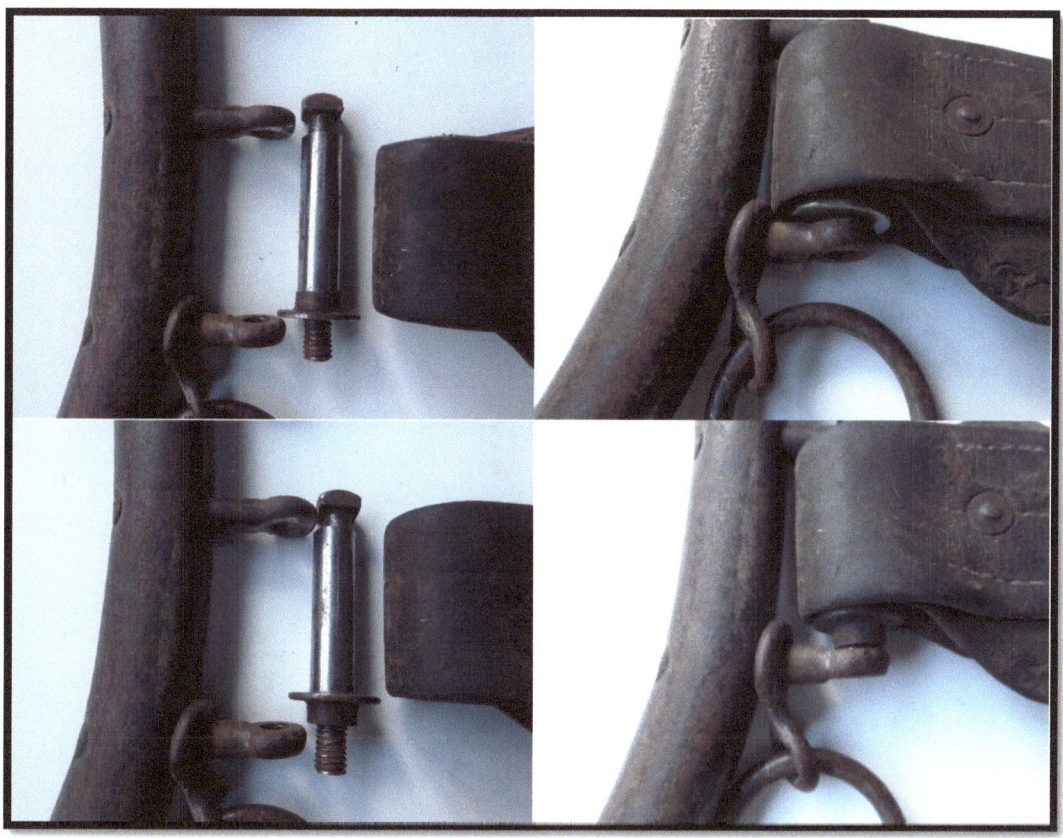

Illustration #13: Adjustability on the hame bolt with a flanged spacer allows for movement of the point of draft up and down by 1/4".

Illustration #14: This collar is too long, causing the hames to be set too low, causing the point of draft to be too low. There is no marriage at all of the three points of draft.
J.C. Allen Photo

Illustration #14 shows a situation where none of the points of draft are properly positioned. Because the collar is too long, its draft area is too low. The point of draft on the hames aligns with that of the collar, but they are both well below the ideal point of draft on the mule's shoulders. Doc observes, "This puts the draft area of the collar and therefore the forces of draft directly on the bony shoulder and associated structures which are easily damaged."

Doc continues, "How the collar lays on the collar bed is going to determine the angle of the hame on the shoulder. I don't worry about the 90 degrees with the trace initially. What I go for first is getting the collar fit with the hames so that the collar is laying on the collar bed properly. When you get the collar to fit right with the hames, then you may find it's not difficult to get the ideal point of draft on the hames. Or you may find you cannot get the point of draft where you need to have it.

"For example, if you took the mule collar and hames in illustration #14, if you took those hames, if you put a collar that fit the mule on and then took the same hames and tried to put them on the smaller collar, you would probably be able to lower the top hame strap at the ratchet to effectively make the hames shorter to go with the shorter collar. Because the hame was designed for a longer collar, though, the distance from the bottom of the hame to the trace might or might not work out."

Doc continues, "The ideal point of draft on the hame is the point on the collar-and-hame-combination where the pull is balanced on the collar up and down and distributed across the collar bed. It's not just a point equidistant from either end of the hame like balancing a stick on a finger. It has to do with how the force of the load is distributed across the collar face to the collar bed. You can't just measure it because the collar bed is much narrower at the top and much wider down below. If you're too low on the balance point, we're going to put more force on the low part of the shoulder from the load. If you are too high on the balance point too much of the load will be carried by the narrow part of the collar bed up on the sides of the neck."

In Motion

All of our considerations so far have been with the horse standing idle. Of course work gets done with the horse in motion, which introduces another consideration for why the point of draft needs to be right. As we've seen, the load is predominantly carried on the collar bed of the draft area of the horse. Also as we've seen, underneath the collar bed and underneath the muscles is the scapula or shoulder blade. Now consider the following:

"To move forward, the horse must advance his front leg and also his shoulder blade. Therefore, when he is pulling a weight, he must displace the load, for a brief moment, solely through movement of this shoulder…Evolution has not adapted the horse's shoulder for this purpose. This means that our training program and our driving equipment must allow for as much shoulder freedom as possible…. If we don't make these allowances, we will destroy the horse's shoulder movement." (2)

Doc adds, "While it's true that the shoulder blade moves, most of the motion of the shoulder blade is at its lower extreme near the point of the shoulder. It's because most of the motion of the draft area is at the point of the shoulder that we have to be so careful to keep the collar up and away from there as much as practical. A collar properly sized and seated on the collar bed with the proper point of draft that distributes the load evenly across the collar bed minimizes the work the horse has to do to move his leg and the load forward. Conversely, when a collar is too long or a collar is too wide, the horse has to work harder to move his leg and the load forward, and the risk of injury is increased."

Now consider the case of the point of draft being too low on the collar bed, as in Illustration #14. Doc explains, "A point of draft too low also interferes with the horse's stride because we're overloading the lower portion of the draft area and constraining the leg moving forward more than necessary."

Illustration 15: When an equine is working, it is pushing into the load with its shoulder. To move its shoulder, it has to move not just its leg but the weight of the load, too.
J.C. Allen Photo.

Illustration #15 shows a four-abreast of mules in motion. Note how the collars on the right two mules in the photo are oriented differently because the two mules are at different points in their strides. The collar on the second mule from the right is well seated on the collar bed, yet it is tipped back at the bottom above the mule's left leg because the other side is pushed forward by the mule's striding forward with its right leg. The collar on the rightmost mule in the photo, on the other hand, is up and forward on the left side because that mule is striding forward with its left leg. The difference in the position of these two collars is due to the different positions of the points of the shoulder which is the part of the draft area that moves forward and backward the most when an equine is in motion.

Of course, we're more accustomed to seeing the singletrees move than the front of our horses because of where we typically are when we work. Singletrees ideally equalize the alternating side-to-side rocking of the collar in forward motion as movement is transferred from the horse's draft area to the load. Doc cautions, "If we hitch a horse to a load without an equalizer such as a singletree, when one shoulder goes forward, most or potentially all of the force of the load is transferred to that one shoulder. Rather than two shoulders sharing the load equally at all times, each shoulder is alternately overloaded and unloaded as the animal moves forward. The effect produced is one of up to twice as much pressure on the shoulder and leg being advanced forward as compared with when a singletree is used that equalizes the load between the two shoulders. Working without an equalizer like a singletree throws the animal off balance, leads to discomfort and fatigue, and increases the likelihood of physical damage and psychological problems. The equalizing effect of singletrees is vitally important."

Doc continues, "When you look at equines in motion, and you consider if the collar is not well-seated on the collar bed or the point of draft on the hames is not well married to the point of draft on the horse, it's easy to imagine that the structures of the shoulder could be damaged by the forces of the load being applied to sensitive areas. On the other hand, when we have the three points of draft well married, it takes much less effort for the horse or mule to move the load forward.

"We have to keep in mind that points of draft can be impacted by the type of work we're doing. I fit collars differently if I'm pulling a light load versus a heavy one. If we have the weight of a neck yoke and pole on the collar, we need to consider if and how that's affected the ideal point of draft that we've worked so hard to achieve. How does it change when we're hitched to a mower and then does it change again when we sit on the mower seat? Finding the ideal point of draft is part art, part science, with a good measure of attention to detail and constant diligence thrown in as well."

Putting It all Together

We are searching for the elusive ideal point of draft because we know it is the most comfortable for our horses and allows them to work at their best efficiency. That the ideal point of draft is actually three ideal points of draft married together explains why many consider finding it an art rather than a science.

The 1900 article states:
"The adjustment of the hame-tugs, so as to bring the draught on the shoulder at the proper place, is also a very important matter that deserves the closest attention. If the draught is too low, the movement of the shoulders in walking gives too much motion, back and forward, to the collar, and is almost certain to cause soreness, both at the points of the shoulder and at the top of the neck; and if the draught is too high, the injury will be equally as great.

"When the hame-tugs are just at the proper place, there will be but very little motion at the top of the hames, as the horse walks along: but when too low there will be seen a weaving back and forth of the hames at the top, which shows that the draught is too near the point of the shoulders and the collar is kept in constant twist, one way and the other, which is very injurious to the shoulders and top of neck. This is generally the condition when the top of the neck and points of the shoulders are sore at the same time."

Clearly, given the propensity for soreness that accompanies ill-fitting harness, we need to keep striving to find the ideal point of draft. Doc shares, "The ideal point of draft is an anatomical and kinetic balance point in the area of the shoulder of the horse. While the ideal point of draft can differ from horse to horse, the point of draft on a particular horse remains constant. It is the point of draft on the collar and most importantly the fit of the collar and the point of draft on the hames that must be monitored and adjusted to ensure our horses' comfort."

Doc concludes, "Our horses are safer to work when they are comfortable. Behavior issues related to ill-fitting harness can become safety issues very quickly if not addressed. I am constantly reminded how hard my mentor Addie worked to achieve the ideal point of draft. He knew that ensuring the comfort of the horses meant more work, better work, and safer work. It's a lesson I think about every day that I work horses."

1) "To Properly Fit a Horse Collar," *West Gippsland Gazette*, Warragul, Victoria, Tuesday, 14 August 1900 as available at http://trove.nla.gov.au/ndp/del/article/68700231
2) Bean, Heike and Sarah Blanchard. *Carriage Driving: A Logical Approach through Dressage Training.* Wiley Publishing, Hoboken, New Jersey, 2004, p. 25-6

The black and white photographs in this chapter are from America's Rural Yesterday, Volume I: Fieldwork *published by Mischka Press and used with permission.*

The author appreciates consultation from Bernie Samson of Samson Harness Shop, Inc.

Measuring for a Collar

Collars were in abundance in all the west coast barns. Must have been a hundred in my dad's barn.
– Dale Wagner (1)

It would be nice if you had a neighbor or friend who had a couple of collars you could try on.
- Mooney Ranch (2)

Even if you have to haul your animal a considerable distance to a shop that has collars, you will end up spending less money.
- Vince Mautino (3)

So you have a horse you want to work in harness. You may even have a harness. But you need a collar. Where do you start? Hands down the best answer is to find someone who has a collection of collars and a comparable collection of experience with working horses successfully in harness. This person may be a neighbor who's a teamster, or if you are so fortunate to live close to one, a harness maker or a proprietor of a collar shop. Then take your horse to the collar collection and knowledgeable horseman (or woman) and have them find a collar that fits your horse. (While you're with them, learn as much as you can; it will serve you well, as you'll see below.)

Lynn Miller, in *Work Horse Handbook* emphasizes, "[There] are so many variables involved in the size and shape of a horse's neck that the only accurate and easy way to size the neck is to use several collars and put them on one at a time until fitting is found." (4) Doc admits that he and his partner Cathy have over fifty useable collars in their barn, accumulated over many years of fitting their horses and mules comfortably.

A farmer drills wheat in a field from which a corn was cut for silage at the Purdue Experimental Livestock farm, Lafayette, Indiana. J.C. Allen photo

So let's say your friend picked out a collar that is just right for your horse. But the collar isn't for sale. What do you do next? Or what if you don't have access to a collection of collars and a knowledgeable neighbor? What do you do next? In either case you need to understand the different styles of collars and what their critical dimensions are and why all of this is important.

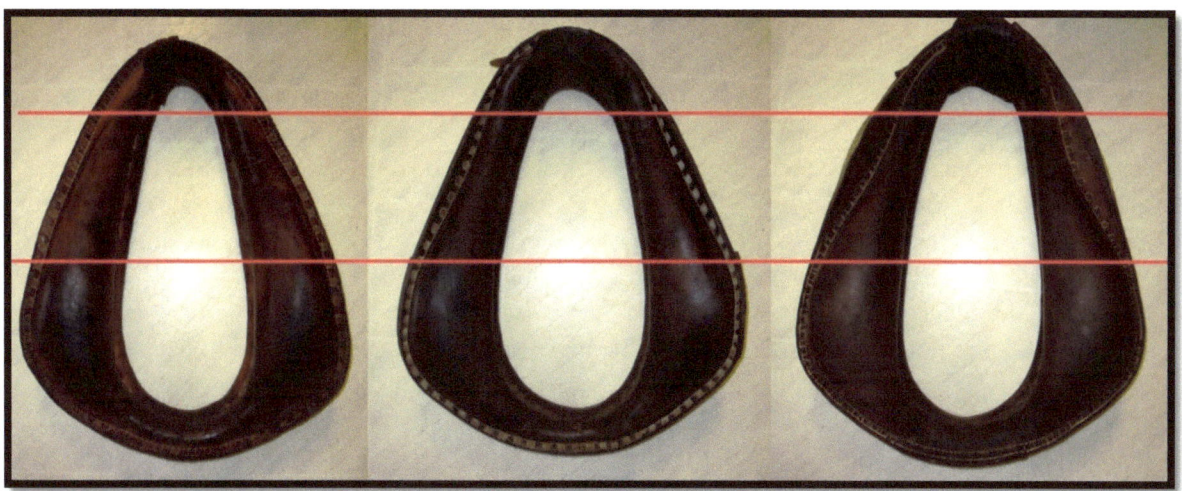

Illustration #1: Collar styles, from left: Full face, half sweeney and full sweeney. The difference is in the amount of stuffing in the area between the red lines. Photos courtesy Doc Hammill

Collar Styles

If you've decided to work equines in harness, then you've probably seen discussions of collar style. In *Work Horse Handbook*, Lynn Miller aptly describes why different styles of collars are needed: "[Horses] and mules have different shaped necks with mules commonly being more flat-sided. Stallions have thick necks with big crests and require larger-wider collars in order that they set back against the shoulder in the required manner." (5)

The vast majority of collars are of one of three styles: full face/regular cut, half-sweeney, and full sweeney. In illustration #1, the three styles are shown. If you've found a collar that fits your horse, you need to look at its face to determine its style. The 'face' of a collar is the surface that touches your horse's neck. What differs in the three styles of collars is the amount of stuffing in the collar above the draft of the collar. For thin necked animals, more stuffing is needed in this area and is provided in a full face collar. For very thick necked animals, less stuffing is needed in this area, which is addressed by a full sweeney collar (with less stuffing, there is more flexibility to shape to a bulkier neck). Most of today's horses and ponies of draft type need a moderate amount of stuffing in this area, which is why most collars today are the half-sweeney style. Bernie Samson of Samsons Harness Shop, Inc. in Gilbert, Minnesota sums up the importance of collar style this way: "A collar needs to be thick where a horse is thin and thin where a horse is thick."

The red lines in illustration #1 bound an area where we can compare the amount of stuffing in the three types of collars. All the collars are 21" in length. The thickness of the padding in the full face collar between the red lines is 2 ½"; the thickness of the padding of the half sweeney collar is 2"; and the thickness of the padding of the full sweeney collar is 1 ½".

The late Steve Bowers, in *A Teamster's View*, shares this anecdote about the different styles: "Regular cut or full face collars are made for narrow-necked animals. Many mules, mares and geldings which are being worked hard, and younger animals, wear regular cut collars. Half sweeney collars are made to fit horses with a bit more width and roundness to their necks. Fatter, underworked mares and geldings, and older animals, often use half sweeney collars. Collar manufacturers tell me that before the invention of the tractor, most of the collars in use were regular cut collars. Now, most of the collars being made are half sweeney collars. I bet the same sort of thing has happened to the pants size of the farmers since the invention of the tractor!" (6)

Doc explains, "An important reason for having full face, half sweeney, and full sweeney collars is the need to have a collar that will seat well on the shoulders of a specific equine. We need a well-seated collar that not only fits the neck and shoulders in a way that distributes the load properly over the collar bed, but we also need the collar to position itself, and therefore the hames, at an angle that will create the correct angle of draft. For example, on some thick horses with a certain type of wide upper neck, a half sweeney collar might be held too far forward at the top (at too vertical an angle), even though the collar fits in terms of length and width measurements and does not put pressure on the windpipe or pinch on the sides of the neck. A full sweeney collar of appropriate size because of its design may seat farther back on the upper part of the neck and thereby be carried at a more laid back angle and improve the angle of draft.

"For equines with the upper half of the neck very narrow and/or with very laid back shoulders, a half sweeney collar will sometimes be carried too far back at the top. This will cause the angle of the collar to be too laid back and cause an angle of draft problem. In such cases a full face collar of appropriate size and shape tends to hold the collar in a more vertical position that will improve the angle of draft.

"Sometimes a collar seems to be the right size and shape but does not seat well on the collar bed and neck; you can teeter-totter it forward and backward over a contact point somewhere between the top and bottom. In such cases, experimenting with the three collar styles (full face, half sweeney, and full sweeney) may provide the solution."

While the three styles described above are the most common, there are variations available, as this post on the *Rural Heritage* Front Porch illustrates: "I sell a collar made for mules, half sweeney but made narrow to better fit a mule.... A mule ain't a horse, only half one." (7)

Eight beautiful mules with two sulky plows create perfectly straight furrows on the Charles Kelly Ranch near Monon, Indiana.
J.C. Allen photo

Critical Collar Dimensions

The style of the collar is not as important as the size.
- Klaus Karbaumer (8)

If you have identified a collar that fits your horse and you know its style, you need to measure it so that you have the best chance possible to find one just like it. There are two common dimensions to measure, and there are two additional measurements that can be helpful.

The two common dimensions of the collar that you need to measure are its length and its draft. The length of a collar is measured on the inside of the rim, where the equine's neck will be, as shown in illustration #2. The draft of a collar is the circumference of the collar at its largest point. Measuring the draft of a collar is also shown in illustration #2.

Doc describes the importance of the draft of a collar this way: "The larger the draft the more surface area that the forces of the pull are distributed over. Buggy collars have a very small draft. They're designed to pull very light loads. Farm or field collars have a larger draft. Collars for logging, pulling contests, and other exceptionally heavy work have even larger drafts for the comfort and safety of the horse."

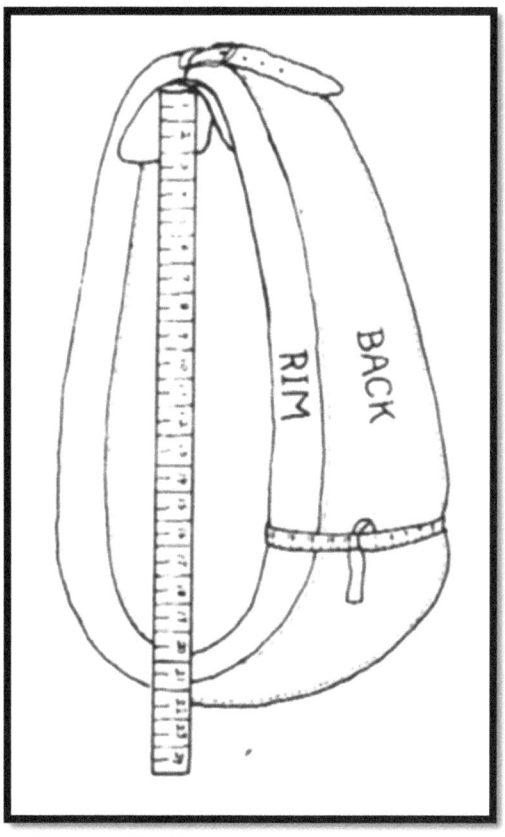

Illustration #2: Two of the common dimensions for measuring a collar are shown: the length and the draft.
Image courtesy Mari Leedy,
Stitch-n-Hitch Harness Shop

Grey, on the *Rural Heritage* Front Porch, gives this advice about choosing the draft dimension of your collar, "[The] wider the draft you can find, the more well-suited the collar will be for any type of farm work." (9) Doc elaborates, "I agree in general, but it depends on the size and angle of the collar bed of the animal. In animals with narrower, less flat collar beds, a collar with a very large draft could well extend beyond the collar bed and come too close to or even contact the bony structures and sensitive areas which should not receive forces of draft."

Two Additional Important Measurements

Let's say you have a piece of string that is four feet long. You can lay that piece of string onto the ground and form a circle, a rectangle or a triangle but the perimeter of the shape will still be four feet long.
Same thing with that 24" collar. You can make it be 24" long by 10" wide at the draft and 6" wide at the top of the neck. Or adjust your hame straps and the hame rachet and make the collar be 23" long by 11" wide at the draft and 6" wide at the top of the neck.
– Grey (10)

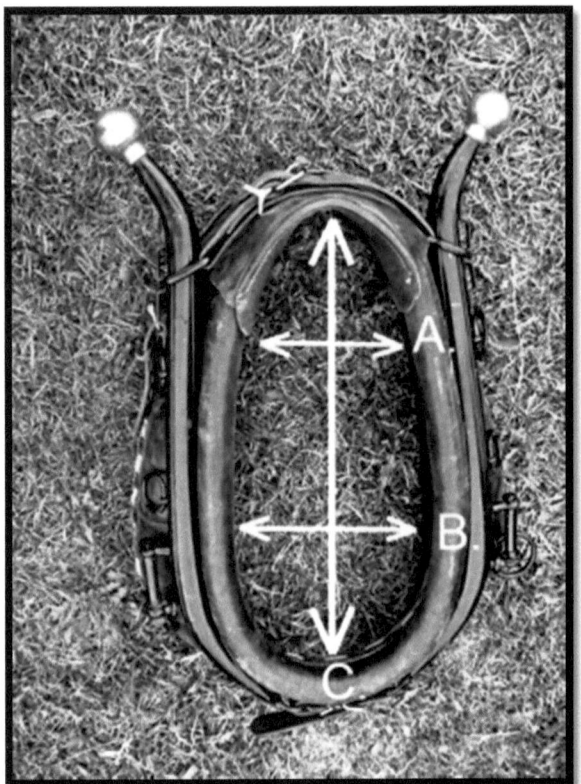

Illustration #3: Two additional measurements, beyond the length, that greatly improve your chances of ordering a collar that fits are the width in two places.

The two additional measures you can take that are helpful in finding an appropriate collar are the width in two places as shown in Illustration #3. By measuring the width of the collar a third of the way up from the bottom and a third of the way down from the top, you will be able to give the collar shop useful information for choosing a collar that's right for your horse.

Doc explains, "New collars come to us with various lengths and drafts, but from a given collar maker the patterns used to produce collars result in a very consistent shape of hole in the center of the collars. Collars of different sizes with this consistent shape of hole are then purchased by a length measurement and placed on horses with an almost infinite number of shapes to their necks – most of which are unlikely to be the same as the shape of the hole in the collar as it comes to us. If we purchase a collar by length measurement only, it can easily be too wide or too narrow at some point up and down the sides of the neck. Of course we can adjust the hames to reshape the collar to fit the sides of the neck better, but doing so will change the length which may then be incorrect.

"For example, look at the collars in illustration #4. Specifically pay attention to the shape of the center of these collars where the horse's neck goes. The one on the left is new from the collar shop. Inside it is 23" long, 7" wide one third down from the top and 8 ½" wide one third up from the bottom. The collar on the right started as a 25" with an "inside neck hole shape" like the one on the left. After being reshaped to fit by hame adjustment and years of work on a heavy-muscled horse with a wide neck (always on the 25" adjustment), it measures 23" long, 10 ½" wide one third down from top, and 12" wide one third up from bottom."

Illustration 4: Note the different shapes of the hole in the center of these collars where the equine's neck goes. The collar on the left is new; the collar on the right started with the same hole in the center but has been shaped and molded by years of work, being widened and also shrunk in length by two inches.

Doc summarizes, "It's very unfortunate that for the most part people talk about, measure for, and purchase collars by only one measurement, that being the length. The odds of choosing the right collar for a specific equine with just one measurement are very slim. By having the two width measurements, we have a much better chance of obtaining a collar that has the proper inside circumference measurement to allow it to be molded into the shape that will fit our horse."

When You Can't Try One On

What if you don't have access to a seasoned teamster with a sizable collar collection? You need to start by measuring your horse in its draft area.

The problem with just about any method is that you can only get close with measuring.
— Vince Mautino (11)

*Most times [when] I've measured the neck for a collar, instead of trying a collar to see,
I've been too big in the measurement.*
- Mooney Ranch (12)

*Depending on the shape of his neck, you might get it right the first time,
but probably you will need to try several different collars.*
- Wally B (13)

There are three common measuring methods:
1) laying a measuring tape where the collar lays;
2) Using a collar measuring tool, either purchased or home-made
3) Measuring around your horse's front leg.

To use a measuring tape, lay it along the draft area in a straight line, keeping in mind that the measurement you want isn't where you have the tape laying. You need to estimate where one end is at the base of the neck where it enters the chest and the other end is in front of the withers, keeping the measuring tape straight. The number of inches is the size of the collar.

The problem with laying a measuring tape is that you need a straight-line measurement because that's how collars are measured, but your horse's body won't allow you to lay the tape in the exact location needed for the measurement, so you are estimating the size from the very beginning. That's why we're always looking for better ways to measure.

Using a Collar-Measuring Tool

Many collar shops offer a collar measuring tool for sale. It's also possible to improvise at home.

I haven't had real good luck using a tape measure to measure a horse's neck for a collar. I like to use two framing squares, laying one over the other to make a C shape. Put one end over the neck and one under the neck where the bottom of the collar should be and then look at the measurement on the side along the neck.
- Jerry Hicks (14)

Illustration #5: A collar measuring tool can be improvised from two framing squares.

Illustration #5 shows how to take two framing squares and make a measuring tool. While not everyone necessarily has two framing squares laying around, they can be found for less than $10 each (sometimes just a dollar or two) and are a worthwhile investment given the cost of a collar, the length of time you'll own that collar, and the importance of proper collar fit. A ready-made collar measuring tool from a collar shop is likewise a worthwhile investment.

The Square method works [but] you need to know where to place them for the right reading.
- Dave W (15)

As with any tool, using the collar measuring tool/framing square method of measuring for a collar requires that you do it correctly. First, when you measure, your horse's head needs to be in the position that it will be in while working. It shouldn't be to one side or the other, looking for its friends. It shouldn't be up high because it's afraid of the framing squares, and it shouldn't be low because it's reaching for a bit of green grass.

Second, when you measure, you need to put the arms of the collar measuring tool/framing squares exactly where the extreme ends of the collar's rim will be. Keep in mind that putting the measuring tool at the base of the neck and in front of the withers on the collar bed isn't the right place. The reason is that collars are measured at the inside of their front rims and putting the measuring tool at the base of the neck and in front of the withers is farther back than where the rim of the collar will be and may result in a measurement that's too big by an inch or more.

Illustration #6: The collar measuring tool needs to be put forward of the collar bed at the depth of the collar. Two ways to estimate the right location are shown: using your hand to measure and using an oversized collar.

Bernie Samson suggests the following: Stand on the near side of your horse. Place your left hand on the horse's neck with your thumb towards the point of the shoulder and your pinky finger towards the head. Now slide your hand down the neck until your index finger rests on the collar bed. Approximately between your ring and pinky finger is where you want to take a measurement with your collar measuring tool. Or, if you have a collar that you know is too big, you can still put it on your horse and use its rim to help you locate where to put your collar measuring tool. These techniques are shown in illustration #6. Bernie emphasizes again that using a collar measuring tool and these techniques to properly place it still only give you an estimate of proper collar size.

Depending on the size of the squares you have, you may be able to read the measurement you need right off one of the squares. More likely, you'll need to hold them together and use a measuring tape to determine the inches between them, as shown in illustration #7.

Illustration #7: If you can't use the framing squares to get a measure directly, you'll need to hold them at the right size and use a measuring tape.

Taking Width Measurements on Your Horse

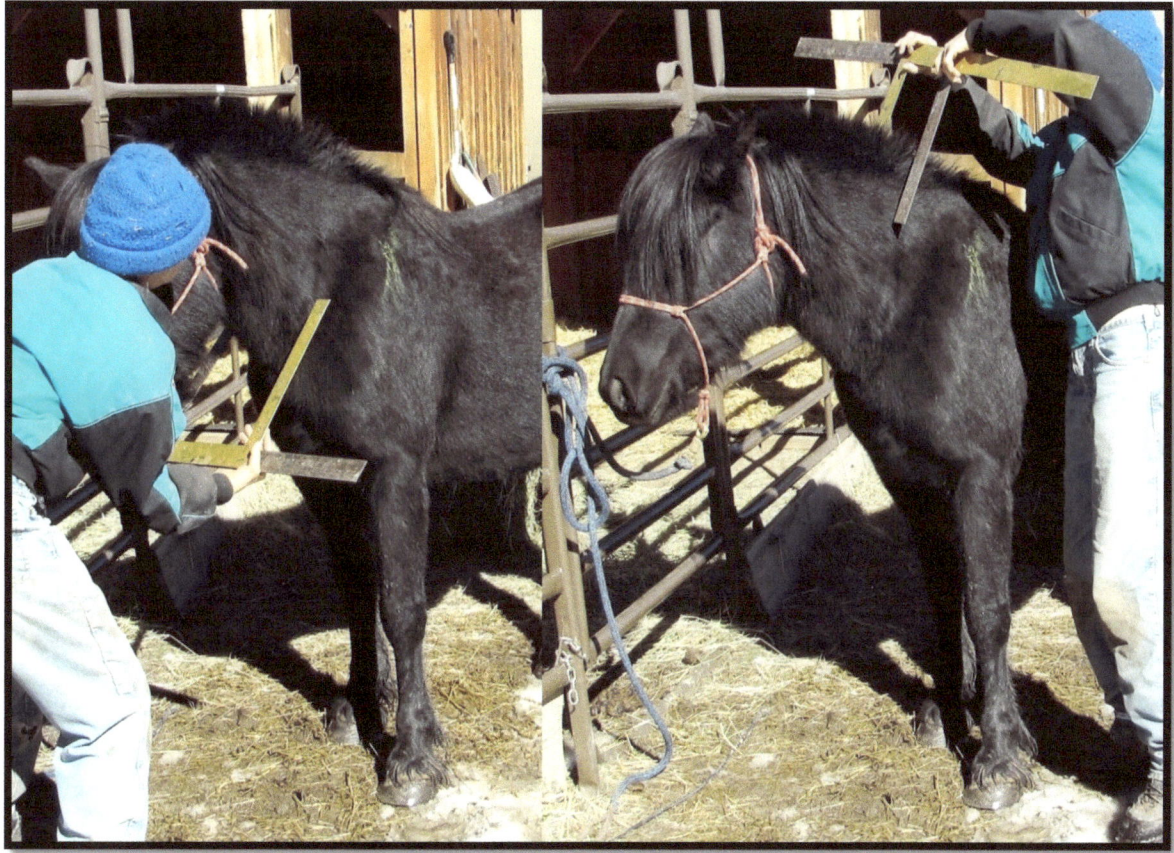

Illustration #8: By taking two additional measurements with a collar measuring tool- the width in the two widest places - you can provide even better information to a collar shop for a proper collar fit for your equine.

You can also use the collar-measuring tool to take two additional measurements that are helpful in getting the right collar to fit your horse. Doc Hammill credits his friend and fellow teamster John Erskine for showing him this technique. These two measurements are taken at the thickest point of the two most thickly muscled areas of the neck – one up high just below the crest, and a thicker area down lower closer to the base of the neck, as shown in illustration #8. Giving a collar shop these two dimensions, in addition to length, style, and draft, will increase the likelihood that the collar you purchase will fit your horse appropriately.

Doc explains, "For example, assume you accurately measure your horse and get a length of 23" so you order a new 23" collar like the one on the left in illustration #4. When it arrives you try it on your horse and find that the length is okay but it is much too tight on the sides of the neck. You call a friend and learn about taking the two width measurements as well as the length. It turns out your horse has a width of 7 ½" one third of the way down from the top of the neck, and 9 ½" wide one third of the way up from the bottom. You measure your new 23" collar and find that it measures only 7" wide one third of the way down from the top and only 8 ½" one third of the way up from the bottom. The collar can be reshaped by adjusting the hames to force the collar out to the 7 ½" width and 9 ½" width that you need but not without making the length shorter (it would likely end up being only about 22" long). So it would be necessary to purchase a 24" collar in order to get the 23" length, 7 ½" top width, and 9 ½" bottom width that you need.

"Another example is a collar that is the right length and the width on the upper part of the neck works, yet it is too wide one third of the way up from the bottom. Making it fit for width one third of the way up by bringing the lower part of the hames together will result in making the collar too long.

"I recommend that folks ask the harness or collar shop to send a collar of the style and draft they want that can be forced into a shape that produces the three measurements that are needed. It may take a little explaining and convincing, but it will be well worth the extra effort and might save the cost and time of shipping an incorrectly sized collar back and getting a different one."

The Importance of Headset When Measuring

Doc emphasizes that the proper location of your horse's head when measuring is crucial. "If we measure for or fit a collar with the equine's head too low compared to where it is when he normally works, the collar will be too small. For instance, if you measure for or fit a collar with the head lower than when the horse is checked up and then check the horse up to drive or work, the collar may end up being too tight and choking. If on the other hand, the head is too high when measuring or fitting, the measure will be too large and the collar is likely to be too loose and ill fit when the head is lower at work."

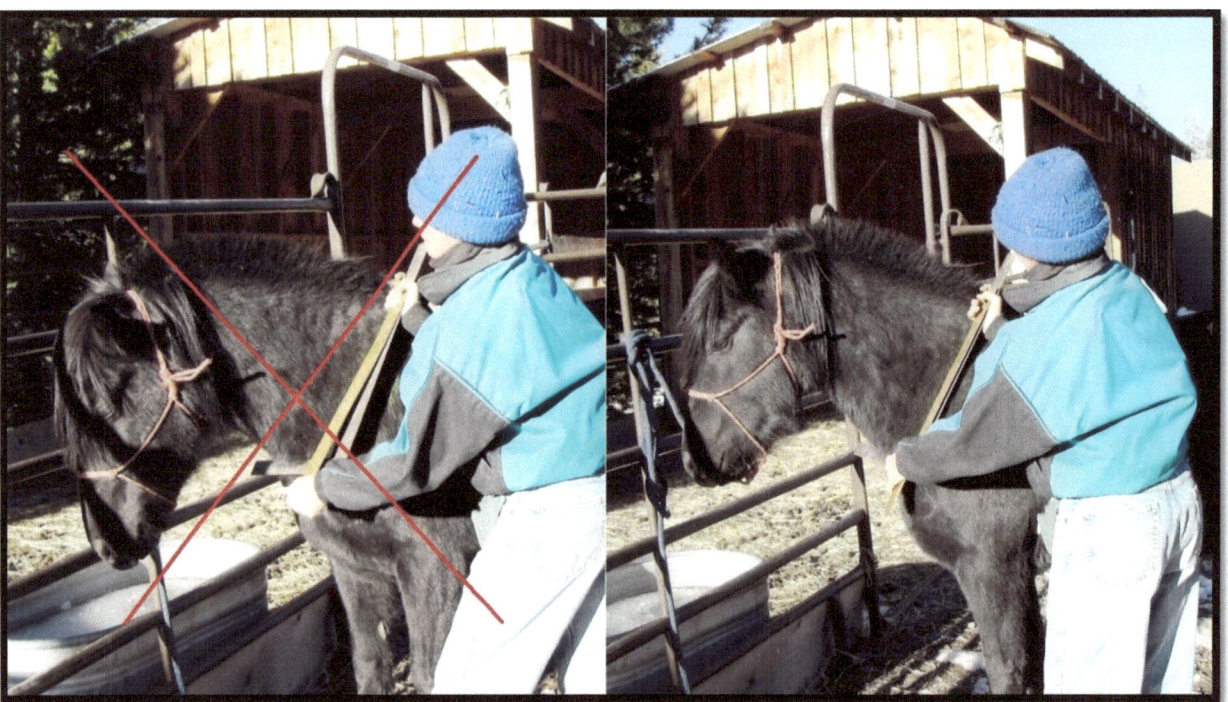

When we measure with a collar measuring tool, the position of the horse's head MUST be in the position in which it will be worked for a measurement to be close.

Doc continues, "I can't emphasize enough the potential for error if we're not extremely careful in measuring. It's very easy to measure at points too far forward or too far back on both the top and the bottom of the neck. We must also be aware that there needs to be room at the throat of the collar for the windpipe, so we need to estimate and add a little extra length so the throat of the collar does not make contact over the windpipe.

"Even with all three measurements – length then width in two places – measuring using a collar measuring tool is only an estimate because there can be so much variation in the curved lines between the measuring points on various horses' necks due to different conformation."

Measuring Technique #3

...if you measure around the thickest part of a front leg (right near the top), it will be within about an inch of collar size. I was skeptical of this fact, so I have measured all 10 drafts on my place and several others...low and behold it is always within two inches. If I rule out the horses with freakish features (2100 lb horse, 23" collar), I found that it is probably within about a half inch!
- Jason Mac (16)

Jason Mac isn't the only one that has found this technique reasonably accurate. Bernie Samson, who as a harness maker regularly coaches people on buying the right size collar, says, "It's amazing how close this measurement comes to estimating the correct size for a collar. It works for ponies all the way to drafts. Anyone can do it. The only time I've seen people run into issues is with, for instance, some quarter horses that have a bulge in their leg that throws off the measurement."

Will Beattie, on the *Rural Heritage* Front Porch, wisely suggested that this method can be used to double-check the other measuring methods; if they give wildly different answers, you'll want to make sure you are doing the measuring correctly. (17) Doc concurs: "I measured the horses in my herd, and the leg measurement did typically come within an inch of the collar length measurement. But, and this is important, for the horses in my herd, the length measurement would never be adequate on its own for estimating correct collar size. The variations in the width of the horses' necks will cause changes in the needed length measurement that this technique just can't predict. You saw exactly what I mean in illustration #4."

In the Internet Age

If you are one of those horsemen (or women) who don't have access to a seasoned teamster with a sizeable collar collection, you may feel daunted by the measuring techniques available and their accuracy (or lack thereof). A middle road might be to take advantage of the internet. By taking photos and/or videos and sharing them with someone knowledgeable, you might be able to get measurements that you feel more confident about.

Doc shares, "I'm doing more long distance consulting and coaching by phone and computer all the time. It's a great option when someone doesn't have access to an expert or a mentor in person. Like all other aspects of driving and working horses in harness, doing a good job of sizing and fitting collars is an art -part science, part numbers, and a lot of tinkering and fussing to get it right and keep it right. I encourage folks to get help from someone who is truly knowledgeable one way or another. Trial and error is usually a tough way to learn."

You're Not Done Yet

In the chapter "The Elusive Ideal Point of Draft" we learned about the anatomy of the shoulder area of the horse and how important proper collar and harness fit are to protecting the sensitive structures of this area. Ensuring the comfort of our horses not only protects them from injury but also makes our work safer and more efficient. Going from understanding the importance of proper fit to getting proper fit is, of course, not easy. A quick search of the *Rural Heritage* Front Porch brought up 55 strings on 'collar fit' over a period of ten years, with sixteen of those strings explicitly about fitting a collar; the rest were about the many ways that getting the right collar fit impacts our horses' comfort and ability to work well in harness.

Collar fit is often compared to fitting human boots. You wouldn't attempt to climb a mountain in a pair of boots that were too big or too small, just as you shouldn't expect your horse to work with a collar that's improperly fit. Doc was recently on a website looking at work boots. "There was a chart comparing foot measurements to boot size. On a diagram of the foot, the measurements required were length from toe to heel, greatest width at the front of the foot, and greatest width at the heel. It was very similar to the three measurements I use when measuring for collar size. In my opinion, any measurement system using a single measurement is pretty much a shot in the dark."

At this point you may have measurements and you may know the style of collar you need, but you're still not yet ready to buy a collar. You still need to make some additional decisions that will significantly impact the size and style of the collar you choose. For instance, you need to think about using collar pads or not, adjustable collars or not, and the impact of working condition.

Once you do buy a collar, there's even more that must be considered before you can work your horse. Doc explains, "Collars rarely come off the production line with the measurements we need. Rather, they typically need to be reshaped and molded into the perfect size and shape for your animal. This can be accomplished first by way of proper hame adjustment, and second by the animal doing some relatively light steady work in the collar after hame adjustment has it fitting close to ideal. The secret ingredient is a collar that has the correct inside circumference distance to be molded into the specific size and shape of a cross section of the neck at the proper level and angle on the neck where the collar should rest." So, there's more to come!

1) Response by Dale Wagner at 2009-10-20 10:44:58 at
   http://www.ruralheritage.com/messageboard/frontporch/12385.htm
2) Response by Mooney Ranch at 2007-08-01 23:06:11 at
   http://www.ruralheritage.com/messageboard/frontporch/9461.htm
3) Response by Vince Mautino at 2007-07-31 14:58:51 at
   http://www.ruralheritage.com/messageboard/frontporch/9461.htm
4) Miller, Lynn R. *Work Horse Handbook*. Sisters, Oregon: Small Farmers Journal, Inc., 1981, p. 81
5) Miller, p. 80.
6) Bowers, Steve. *A Teamster's View: More and Different*. Fort Collins: Bowers Farm, 2001, p. 38.
7) Response by Buggy at 2008-10-20 13:32:33 at
   http://www.ruralheritage.com/messageboard/frontporch/11126.htm
8) Response by Klaus Karbaumer at 2012-03-06 21:43:13 at
   http://www.ruralheritage.com/messageboard/frontporch/15903.htm
9) Response by grey at 2012-10-30 12:39:55 at
   http://www.ruralheritage.com/messageboard/frontporch/16688.htm
10) Response by grey at 2013-08-29 09:50:14 at
    http://www.ruralheritage.com/messageboard/frontporch/17798.htm

11) Response by Vince Mautino at 2007-07-31 14:58:51 at
http://www.ruralheritage.com/messageboard/frontporch/9461.htm
12) Response by Mooney Ranch at 2010-03-31 23:43:24 at
http://www.ruralheritage.com/messageboard/frontporch/13042.htm
13) Response by wally b at 2007-07-29 21:36:35 at
http://www.ruralheritage.com/messageboard/frontporch/9461.htm
14) Response by Jerry Hicks at 2011-08-01 06:45:19 at
http://www.ruralheritage.com/messageboard/frontporch/15031.htm
15) Response by Dave W at 2010-04-09 01:31:21 at
http://www.ruralheritage.com/messageboard/frontporch/13070.htm
16) Response by stuck in the past alberta canada at 2012-05-29 21:14:41 at
http://www.ruralheritage.com/messageboard/frontporch/16212.htm
17) Response by Will Beattie at 2010-03-31 22:59:58 at
http://www.ruralheritage.com/messageboard/frontporch/13042.htm

Bernie Samson is the proprietor of Samson Harness Shop, Inc., 218-865-4602. The author is grateful to Mari Leedy of Stitch 'N Hitch Harness Shop, www.stitchnhitch.com

The historic black and white photographs in this chapter are from America's Rural Yesterday, Volume I: Fieldwork *published by Mischka Press and used with permission.*

To Pad or Not to Pad (a Collar)

I've had horses that wouldn't tighten the tugs without pads. The shoulders needed a cushion. – Dale Wagner (1)

I'm more a minimalist and don't believe in cushioning the cushion. - Ken (2)

Myself, I would never deliberately buy a collar that was too big for my horse with the intention of padding it out. (see addendum to this comment below.) – Grey (3)

**Collar pads can be used to improve a horse's ability to work comfortably.
Allen photo.**

As the above comments from the *Rural Heritage* Front Porch illustrate, collar pads generate a spectrum of opinions. Some have found that their collar provides all the cushion on the shoulder their equine needs; others have found that collar pads make sense for their situation. The key of course is that the collar should properly fit the horse to maximize their ability to transfer their movement to movement of the load. If a collar pad helps a collar fit properly and improves the comfort of the horse, then a collar pad is probably a good idea. And just like everything when it comes to working equines, a collar pad can also be used in a way that is uncomfortable for the horse and therefore has the potential to cause emotional and physical damage and therefore safety issues. In addition, while collar pads can help with some mis-sized collar problems, they can't make up for all of them, so we must never lose sight of our goal of a properly fitted collar.

The Purpose of Collar Pads

I may be in the minority here, but I still feel that if you have just the right collar fit then a bare collar works best, particularly with heavy work... That said, my horses do gain and lose over the season and I have a limited number of collars to use so I too have multiple pads to accommodate the changes in sizing during the season.
– Brad Johnson (4)

Some pad to make a collar fit right. Some to protect the face of a high dollar collar. And sorry to say, some just to be able to claim their horse wears a bigger collar than he does. - J.L. Holt (5)

As J.L. Holt suggests, collar pads are used for several reasons. The most typical are:
1) they provide extra cushion;
2) they are used to shim out a collar that is a little too big so that it fits the horse properly;
3) they can protect the horse from rough spots on a used collar that is otherwise serviceable;
4) they are used therapeutically to protect an injured shoulder; or
5) they are used to create more space at the throat to protect the windpipe.

A variation on #2, as Brad Johnson suggests, is that they are used to take up space in a collar that formerly fit well but is now too large because the horse has slimmed down with work or for other reasons.

Doc describes another variation: "I know a teamster who worked an Appy mare with a half pad on one side because that's what she needed to work comfortably. I relate this story with caution; doing something like this – a one-sided pad – has the significant potential for creating a problem. It must be done with care; in that case it worked."

Pads and Collar Sizing

If we are setting out to buy a collar for our working equine, then we do need to think about whether we intend to use a collar pad at the outset because it will impact the size of collar that we buy. Depending on the pad, the collar may have to be as much as 2" larger than the size we arrive at through measuring.

If you think a collar pad makes sense in your situation, Doc explains some considerations: "If you anticipate ever using a collar pad under a collar, doing so will effectively reduce the size of the collar, so the space the pad takes up inside the collar must be taken into account in your calculations for collar size. Keep in mind that collar pads not only come in various thicknesses but when made of the same components they can even vary in thickness from different manufacturers, and sometimes they can vary from the same manufacturer or distributor at different times."

If we are fortunate enough to have access to a collar collection and pad collection and a knowledgeable friend, then we may not have any trouble buying a collar that fits. Many of us, though, will be buying a collar sight-unseen so we need to think about what to do if a collar arrives that doesn't fit. Even if we don't intend to use collar pads initially, they may end up helping us improve the fit of a collar that is otherwise too large.

Strategies for Adjusting Collar Size After Purchase

Sometimes I got [the collar shop] to send me two; I chose the one I wanted then sent the other back with payment for the one I kept. Yes, there is a little shipping cost involved, but you will use the collar for years so you want a very good fit. – Will Beattie (6)

You can't make a collar that's too small bigger, but you can pad a collar that's a little big. In the end, the right size is the best one. – Bret (7)

My aim is to fit the collar to the horse. If I can't get an exact fit with a naked collar, I will pad to try to adjust the fit. – Grey (8)

Let's say we plan to purchase a collar sight-unseen. What are our options if it doesn't fit when it arrives? As Will Beattie suggests, ordering more than one then returning the ones you don't want is a possible strategy. If the collar is too small, unfortunately, there is only one choice, as Doc explains: "If you end up with a collar that is just too small to reshape to fit your horse, you have no option but to get a larger collar. Or a smaller horse!"

Grey and Dale Wagner suggest that collar pads can be used to adjust collar fit. Doc concurs, "It would be better to end up with a collar that is a little too large and make up the difference with a pad than to end up with one that is too small. Pads are much less expensive than collars and are lighter and therefore cheaper to ship."

A collar measuring tool, used before ordering, can also help you end up with a properly sized collar. Such a tool costs about the same as the price of returning a collar so it can be a worthwhile investment.

Collar Size and Working Condition

A good fit collar does not need a pad. However, if the critter goes to sweating and drops a few pounds, then a pad comes in handy, to my way of thinking. – Buggy (9)

If the collar fits the horse; if it loses weight or muscle, then add the pad. – Don McAvoy (10)

Some horses can wear the same size all the time but some the neck just keeps shrinking as you work them. – Dale Wagner (11)

I like to have three pad options for when they sweat off a lot of water during haying or the wagon train. – Grey (12)

Another consideration when planning to purchase a collar is an honest assessment of our horse's current and anticipated future working condition. If the horse is already work-hardened and you anticipate keeping it that way, then ordering a collar that fits correctly is a good answer. However, if your horse is out of condition and you anticipate getting it into working condition, you will have to adjust collar fit over time. You'll have to decide whether to buy a collar now that fits and then one later that fits if necessary or to buy one that fits now and then pad it out later if necessary. (Adjustable collars may be another option in this situation and are the subject of the next chapter.)

Collar Pads and Age

Let me add a quick addendum to my previous statement [about never buying a collar that I know is too big.] If I had a growthy young animal, I might buy a collar a bit too large and pad it if I expected the horse to grow into it quickly. So I shouldn't have said "never". But for an adult animal, I buy collars to fit the horse, not to shim the horse out with a pad. – Grey (13)

Bringing on a young animal, as Grey suggests, is another situation where collar pads can play a role in collar fit by allowing you to possibly purchase a single collar for the life of the horse. However, some horses may not change much as they age, so purchasing a collar you know is too big should be done cautiously.

Some teamsters have found that mares with foals at foot will lose mass in their necks while lactating and then regain it when the foal is weaned. Collar pads may be helpful in shimming out the collar during the period when the mare's neck slims down.

Doc has found that collar pads are also useful at the far end of the age spectrum. "I've had older horses that lost some muscle mass and had less natural cushion, so we started using pads on them, just for cushioning. They were doing work similar to that they'd always done but with less protective muscle under the collar. A little extra padding was good insurance they would be comfortable in their work."

Types of Collar Pads

A thin felt pad, a thick deer hair pad, and a thick deer hair top pad are the three pad types I like to keep around to adjust collar fit when necessary. However, I also have several sizes of collars in my barn.
– Grey (14)

If you buy good collars you won't need pads unless they lose a little weight from working in summer. I've done both ways and when you don't have pads you can wipe the collars and go. Anything other than vinyl pads get wet and have to dry or they go on the horse dirty. – Mooney Ranch (15)

I have 2 sets of vinyl pads for each horse. I have both thick pads (2") and thin (1"). This helps insure perfect collar fit as they change their weight/body condition over the year. Even with consistent summer work, my horses tend to put on weight when they are on fresh grass. - George (16)

I have used vinyl pads for about 4 years. I agree, they are great for horses that you don't use as much as you would like. I have a couple of different attachment versions. A clip on the collar version and a velcro version. I prefer the velcro attachment, hands down. However, you do get an interesting reaction from the horses the first few times you rrrrip that velcro strap apart taking it off! – Tim (17)

There are three common materials from which collar pads are made: deer hair, felt, and vinyl. Deer hair pads (technically cotton ticking/fabric stuffed with deer hair) tend to be thicker. Felt pads tend to be thinner. Vinyl pads are often preferred because they don't soak up sweat and therefore are less likely to get dirty and chafe. Also, because they don't get wet, vinyl pads don't have to be dried out between work sessions like the other types do. Some vinyl pads have vinyl on the horse side and ticking on the outside.

Different materials perform differently in different situations. For instance they each respond differently to moisture, whether from sweat, rain or snow. Doc shares, "There can be either advantages or disadvantages to having moisture soaked up by a pad, and the same can be true for it not being soaked up. Humidity and temperature play a role that is not always predictable. At times a specific

Collar pads come in different materials and thicknesses. From the outside in: cotton-covered deer hair, vinyl, and felt.

pad may be an advantage in dealing with heat and/or moisture and/or friction then again under somewhat different conditions it may not. Sometimes it's specific to an individual horse, not the pad type or material necessarily. In some animals, skin and other tissues are inherently more sensitive and less durable. In general, heat and moisture are not our friends in terms of working horses."

Collar pads consist of both padding and the mechanism that attaches them to the collar. Most collar pads have clips. Doc notes, "The clips on collar pads are prone to coming loose and pulling out or breaking off if not well cared for and handled gently. Some are better attached than others at the factory. We need to check the clips and rivets

The clips and rivets on collar pads need to be checked regularly to make sure they are secure and don't have potential to injure our horses. Here the clip on the left has come loose.

they are attached with frequently so if they don't hold up, they don't cause injury to our horses."

Top Pads

There are top pads for just the top of the collar if the collar is too long and the width is just right. You can get thin pads or thick ones. The felt ones are only about 1/2" to 3/4" thick. – Grey (18)

If you think you only need to take up space on the bottom and your sides fit well, they make top pads that go under the flap to lift the collar up about an inch. – Dennis Decker (19)

Top pads provide cushioning and take up length. They come in various materials and thicknesses, from left to right: deer hair, felt, vinyl.

Top pads, as Grey and Dennis indicate, fit under the collar cap and are often used to take up collar length. Top pads are made of various materials resulting in different thicknesses. Top pads also protect the horse's neck from extreme tongue weight, as may be experienced with mowers and other equipment.

Doc adds, "I did research for an article once on tongue weights, and I was shocked. My old dump rake with a person on the seat had the heaviest tongue weight of all – almost twice as much as a #9 mower. So we need to not make assumptions about what types of equipment have heavy and light tongue weights; instead we need to assess when a top pad might be important to help our horses be comfortable."

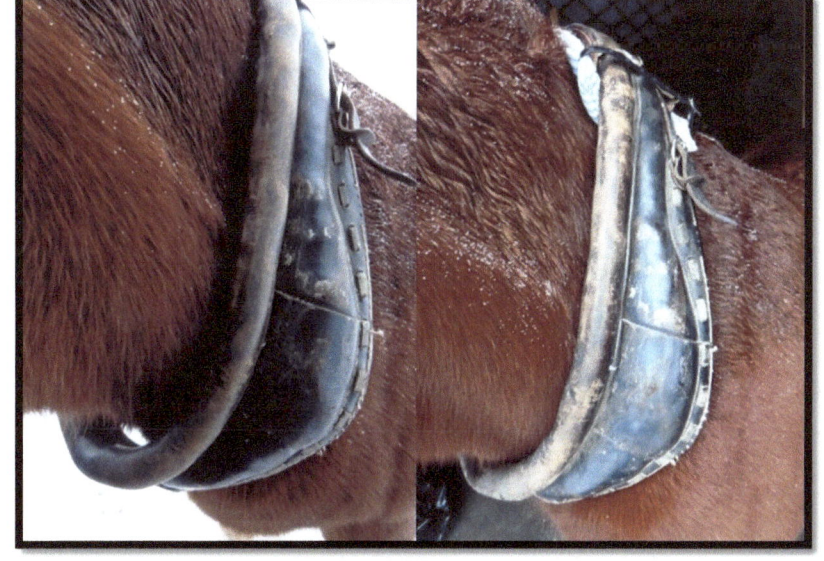

On the left is a collar that is too long but is okay on the sides. On the right is the same collar with a top pad taking up the excess length.

Pads as Cushion

As Dale Wagner suggested in the first quote in this chapter, some horses need the extra cushion of a collar pad on their shoulder to be comfortable doing their work. The padding in a collar pad is softer than that in a collar, so collar pads do play a different role from a cushioning standpoint than collars do.

Doc adds, "I'm not for or against collar pads. My goal is always to make the horse comfortable in its work – both physically and psychologically comfortable. In most situations a well-fitting collar without a pad can accomplish that goal. However, if I suspect that a specific pad option has the potential to provide more comfort or protect the horse better I will try it. The horse will tell me if it works better for him or not. The heavier the draft demands of a job, the larger the draft area should be and the greater is the need for cushioning to protect the animal from pressure and concussion. This is doubly true if there is any chance that the animals will be jerked by the load hanging up."

Pads as Shims

The sides of the collar, you should not be able to get your whole hand in between the rim of the collar and your horse's neck (proper fit). Just your fingers. So, before you order a full pad, estimate that most are an inch thick. That will add an inch to both sides of the collar. If you think that will be a good fit, then you are on your way.
– Will Beattie (20)

A pad is like a half size. They don't make collars in half sizes so use a CLEAN pad to make it fit right.
– Dale Wagner (21)

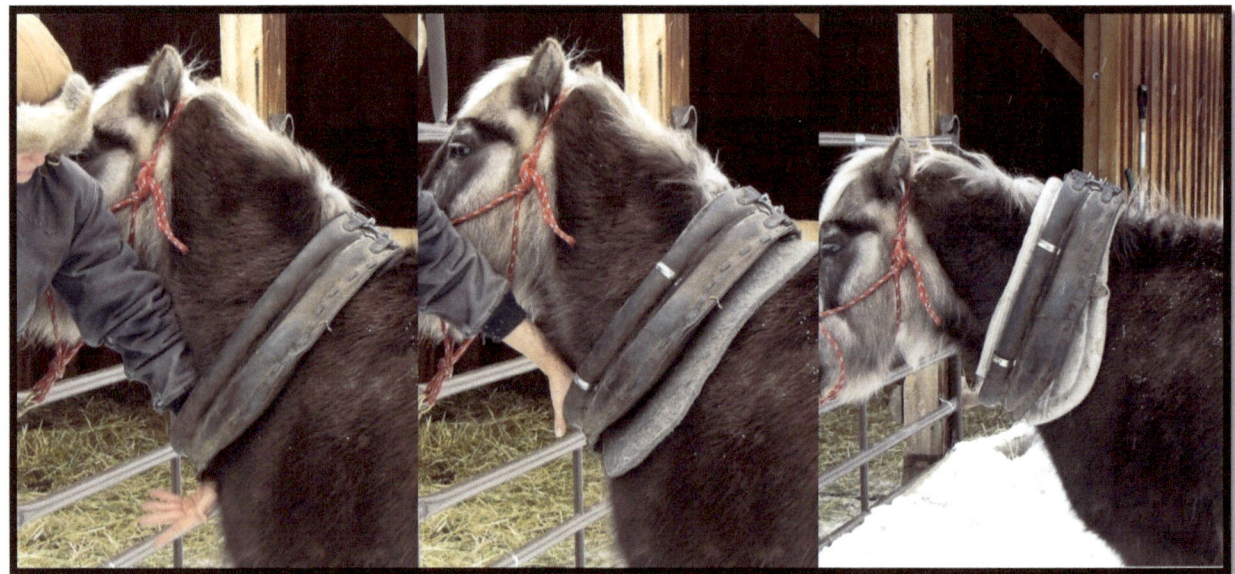

A primary use of collar pads is to shim out a collar that is too large. On left, the naked collar is too long and too wide; in center a felt pad makes it fit properly; on right a deer hair pad makes the collar too small and keeps the collar from sitting on the shoulder properly.

A primary use of collar pads is to create a properly fit collar by shimming. If you have a collar that you suspect is too big, you need to figure out where the extra space is. Is it on the sides? Is it the length that is the problem? As Will Beattie suggests, different pads are needed to solve different problems. Top pads take up length, while full pads take up both length and width. Both come in different thicknesses to take up different amounts of space.

On the other hand, Doc cautions, "If a collar isn't shaped like the horse's neck before you put a pad in it, the pad can potentially cause more problems than it solves. If you have a collar that's too long and you put a full pad in, you may have corrected the length problem only to find that the collar is now too narrow and pinches along the sides of the neck or won't sit all the way down on the shoulders. A top pad may have been a better choice, or perhaps a thinner full pad combined with adjusting the hames to reshape the collar so that with the thinner pad it has both the right length and enough width."

The Importance of Cleanliness

Dale Wagner makes an important point when he says pads should be clean. Doc explains, "After ill-fitting collars, most of the shoulder sores I've seen were due to dirty, wet, or damaged pads causing chafing. In my opinion it takes more effort to keep pads clean than to keep the face of a collar clean because pads tend to pick up dirt, sweat, hair, and debris faster than leather collars do, and they wear out many times faster. The ultimate job of a pad is to in some way help the horse do its work more comfortably. Dirty, worn, or wet pads will cause more problems than they solve."

Some collars have tick faces rather than leather faces. Those tick faces get sweaty and dirty just like pads do so must be managed similarly.

Collar Pads and Used/Worn/Defective Collars

Many of us have seen them or even put them on a horse: a used collar, worn from use that is mostly serviceable. Collar pads can come in handy with these sorts of collars by protecting the horse from rough spots or defects. Doc explains, "I've seen collars with small cracks or roughened-up leather or a collar cap that isn't smooth. I've had collars like that, and I wouldn't put them on a horse's shoulder the way they were, but with a pad they are structurally sound and perfectly usable if the pad is what's in contact with the shoulder."

Therapeutic Use of Collar Pads

I ordered some vinyl pads…. They were advertised to heal collar galls and I'll be darned if it is not true. I have had no trouble since. – Dave (22)

One use of collar pads is to prevent or protect a sore shoulder, or in the case of top pads, a sore on the top of the neck. Pads of all material can be used in this manner, but vinyl pads seem to be especially valued, as Dave indicates in his Front Porch comment.

Doc demonstrates on one of his videos how a collar pad can be used therapeutically. While his demonstration is on a deer hair-type pad, you can also use the same technique with felt or vinyl. "First you locate the exact spot on the pad which will lie directly over the inflamed area or sore on the shoulder or neck. Then on the outside of the pad at that spot, you cut the fabric and remove enough deer hair to create a deer hair-free area. This creates a pocket over the lesion where little or no pressure or friction from the draft is transferred to the shoulder. Of course it's best not to work a horse that has a bruise or sore, but if you have to, using a pad modified this way may prevent further damage and speed up healing." (23)

Protecting the Windpipe

Occasionally, on pulling competition horses and logging horses, you will see multiple pads. Here the pads are serving an additional purpose beyond cushioning and shimming: they are keeping the rim of the collar at the throat away from the windpipe under the extreme exertion required in heavy pulling situations.

Doc explains, "Push on your own trachea with your thumb and see how very little pressure causes pain. You will understand immediately how painful it can be for a horse to push into a collar that makes contact with his trachea.

Sometimes collar pads are layered to provide additional space at the windpipe, especially on pulling or logging horses. For instance, the far horse in this photo has a black and a red pad. Mischka photo, used with permission.

Relatively little pressure from a collar on the windpipe (trachea) causes pain and is a sure way to sour a horse on pulling. The extreme forces generated by heavy pulling compresses collars back on shoulders and necks much harder than we could ever push them back to check collar fit. The gap between the bottom ends of properly fitting collar pads creates extra distance between the collar and the trachea and thus tends to protect the trachea better on hard pulls."

When we add collar pads, it's important (as it always is) to check how the collar seats on the collar bed not only when the horses are standing still but during movement of a load and between trips. Allen photos

Collar Pads and Point of Draft

Doc cautions, "When a collar pad or top pad is added or removed it causes the collar to be raised or lowered on the horse's neck. In either case there can be a change in the way the draft area of the collar is positioned on and/or fits the collar bed, and also potentially a change in the relationship between the correct point of draft on the shoulder and the point of draft on the hames. Always evaluate carefully the fit of the collar after any change is made, before attaching the hames, after fastening the hames, after any adjustment of the hames, after the horses are hitched, pulling a load, and frequently thereafter."

Crooked Pads

Collar pads are usually connected to the rim of the collar with clips. The clips cannot be trusted to keep the pad in the same place over time; pads can migrate during storage, for instance. It's therefore very important to check the position of the pad whenever a collar is placed on a horse to make sure the pad is where it is supposed to be. A crooked collar pad has the potential to cause discomfort to the horse, which may lead to safety issues.

The collar pad on the near horse is crooked. Care must be taken with collar pads to make sure they stay even in length on each side of the collar so they don't cause discomfort and lead to safety issues. Mischka photo, used with permission.

Doc shares, "It is rare when I go through draft horse magazines to not find a picture of a horse with a crooked collar pad. You'd be surprised how common this problem is. Pads can shift and migrate during work, when collars are put on and taken off, as well as when they are hanging or transported. Crooked pads place unequal forces on the two shoulders and thus distribute the forces of draft in different places on each side of the neck. Horses are very sensitive to this and will adjust their posture in an attempt to equalize the pressures. This can lead to discomfort, physical problems, irritability, and behavior problems. In the photograph showing the crooked pad, the horse with the crooked pad is showing some unease. Whether or not this reaction is actually caused by the crooked pad, what we're seeing in the horse is the type of behavior that can result from unequal feel on the two shoulders.

"The process of putting collars with pads on and taking them off is a time when pads are prone to move, especially when one side of the pad is unfastened so the collar can be opened up and slipped around the neck. Check pads often to make sure they are even at the bottom, and smooth, flat, and in contact with the collar throughout their full length."

Conclusion

I think most people don't have a collar fitting near as tight as they think they do. What most people think as fitting correct, I would add a pad. – Dale Wagner (24)

I prefer not to use a pad whenever possible. The more you ask of them, the more crucial it is to have a good-fitting collar. – Grey (25)

I didn't grow up farming. I had no set paradigms. The biggest problem I had learning was that everyone had their own ideas on every aspect and there was never one right answer. – Ken (26)

Many teamsters use pads, and many others do not. Doc notes, "I typically don't use a collar pad unless I feel there is a good reason to do so. The good reason is usually my belief that using the pad will in some way improve the horse's comfort and well-being. Equines are extremely sensitive animals both physically and emotionally/psychologically. It's amazing what tiny little changes can make them uncomfortable or, better, comfortable.

"The horse is the ultimate judge. With equines anytime I change something it's a test. I ask and keep asking: is this working better for the animal or not? If we pay attention, they tell us what works for them and what doesn't. Comfort and well-being are what it's all about. Many respected and knowledgeable horsemen and women and equine behaviorists believe that around 80% of behavior problems in equines are due to physical discomfort. So I feel we have a huge responsibility to help our horses drive and work comfortably. Take every opportunity to evaluate and improve collar fit and function whether it involves using pads or not."

Whether we intend to use a pad with our collar or only plan to use one as a last resort, we need to make that decision before buying a collar for our horse. As Ken concluded, there is not a single right answer, including regarding collar pads, because we all work different horses in different places in different situations. We each, then, have a unique responsibility. It is up to us to ensure our equines are working as comfortably as possible, for their safety and for ours. Collar pads have the potential to help with that goal.

The black and white photographs in this chapter are from America's Rural Yesterday Volume 2, *published by Mischka Press.*

1) Response by Dale Wagner at 2006-08-12 10:10:16 at
   http://www.ruralheritage.com/messageboard/frontporch/7804.htm
2) Response by Ken at 2006-08-14 06:20:16 at
   http://www.ruralheritage.com/messageboard/frontporch/7804.htm
3) Response by grey at 2012-10-29 14:36:51 at
   http://www.ruralheritage.com/messageboard/frontporch/16688.htm
4) http://www.draftanimalpower.org/forums/topic/collar-pad/
5) Same as #4
6) Response by Will Beattie at 2012-03-06 22:54:32 at
   http://www.ruralheritage.com/messageboard/frontporch/15903.htm

7) Response by Bret4207 at 2012-03-08 07:10:29 at
http://www.ruralheritage.com/messageboard/frontporch/15903.htm
8) Response by grey at 2012-10-29 14:36:51 at
http://www.ruralheritage.com/messageboard/frontporch/16688.htm
9) Response by Buggy at 2006-01-18 17:14:59 at
http://www.ruralheritage.com/messageboard/frontporch/6906.htm
10) Response by Don McAvoy at 2012-11-07 09:17:18 at
http://www.ruralheritage.com/messageboard/frontporch/16718.htm
11) Response by Dale Wagner at 2013-08-29 09:52:16 at
http://www.ruralheritage.com/messageboard/frontporch/17798.htm
12) Response by grey at 2012-10-29 17:47:51 at
http://www.ruralheritage.com/messageboard/frontporch/16688.htm
13) Same as #12
14) Same as #12
15) Response by Mooney Ranch at 2012-10-29 14:38:05 at
http://www.ruralheritage.com/messageboard/frontporch/16688.htm
16) Same as #4
17) Response by Tim...Central IL at 2007-03-30 00:05:12 at
http://www.ruralheritage.com/messageboard/frontporch/8930.htm
18) Response by grey at 2013-08-29 09:50:14 at
http://www.ruralheritage.com/messageboard/frontporch/17798.htm
19) Response by Dennis Decker at 2005-05-02 20:14:18 at
http://www.ruralheritage.com/messageboard/frontporch/5944.htm
20) Response by Will Beattie at 2010-04-06 10:15:19 at
http://www.ruralheritage.com/messageboard/frontporch/13070.htm
21) Response by Dale Wagner at 2013-08-29 09:52:16 at
http://www.ruralheritage.com/messageboard/frontporch/17798.htm
22) Response by Dave at 2003-08-03 09:21:31 at
http://www.ruralheritage.com/messageboard/frontporch/3347.htm
23) Hammill, Doc and Don Hill. "Managing Collar Sores," Fundamentals 3 and 4: Gentle, Effective Techniques for Driving and Working Horses in Harness, DVD, 2003.
24) Response by Dale Wagner at 2010-04-11 11:17:59 at
http://www.ruralheritage.com/messageboard/frontporch/13093.htm
25) Response by grey at 2011-08-03 11:34:19 at
http://www.ruralheritage.com/messageboard/frontporch/15031.htm
26) Response by Ken at 2006-08-14 06:20:16 at
http://www.ruralheritage.com/messageboard/frontporch/7804.htm

Adjustable Collar Considerations

I like my adjustable collars. My horses are still growing and they fit well. I slip them over the head so I don't have to undo them. They cost a bit more, but from 2 yrs to 4 yrs in the neck they have saved me money.
- Mooney Ranch (1)

We do not believe in adjustable collars but have a rack of sizes with pads and half pads to make good fits.
- Dave W (2)

Adjustable collars obviously have their enthusiasts and their critics. If we are in need of a new collar for our equine, our goal is to ensure a comfortable and effective working situation for them, so we need to understand adjustable collars enough to determine if they might be an appropriate option before we either adopt them or cast them aside completely.

Doc Hammill admits that his opinion of adjustable collars has changed. "Many people have felt over the years that adjustable collars are a poor substitute for one-size collars. I too assumed that was the case for years without really questioning why. I have used and experimented with adjustable collars a lot more in the past 20 years or so. What I've learned is that like most things, including one-size collars, adjustable collars have their advantages, disadvantages, and limitations.

One teamster's preferred method of adjusting collar fit.
Courtesy John Erskine

"Adjustable collars do give us the option of changing the size of the collar, however, it is important to understand precisely how, where, and how much size-change occurs. When an equine that an adjustable collar fits at one setting happens to gain or lose weight, it may or may not be possible to get that collar to meet all the requirements of perfect fit on the animal at a different setting. Likewise, as a young animal grows and matures, anatomical relationships in the neck and shoulders change in ways that the adjustable collar it wears might or might not be able to accommodate simply by adjusting the collar to be longer or shorter. Each case is unique and must be dealt with on an individual basis.

"Cathy and I have been able to use both one-size collars and adjustable collars very successfully. If we can get better overall fit, comfort, and results with an adjustable collar, we use it. If a one size collar will meet our criteria and fit better, then it will be our choice. The important things are that the collar precisely fits the individual horse in his or her current condition, that the draft area of the collar is appropriate for the specific horse and for the work to be done, and that the ideal point of draft on the collar, hames, and horse all can be, and are, matched up. Once we fulfill these requirements and ensure a correct angle of draft and a straight line of draft, the system should work and ensure the animal's psychological and physical comfort and wellbeing."

What is an Adjustable Collar?

I think I was around 60 before I even knew there was an adjustable collar. Had 5 sizes of collar for one horse and at least 2 for every other horse I owned.
- Dale Wagner (3)

I'm a big fan of adjustable collars. The alternative of course, and it's a better one, is to have a shed full of collars. But that is beyond the economic reach of most people I work with.
– Rob Johnson (4)

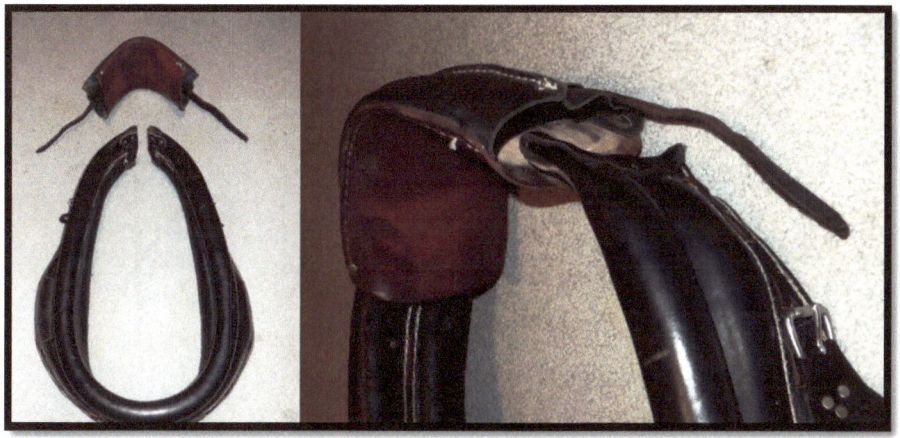

Illustration 1: Adjustable collars typically are u-shaped with a cap and strap-and-buckle assembly that allows for length adjustment.

An adjustable collar has a means for changing its size; initially it is the length of the collar that varies. When you purchase an adjustable collar, it's usually recommended that you purchase the collar to fit your animal at its center length (with or without a pad as you choose), and then you can shorten it by an inch or lengthen it by an inch if needed. Some latch-top collars have the ability for small adjustment, but today's adjustable collars usually have a cap and strap-and-buckle assembly as shown in illustration #1. The collar is u-shaped, with the two top ends of the 'u' fitting up into the sleeve-like cap and being held in the desired position by the straps and buckles.

Illustration 2: An adjustable collar of an old and different design.
Courtesy John Erskine

Illustration 2 shows an uncommon adjustable collar design. The collar is u-shaped but instead of the cap being a sleeve into which the two ends of the u fit, the 'cap' is a separate piece of leather with 2 metal loops permanently affixed. The metal loops are inserted through appropriate slots built into the top of the collar sides. A keeper strap, which is permanently attached to one side of the collar, is inserted through the metal loops to secure the cap to the collar in the right position to achieve the desired length. This type of adjustable collar has less bulk at the top, addressing a complaint that some have about the typical adjustable collar design.

The Cap Seam Ridge

One of the things that varies between different styles of modern adjustable collars is the location and style of the cap seam ridge. As discussed above, most adjustable collars today have a sleeve-shaped cap into which the two ends of the u-shaped collar slide. The construction of the cap requires that there be a seam in the leather, and to keep the horse-side of the cap smooth, the seam should be on the upper side of the cap. How this seam is finished varies between collar makers, as shown in illustration 3.

The cap seam of the collar on the upper left, for instance, forms a distinct ridge behind which the hame strap is seated. The cap seam of the collar in the upper right does not have a very high or functional ridge. In the collar on the lower left, the cap seam is high but the hame strap sits in front of it. Finally, in the collar on the lower right, the cap seam ridge is again behind where the hame strap sits, but the front of the collar cap is built up into a horn which provides a very distinct bed for the top hame strap.

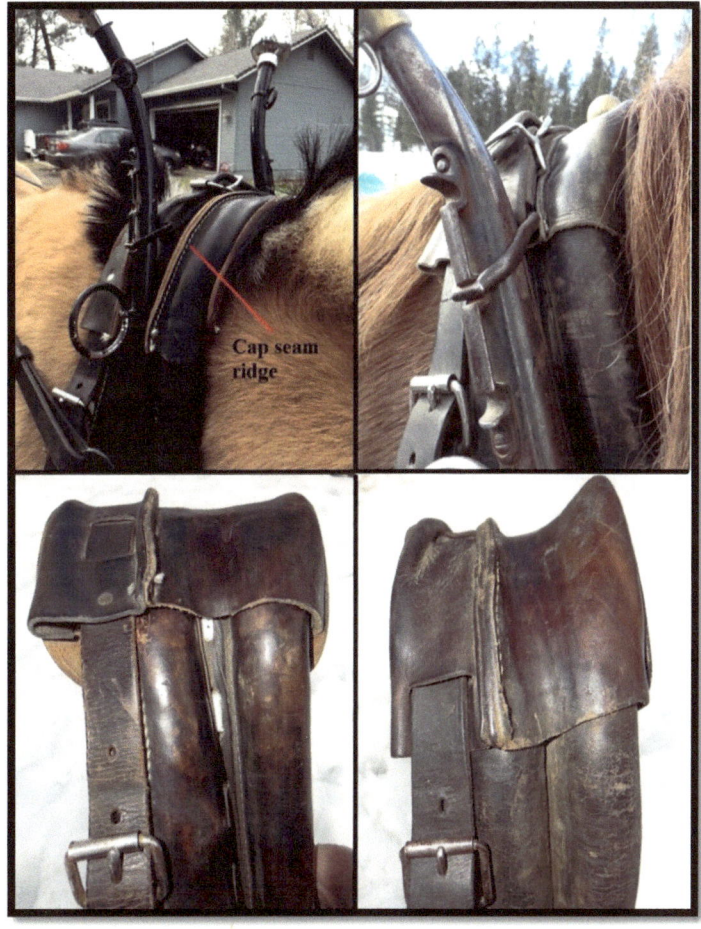

Illustration 3: Four different styles of adjustable collar are shown. Upper left: Note the distinct ridge of leather up against which the hame strap rides. Upper right: the cap seam is folded and doesn't form a distinct ridge. Lower left: the cap seam ridge sits behind the hame strap bed. Lower right: the cap seam ridge sits behind the hame strap bed but a horn of leather forms a distinct front for the hame strap bed.

Doc prefers the type of adjustable collar that has the hame strap seated behind the cap seam ridge because it provides an obvious bed for the hame strap. Doc says, "While I have used both types successfully, I prefer the stitched ridge created by the cap seam being in front of the top hame strap rather than behind. I prefer the seam to have enough thickness and height to keep the hame strap from working forward. Although I have never had a set of hames work forward on the top of a collar and threaten to come off with either an adjustable or one-size collar, it doesn't hurt to have the extra security if you have a choice. The collar in the lower right of illustration 3 has something even better than a distinct cap seam ridge. This is a collar that came from my stepfather's father and has been used since very early in the twentieth century. It has a horn built up in the front and the cap seam ridge behind to form a very secure bed for the top hame strap".

Differences in Adjustable Collar Manufacturing

There are obviously those that don't care much for adjustable collars. There are obviously those that do like them. I have used nothing but adjustable collars for 11 years now on my Belgians... I have never had a single collar sore on any of the horses in that time... My reasons for liking adjustable collars: starting a young horse and as its neck grows the collar grows with it, don't have to buy 3 regular collars for the growing youngun. Second: mares having babies, their neck is full to begin with, it shrinks over the next 6 months while the mama works and the foal nurses, same collar shrinks and stays with the mama right on through the whole season. Then as her neck fills back out, same collar gets larger. So I will stick with my adjustable collars and hope they continue to work as well as they have for the last 11 years.

- Brabant owner in SC (5)

As the above quote from the *Rural Heritage* Front Porch suggests, adjustable collars do work well for many people in many situations. Doc adds some words of caution, though: "All adjustable collars are not equal. There are high quality, and there are the others. For instance, sometimes the top hole on the straps is too close to the bottom edge of the collar cap; this makes it very difficult to buckle and unbuckle in the top hole setting, especially in cold weather when things are stiff. Another thing to watch for is to make sure the top ends of the collar slide

Illustration 4: Not all adjustable collars are created equal. Notice the slop in the cap sleeve in the collar on the right and the preferable fit of the collar into the cap on the left.

into the cap without being loose or sloppy but also not too tight at any of the settings. Some caps are too loose in the long setting and too tight in the short one.

"Notice on the collar on the left in illustration 4 that the end of the collar inside the cap basically fills up the diameter of the cap. By comparison, the cap on the collar on the right has a larger diameter than necessary as shown by the extra space inside the cap which is not filled by the collar end. For stability and ease of buckling and unbuckling adjustable collars, it's important for the collar ends to fit into the cap without being too loose or too tight at any of the settings."

Doc continues, "The inside or horse side of the cap must be smooth and free of damage, irregularities, and abrupt or sharp edges. Also, on the longest setting, the end of the collar needs to be far enough up into the cap to be stable. Illustration 9 below shows what can happen when this isn't the case. In addition, some collars are made to have more of the collar up into the cap at all lengths, and this type of collar is preferable."

Adjustables and the Point of Draft

While a collar that adjusts is in theory helpful, the reality is of course much more complicated. A complaint that some have is that adjustable collars only adjust in length above the point of draft. Illustration 5 shows the same 23" adjustable collar in each of its three adjustment positions. Small white dots (and red lines between them) indicate the center of the draft area of the collar.

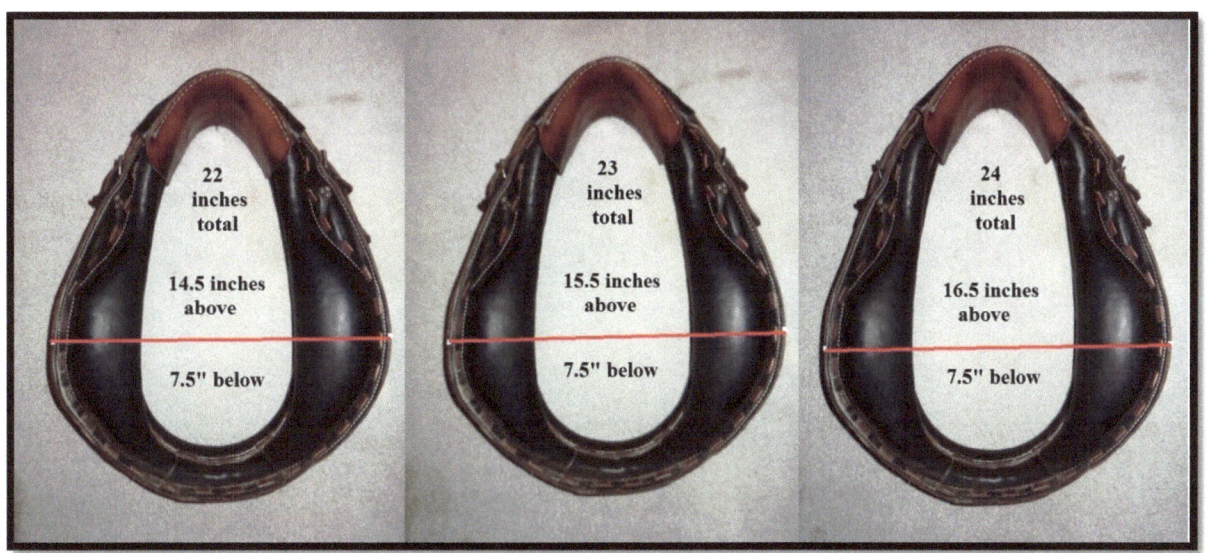

Illustration 5: A 23" adjustable collar is shown at left in its 22" position, in the center at 23" and at right at 24". Measurements above and below the collar's draft area are shown, demonstrating that the length of the collar only changes above the draft area.

Measurements from this line up and down are shown. In each case, the distance from the draft area to the throat remains the same at 7.5". With the collar set to 22", at left in the illustration, the measurement above the red line is 14.5 inches. With the collar set to 23", in the center of the illustration, the measurement above the red line is 15.5 inches. With the collar set to 24", at right in the illustration, the measurement above the red line is 16.5 inches. All of the increase or decrease in length of the collar happens above the point of draft of the collar.

Let's say, for instance, that our horse has lost weight, so we decide to cinch up our adjustable collar, making it shorter. As the illustration shows, we are only shortening it above the point of draft. As long as our horse has lost its size above the point of draft, it's possible the collar will fit fine, but what if our horse lost size low on its shoulder or in the throat area? The draft area of the collar will now be higher on our horse's shoulder and may no longer marry well with our horse's point of draft.

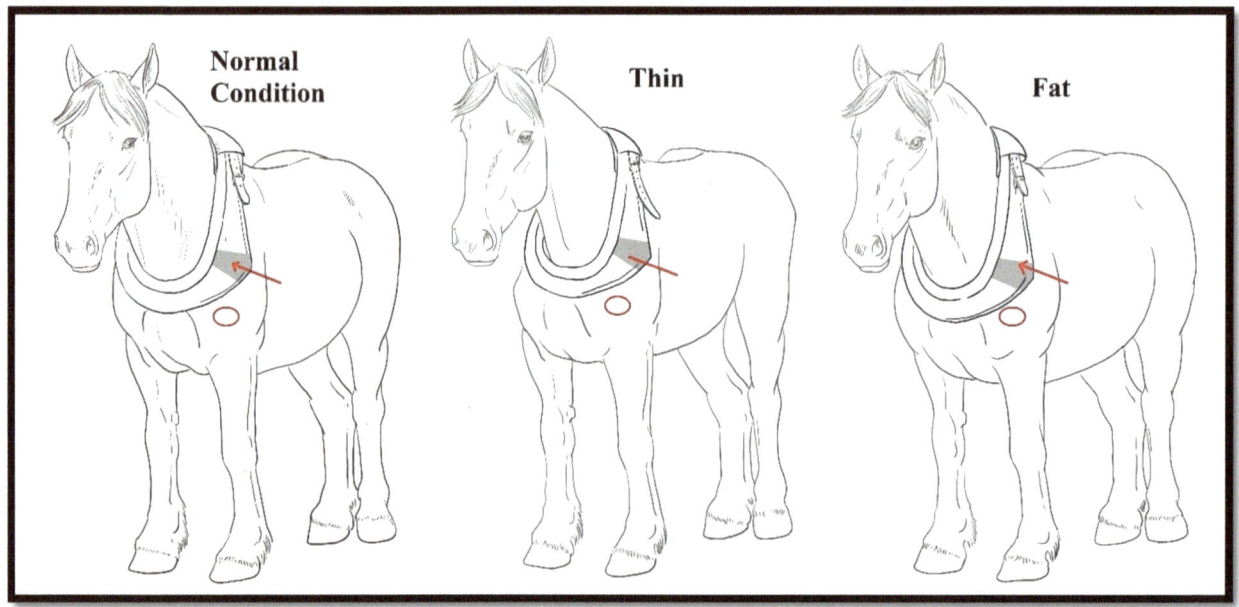

Illustration 6: At left is a collar properly fit on a horse in normal condition; the horse's point of shoulder (red circle), the horse's ideal point of draft (red arrow), and the collar's draft area (gray shading) are shown. In the center is the same horse that has lost weight. The adjustable collar has been shortened; the draft area of the collar is now above the horse's point of draft. At right is the same horse that has gained weight. The adjustable collar has been lengthened; the draft area of the collar is now below the horse's ideal point of draft.
Illustration © Bethany Caskey

Illustration 6 shows a horse wearing an adjustable collar. In the left drawing, the horse is in normal flesh and the collar fits properly. The horse's point of shoulder is shown as a red circle and the horse's ideal point of draft is shown at the end of the red arrow. The draft area of the collar, which is shaded in the drawing, is centered over the ideal point of draft of the horse.

In the center drawing, the horse has lost weight so the collar has been shortened. Note that the center of the draft area of the collar, the shaded area, is now above the ideal point of draft on this horse's shoulder because all the shortening of the adjustable collar occurred above the collar's point of draft. This situation is what makes teamster John Erskine state, "An adjustable collar usually will only fit a particular horse well at one length. After that it's a compromise because the two ideal points of draft (collar and horse) usually can't be well married. That same collar might fit another horse well set at the same or a different length, but it's unlikely it will ever fit the same horse well at any but one length."

In the right drawing of illustration 6, the same horse has gained weight. The adjustable collar has been let out to its longest setting. Again, if the horse has changed in size both above and below its point of draft but the collar only adjusts in size above the point of draft, the center of the draft area of the collar will be below the ideal point of draft of this horse.

Adjustables, Point of Draft, and Body Condition

Doc explains some of his observations with respect to equines maturing and/or changing body condition: "Equines tend to put on fat in rather specific areas on their bodies. One such place is a localized area on the sides of the neck and upper shoulders. Some also develop a heavy upper neck and crest. Often, when a horse gains or loses weight, the neck and shoulders change most dramatically above the point of draft. That is also where major development will occur in a young stallion as he matures and develops in the neck. Conversely, when equines lose weight they become narrower in their neck and upper shoulders, again mostly above the point of draft. Only occasionally or in select individuals will you see major changes below the point of draft and near the trachea.

"Because most of the change we see is above the point of draft and because adjustable collars have most of their adjustment above the point of draft, adjustable collars can be very useful when body condition changes."

It's Not About Shorter or Longer

While we commonly talk about shortening or lengthening an adjustable collar, Doc reiterates that horses typically change in ways other than length and that those changes must also be accommodated. "We have a tendency to think in terms of changing an adjustable collar to make it longer or shorter to fit a horse that either gains or loses fat or muscle mass. However, in such cases it is not primarily greater or shorter collar length that we actually need. Most horses that gain weight add significantly to the width of their neck and shoulders and add relatively little, if any, to the length. Likewise, they tend to lose more width than length when they drop weight. Consequently, changing the length of an adjustable collar is only the first step in attempting to get it properly resized.

"To resize a collar either larger or smaller, we are actually working to truly fit the 'new' overall length as well as the 'new' width dimensions in multiple places up and down the neck. For instance, to fit a neck that has become thinner but not shorter, we begin by shortening the collar which will cause it to be too short for the horse's neck. But then when we squeeze the sides in, the collar lengthens which adds back the length we lost. Hopefully we end up with a narrower collar of about the original length to fit the thinner neck.

"For a horse that has gained weight, we often have the opposite situation: the neck is wider but again not necessarily longer than it was. We begin by lengthening the collar which makes it too long, but then we reshape it wider which also causes it to become shorter and closer to the length we started with. The next step is fine tuning everything.

"So, rather than thinking in terms of simply changing the length of an adjustable collar, please understand that the goal is to increase or decrease the length in an attempt to get the circumference around the 'neck hole' of the collar to fit properly the circumference around the outside of the horse's neck where the collar sits. Do not expect the shape of the 'neck hole' to necessarily be what it needs to be to fit the horse after simply changing the collar length. If we make an adjustable collar longer when what we primarily need is to have it wider then we must reshape that collar with hame adjustment or by other means to make it fit – and basically hope that afterwards the length ends up being what is needed. If it isn't quite perfect, we tinker with it over the next few days until it fits properly or we determine that a different collar is needed; I describe one such situation below."

A Collar Can And Often Must Be Reshaped

Illustration 7 shows how one collar can have two profoundly different forms depending on how it is shaped with the hames (or other methods). The collar as shown on the left is long and narrow which is sometimes how they come from the manufacturer. On the right, the same collar has been reshaped to be wider and shorter. The center red line indicates the ideal point of draft of the collar. Note how it changes location as the collar is reshaped. When the collar is wider and shorter, the ideal point of draft of the collar is lower relative to the throat.

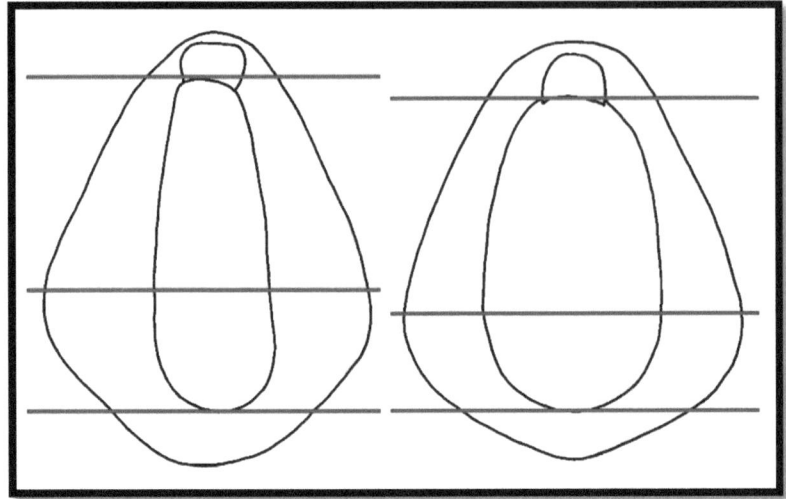

Illustration 7: The same collar can be long and narrow as at left or reshaped to be wider and shorter as at right. The distance around the interior is the same length in both cases. Note how the point of draft changes location relative to the throat.
Illustration © Bethany Caskey

Doc says, "Both adjustable collars and one-size collars come new from the factory with variations in style and shape depending on the manufacturer and the various patterns they use. Most are rather tear drop shaped but some come rather long and narrow like the collar on the left in illustration 7. New collars almost always need to be reshaped to properly fit the animals they are used on. There are nearly infinite variations in the shape of equine necks to which a limited number of sizes and shapes of collars must be fit. The sketch on the left accurately depicts the proportions and shape of a specific new collar that is quite long and narrow. Notice how reshaping the collar to fit a thick necked horse made it shorter in length, much wider throughout, and also lowered the point of draft of the collar.

"It is important to understand that making a collar wider can lower the point of draft of the collar, and that making one narrower can raise the point of draft. Sometimes this effect aids us in getting the point of draft where we need it and sometimes it moves it the wrong way. The difference in point of draft in the diagram looks small, but in real life it can vary from almost nothing to well over an inch on a 24 inch collar depending on how wide or narrow the collar is reshaped. This effect applies to both adjustable and one size collars and should be taken into consideration whenever any changes involving collars, hames, hame straps, or pads are made.

Consequences: Intended and Otherwise

As we've learned, when we adjust an adjustable collar, we are likely changing the location of the collar's point of draft relative to the horse's point of draft. Therefore, we must re-assess the marriage of the points of draft on the horse, the collar, and the hames. (Of course, we should be doing this reassessment anytime anything changes: collar, hames, load/draft, tongue weight, etc.)

Doc explains, "If you change the adjustment on an adjustable collar to make it shorter or longer, you essentially change not only the dimensions but also the proportions and shape of the collar. You will need to start all over on getting the collar to fit the animal all the way around the neck. Then you'll need to match the draft area of the collar to the collar bed of the horse's shoulders, and then match the point of draft on the horse to those of the collar and of the hames. Ensuring that the angle of draft and line of draft are proper will complete the process."

Doc then cautions, "<u>When using adjustable collars, be very careful not to overtighten the hames.</u>

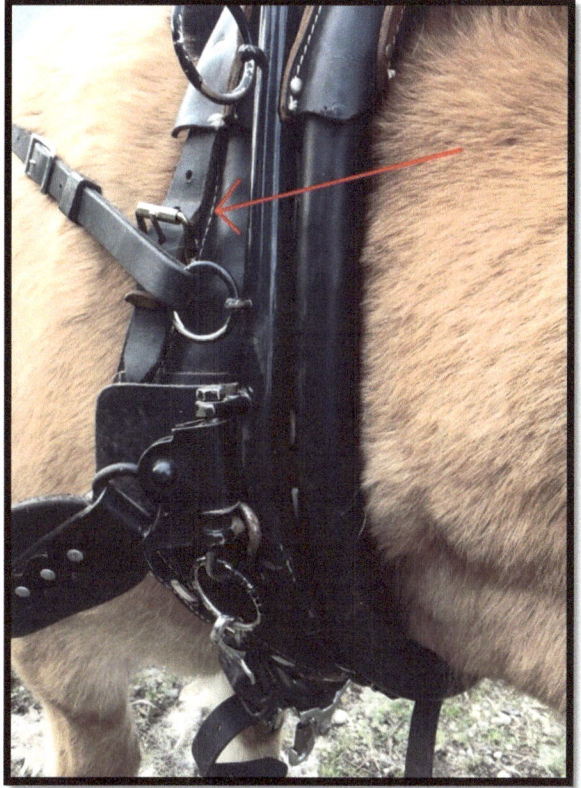

Illustration #8: Note how loose the buckle on the collar is after these hames have been overtightened; the collar sides have been forced up into the cap too far. The strap is loose too.

One indication that you have done this is that the buckle on the hame strap is cocked as in illustration 8. Overtightening the hames can force the collar ends up into the cap too far and make the collar smaller as shown in illustration 8. The collar is now shorter in length than it was after it was fit to the horse and before the hames were tightened. In such cases the overtightened hames keep the collar from returning to the proper length and shape and may cause excessive pressure to be put on the trachea, neck, and shoulders which may result in other problems. Perhaps you also noticed this overtightened hame problem in the upper left portion of illustration 3 earlier in this chapter."

Doc continues, "There's a tendency to feel that the hames should be cranked on as tight as you can get them, but there are a significant number of situations where if you tighten the hames too much, you will lose collar fit. And of course there are other times when you need to tighten the hames enough to help force the collar into a different shape to make it fit right. With adjustable collars there are limitations on doing this; if significant collar reshaping is necessary it may need to be done by other means before the collar goes on the horse and the hames are put on and used."

Punching Extra Holes

Another situation that Doc has encountered is people wanting to get more length out of an adjustable collar by adding a hole or two on the strap past the last hole put in by the manufacturer. The right photo in Illustration 9 shows the consequences: the upper end of the U of the collar is no longer properly seated in the sleeve of the cap and can come out which could cause the hames to come entirely off the collar. Disaster could result of course because connected to the hames are the harness, traces and load. Doc

Illustration 9: Two cases where extra holes have been punched in an adjustable collar strap. On left, holes have been punched between for fine-tuning. On right, a new hole has been added past the last manufacturer's hole and when used it makes the collar loose enough that the top ends of the collar can come out of the cap.

points out, "Even if the top end of the collar cannot come out of the cap completely, the loss of stability can cause problems such as excessive friction and/or heat from movement between the cap and collar ends, or hames working partially or completely off the collar."

The left photo in Illustration 9 shows a different situation. Doc explains, "The two extra holes on the left collar were punched between the original three holes to permit smaller adjustments which is good as long as the holes are far enough apart so as not to weaken the leather. And of course we do not want holes made beyond the original longest hole as shown in the right photo."

Adjustables and Hames

Adjustable collars can be a little challenging to get the hames to seat into the hame bed properly. The cap on the top of the collar tends to shim the hames out at the top and make them more prone to pop out of the hame bed.
- Grey (6)

Adjustable collars are a good idea if you only want to own one collar per horse and ... never have to take the pads out, but I just hate the way the hames fit them.
- Sharon (7)

Doc responds, "When hames do not fit a collar properly, it may be because of the collar, the hames, or the way the hames and hame straps are adjusted. I have not experienced any more difficulty getting hames to fit and stay on adjustable collars than on one-size collars.

Illustration 10: Here are two adjustable collars with very different quality of hame fit. On the left, the hames and hame strap do not sit down well on the collar because the hames are too long. On the right the hames and hame strap sit snugly against the collar.

"For instance, illustration 10 shows two adjustable collars. The one on the right has the hame and top hame strap fitting the collar very well. There are essentially no gaps between the collar and the hame, and the top hame strap is in contact with the contour of the collar all the way from hame to hame. In the left photo, however, there are gaps between the collar and the hame and also between the collar and the top hame strap. Such gaps anywhere around the circumference of the collar increase the chances of the hames coming off the collar – regardless of the style of collar. The reason for the gaps in this case is that the hames are much too long to fit this collar properly. If the hames were the right size for this adjustable collar, then the top hame strap could be lengthened enough to follow the contour of the collar down further, and it could attach to the hame loop right where the hames start to depart from the collar – just as in the right hand photo - without leaving any gaps. As it is, the metal hame loop which attaches the hame strap to the hames is much too high because of the long hames, even though it's in the lowest possible ratchet setting. In my experience, hames not fitting collars properly is more often caused by the wrong size hames for the collar or inappropriate adjustment of the hames and/or hame straps, than it is by the collar. It doesn't seem to matter much whether the collar is an adjustable or not."

Doc continues, "In the interest of safety, I'm compelled to comment on a somewhat unrelated but common reason for hames popping off of collars. When quarter straps and/or pole straps (or side straps) are adjusted too long on team harness, the neck yoke can potentially pull the breast straps too far forward during slowing, holding back, stopping, or backing a load. Too far forward is when the rings on the ends of the neck yoke can get ahead of a straight line along the front edge of the hames that extends down the length of the hames towards the ground. If the neck yoke is pushed forward beyond such a line, the breast straps will be pulled forward and exert a forward pull on the bottom of the hames which can potentially pop the hames off the collar. Of course this whole process can happen easier if the hames are not properly fit to the collar around its entire circumference. Often folks will buckle the bottom hame straps extra tight in an attempt to secure them, whereas what is really required is to shorten the hold back system.

Adjustables and Conformation

Doc has learned over the years that there are particular conformations of equines where adjustable collars have particular value. He explains, "There are an infinite number of neck conformation combinations in equines. The variables involved include but are not limited to shoulder length and angle, muscle conformation, shape and relationship of muscles to bones and other muscles, how and where the base of the neck joins the shoulders (low set necks, high set necks, etc.), width of neck at crest and at each distance between crest and windpipe (trachea), depth of the neck – distance from top of neck to the trachea which translates approximately to length of the collar. Then there is the fact that the head and neck posture when a horse is working may be different than when he's at rest. If you fit a collar and hames to your horse when he's standing with his head and neck in a comfortable, relaxed posture and then check him up high for a show class or plowing match, that collar will become predictably tight and uncomfortable."

Illustration 11: This conformation is a type that especially benefits from an adjustable collar because it often requires extra length above the point of draft that is difficult to get from one-size collars.

Doc continues, "There is a particular conformation of neck and shoulder where I have found adjustable collars to be especially helpful. As shown in illustration 11, the shoulder is quite laid back and the neck exits the chest high and steep. By my calculations, this sort of horse might need as much as 75% of the collar's length above the point of draft. One-size collars that I've checked generally have 65% or less of their length above the point of draft. The adjustable collar in illustration 5 above has 70% of its length above the point of draft at its longest setting. So what is considered by some to be a disadvantage of adjustable collars can actually be an advantage for certain horses."

The "Adjustable Collar Problem"

In "Draft Geometry" above, Doc Hammill told a story about trying to fit, with no luck, an adjustable collar to a horse. That seems a contradiction in terms: how could an adjustable collar not be adjusted to fit a horse properly? We've seen above that in fact there can indeed be situations where an adjustable collar can't be adjusted to fit. In this case, even with his ability to reshape adjustable collars using the hames, Doc still couldn't get the collar to work for that horse.

Illustration #12 shows the challenging collar-fit problem Doc was dealing with. He explains, "The collar fits the shape of the horse's neck fairly well all around the circumference of the neck the way I have it in the photo. Because of that someone without an understanding of point of draft might think that this collar fits the horse. However, the draft area of the collar and point of draft of the collar (green circle) are much too far above the collar bed and point of draft of the horse (red circle). You can see that the portion of the collar at the point of draft of the horse is completely inadequate in surface area and shape to safely transfer the forces of a load to the horse's collar bed. When the collar was lengthened to move its draft area and point of draft down towards the point of draft on the horse, the collar was much too long and rode on the bony point of the shoulder, the red hollow circle. Ultimately this collar could not be adjusted or padded to fit this horse in all necessary respects.

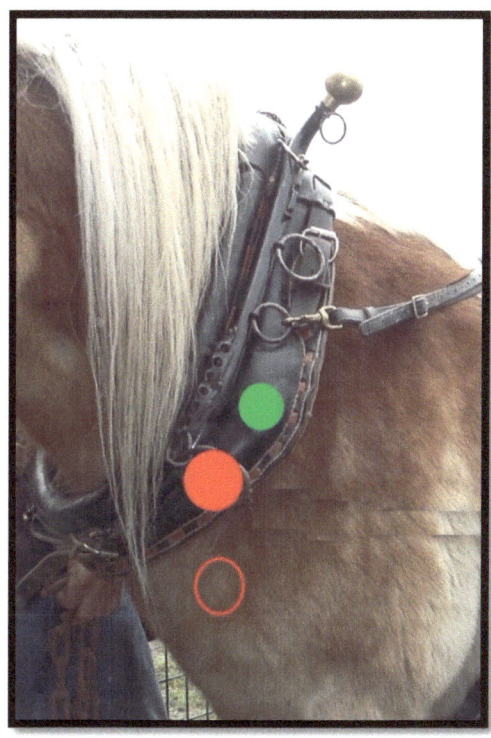

Illustration 12: An adjustable collar whose draft area was so high that it couldn't be made to work for this horse. Point of shoulder on horse: red hollow circle. Point of draft on horse: red solid circle. Point of draft on collar: green circle.

"In the photo, the collar is set at its shortest adjustment and about 60% of its length is above its point of draft (green circle) and the other 40% is below its point of draft. Because of his conformation, this horse would require an adjustable collar with more like 70% or even 75% of the collar length above the point of draft. Adjustable collars set at their longest setting can have 70% or more of their length above the point of draft. Therefore, it's possible that an adjustable collar, of a smaller size than the one in the photo, might fit around this horse's neck nicely when set at its longest adjustment, and such a collar could well have the right proportions above and below the point of draft to work for this horse. I sure wish there had been such a collar there to try on him. For me, adjustables play an important role for hard-to-fit horses."

Adjustables and Husbandry

I have gotten adjustable collars with my big horses, but I found out after awhile that they usually stay on the same notch. Sometimes they are slightly more snug than others, but I typically never change the adjustment as I would have to readjust the hames, hames strap, etc. I'm lazy and like to keep it all fitting so all I have to do is thrown it on and go.
- Will Beattie (8)

Doc notes, "Many people cite weight fluctuations as a reason to have adjustable collars. Cathy and I take managing our horses' weight pretty seriously and consequently seem to have little need to adjust or change collars. We've worked lots of mares with foals, had ponies, saddle horses and all manner of equines, and we've found that we can manage their feed to control their weight so that collar fit doesn't change much, if any, season to season. Like Will, we have adjustables on horses that rarely if ever change settings. Why don't we just switch them to a one-size collar? Because they have been working in their own personal collar for many years, a collar that fits and has taken on the exact shape and feel they need. I have old boots like that – they look bad but they feel oh so good."

The Right Collar is The One That Fits

Teamster John Erskine says, "If it fits the horse, use it; if it does the job, use it." He is not a fan of adjustable collars, but he once used one so much that it wore out because it fit his horse well and they worked until the collar wasn't functional any more.

Doc concurs: "The main thing is whether it works. It's more important that the collar fit the horse than whether it's an adjustable or non-adjustable. We know lots of people who are particular and understand collar fit; both adjustable collars and one-size collars work well for them. Unfortunately we also see way too many collars of both styles that are ill-fitting and causing problems. I feel it's more important that the collar fit the horse properly in all respects than that it be a particular style, make, or type.

"My stepfather and great mentor Tom Triplett tells stories about people coming up to his father, H.P. Triplett, when Tom was growing up and asking his dad if he would check the collars on their team. Tom has said many times that his dad could spot a horse whose collar was bothering him at a distance and tell you just what needed to be changed to make it right. I asked Tom recently if he remembered his dad ever having collar sores on his horses. After thinking about it, he said, "No, I can't remember ever seeing one on his horses." H.P. had several adjustable collars when Tom was young, two of which we are still using. Tom is well up in his eighties now and remembers adjustable collars on his dad's horses when he was just a kid. Tom told me recently, 'What Dad liked was what fit 'em.' Fit 'em didn't just mean length and width, it was point of draft and everything."

The author is grateful to Marion Coblentz of Coblentz Collar Shop in Millersburg, Ohio for his consultation.

1. Response by Mooney Ranch at
   http://www.ruralheritage.com/messageboard/frontporch/9461.htm
2. Response by Dave W at 2014-02-27 10:02:38 at
   http://www.ruralheritage.com/messageboard/frontporch/18327.htm
3. Response by Dale Wagner at 2009-10-20 10:44:58 at
   http://www.ruralheritage.com/messageboard/frontporch/12385.htm

4. Johnson, Rob, email to Jenifer Morrissey, 2/12/15.
5. Response by Brabant owner in SC at 2009-10-19 10:53:34 at http://www.ruralheritage.com/messageboard/frontporch/12385.htm
6. Response by grey at 2009-08-25 14:41:52 at http://www.ruralheritage.com/messageboard/frontporch/12246.htm
7. Response by Sharon at 2012-05-25 17:43:48 at http://www.ruralheritage.com/messageboard/frontporch/16197.htm
8. Response by Will Beattie at 2012-03-06 22:54:32 at http://www.ruralheritage.com/messageboard/frontporch/15903.htm

Too Much Harness?

Does this title mean too much talk about harness or something else? Doc's first thought was of half-harness. "As I've mentioned before, my mentors talked about half-harness: just collar, hames, traces, backpad and belly band. It's really simple and very functional for specific kinds of work."

Illustration #1: Which pieces of harness on these horses are not necessary for the job pictured here? Allen photo.

Do you know which pieces of harness are fundamentally necessary for the work you're doing with your equines? Do you have in your mind a clear understanding of which piece you could do without if you absolutely had to? One of the earliest pieces of advice I received when I started working my ponies in harness was to use an extra hame strap as a shaft tug because it always pays to have an extra hame strap around. Doc confirms this advice: "When we went to the field when we were farming, my mentor Addie never went without an extra hame strap buckled on somewhere in case he needed it."

Illustration #1 shows a team pulling a load of stone. Which pieces of harness on these horses are not necessary for the job at hand? In "Harness Variety and Function," we learned that there are four components of harness: communication, draft, stopping and backing, and support. For the job in Illustration #1, pulling a dead weight in a straight line, a half-harness like Doc describes is sufficient, made up of just the communication and draft components and part of the support system. The stopping and backing component (breeching, etc.) is not strictly necessary.

Illustration #2: What components of harness are present here? Are they all necessary? Are more needed? Allen photo

One of the earliest harness I saw on a pony working in the woods was just collar, hames, and chain traces. A similar harness is shown in Illustration #2, the difference being that one support piece is being used there (the backpad). Doc comments, "For this job, all you're going to do by using conventional harness is to add work to the person putting it on and increase the weight and heat for the mule."

Doc continues, "The Communication Component could be improved here. The lines go through a very high ring on the hames so any pull on the bit will be at an extreme and inappropriate upward angle. I'd like to see the lines go through a ring placed lower on the hames. Also, the point of draft is too high for this mule and the line of draft is broken."

Certainly many of us who work horses want to just get the harness on and go and not be bothered with the myriad detail presented in past articles or contained in Doc's comments here. In a perfect world, we wouldn't ever need to know the details. Unfortunately, we know we don't live in a perfect world, whether we want to admit it or not, so all of us get to a point where safety, comfort, or efficiency needs to be improved, so we have to learn how harness works and especially how it works best in our situation.

As an electrical engineer, my first job out of college had two primary responsibilities: helping existing customers solve problems with my company's product and demonstrating that product to prospective new customers. I quickly learned three things: 1) no product ever works the way it is supposed to, especially at first; 2) no product ever solves all the problems you think it will; and 3) every product has effects on the environment in which it's used that weren't anticipated at the outset. I haven't ever seen a piece of technology that violated these three observations, despite the best efforts of well-intentioned design engineers and sales people.

Harness is, of course, a piece of technology. I got started with a Western style/box breeching harness for my ponies. When I added another pony and needed to buy another set of harness, I pondered how to improve safety, comfort, and efficiency and was attracted to Norwegian Harness. It seemed to solve the problem of proper angle of draft as well as have an easier way to perform collar fit. Ideal angle of draft seemed especially important to get the maximum horsepower from my littler animals, and collar fit as my ponies gained and lost weight seemed easier to address with the Norwegian style than my other harness.

Norwegian harness, like all harness, is a piece of technology and there's no such thing as a perfect solution.

It didn't take long, though, before it was clear that all three things I'd learned in high tech also applied to harness: 1) It took quite a bit of fiddling to get the Norwegian harness to work the way it was supposed to; it didn't work right out of the box. 2) Adjusting the Norwegian harness so it worked optimally wasn't any easier than my previous harness; it was just different. And 3) the Norwegian harness required more changes in the way I hitched than I anticipated. In the end, I learned that a new and 'fancier' harness technology didn't necessarily improve my work situation; it was just different. I still needed to understand the fundamentals of harness to make it work right.

When I was considering the Norwegian Harness, I also studied the New England/D-Ring harness which is similar in how the angle of draft is addressed. One difference between my Norwegian harness and some D-Ring harness, though, is the saddle/backpad. My Norwegian harness has a significant amount of padding to improve comfort for the equine where more weight-bearing exists. I have been told about people who adopted a D-Ring harness for its supposed technical advantages, only to sore their equines' backs because of inadequate padding. 'New' technology such as a Norwegian or D-ring harness isn't necessarily better or the answer to everyone's problem; it still requires attention to detail to make it work safely, comfortably, and efficiently.

Illustration #3: What components of harness are unnecessary in the top image and might improve safety in the bottom? Allen photos

Illustration #3 shows two different workhorse situations. In the top, what component of harness is present but isn't strictly necessary? In the bottom, given that a wheeled vehicle is in use, what component of harness is missing but would increase safety if used?

Doc comments, "One of the things I have on most of my harness is removable hip straps, breeching, and pole straps so I can quickly and easily swap them out for a crupper and go do something that doesn't require braking like the cultivator in the upper part of Illustration #3. For safety and comfort, I would like to see a better stopping and backing component on the harness used on the seed drill in the lower part of Illustration #3."

In the top photo, note the interesting adaptation of the communication component (a mounted teamster.) Doc comments, "When Addie and I farmed in the '70s, we used a saddle horse like this but with the luxury of a saddle!"

Doc continues, "I've known Australians who think we waste a lot of leather on our harness in this country. They're legendary for saving leather; I've seen lots of photos of Aussie's working, and the amount of harness is often really minimal. You can work horses well and comfortably and safely for certain types of jobs with stripped down harness, but you can also get in trouble. Likewise, you can have a full conventional harness and get in trouble if it's not well-designed, well-made and fitting properly. Like any tool, harness can be used well and it can be used unwisely. I feel we have a responsibility to both horses and people to use our harness safely, wisely and well.

"I was at a gathering of farmers once where someone brought their version of draft horse bridles to show and advocate. The bridles had no throat latch or blinders, and as I recall no brow band, nose band, or chin strap. They just slipped the bit in the mouth and put the crown piece over the ears and that was it. Admittedly, it was fast to put on and saved leather and expense, but it was also entirely unsafe in my opinion. I was so uncomfortable with newcomers to horse farming being exposed to this bridle that I forced myself to speak up and express my safety concerns about this bridle that the farmers were so proud of. I have no problem with horses that are comfortable and well trained and accustomed to working without blinders doing so. However, I can cite many examples of disastrous runaways and wrecks because of bridles being pulled or rubbed off. A snug throatlatch plus extra security such as a double crown bridle adapter is essential as far as I'm concerned. Just last week I heard about a buck rake demonstration where a horse rubbed his bridle off not once but twice during the one-day event. I highly recommend Barb Lee's article 'A Bridle Your Horse Can't Rub Off' in the June/July 2011 issue of *Rural Heritage*."

Illustration #4: Note the housings on the hames of the mules to protect them from chaff. What role do the housings you see on equines play? Allen photo.

Illustration #4 shows a crew in Kentucky threshing a legume called Korean lespedeza. Note the housings on the hames of the mules. Doc comments, "Flat hame housings have practical purposes: to keep rain and snow off the collar and neck and keep out chaff and pine needles during threshing, harvesting, or work in the woods. Peaked collar housings are pretty much used to fancy things up; both types are still functional for their designed purpose but they do add weight for the horse."

From a working equine standpoint, Doc also notes, "Show harness and fancy harness often have three hip straps. They're only decorative. There's no reason to have more than two in my mind unless you're trying to cover up an ugly or weak rear end!"

Illustration #5 shows a harness that has spots (metal ornamentation) on the backpad. Doc observes, "Everybody seems to love spots on their harness. My mentor Addie hated spots. Over 40 years ago he asked me if he could take the spots off of the back pad and back straps of a used harness I bought. He wanted to prevent the lines from wearing out from rubbing on the metal spots. Since then I've seen quite a bit of harness with the tops of spots worn off, leaving a circle of sharp metal where the lines slide back and forth. He also didn't like the weight and that the little tabs can get snagged or pried out and dig into the horses' skin."

When teamster John Erskine heard the title of this chapter, his first response was, "You need the best harness you can buy." By 'best,' John didn't mean the harness with the most features or the latest technology. "The best made harness you can buy that's appropriate for the job you're going to do made by a respected harness maker is the cheapest life insurance you'll ever have. When someone whines about paying good money, what's one trip to the hospital worth?" For John, 'too much harness' isn't about having lots or fewer pieces and parts. It's about the quality of the choice we make to ensure safety, comfort, and efficiency.

Illustration #5: Note the spots or metal ornamentation on the backpad of this harness. Spots can wear if not cared for and may cause comfort and/or safety problems. Allen Photo

John often works with people who are new to horses and/or new to working horses. He has found that the idea of 'too much harness' can be useful in the training process. When he's getting equines accustomed to working and needs them to be especially resilient to mistakes that novices make, he may hang extra pieces on the harness or leave adjustments loose just so the horse knows what it feels like and doesn't get concerned. "A lot of times I will not worry too much about harness adjustment; like breeching not at the proper height, maybe a little low, crupper a little loose, so the horses get used to it so if something does happen, they're able to survive it. Never when working though, just in the training process."

Doc's mentors talked about half-harness for reasons of time, comfort for the horse, and economy. With fewer pieces on the harness, it takes less time to put the harness on and take it off. It also weighs less for the teamster and weighs less and is cooler for the equine. It can also be less expensive to assemble a half harness.

Doc describes the time and weight savings for the half-harness shown in Illustration #6. "The time savings of putting on and taking off a half harness versus a full harness for me is about a minute, which turns out to be 40% less than a full harness. Not much in the course of the day but of course it adds up over a year. The real savings is in weight: my half-harness is twenty pounds lighter per horse, so over the course of the year, that's a lot of weight not lifted if I don't need to."

Doc continues, "Work can be done and is done with just collar, hames, and traces. However, my mentors insisted that what they called half harness must include the backpad and belly band system. Can you guess why? Yes, they're part of the support system for the traces, but they don't really keep the traces from dropping to the ground near the hind legs where a horse can step on them or tangle their feet. With half harness, it's the teamster's job to prevent that. The most important reason my mentors wanted back pads and belly bands on their half harness is that proper backpad and belly band adjustment sets and maintains the ideal angle of draft, the angle at which the

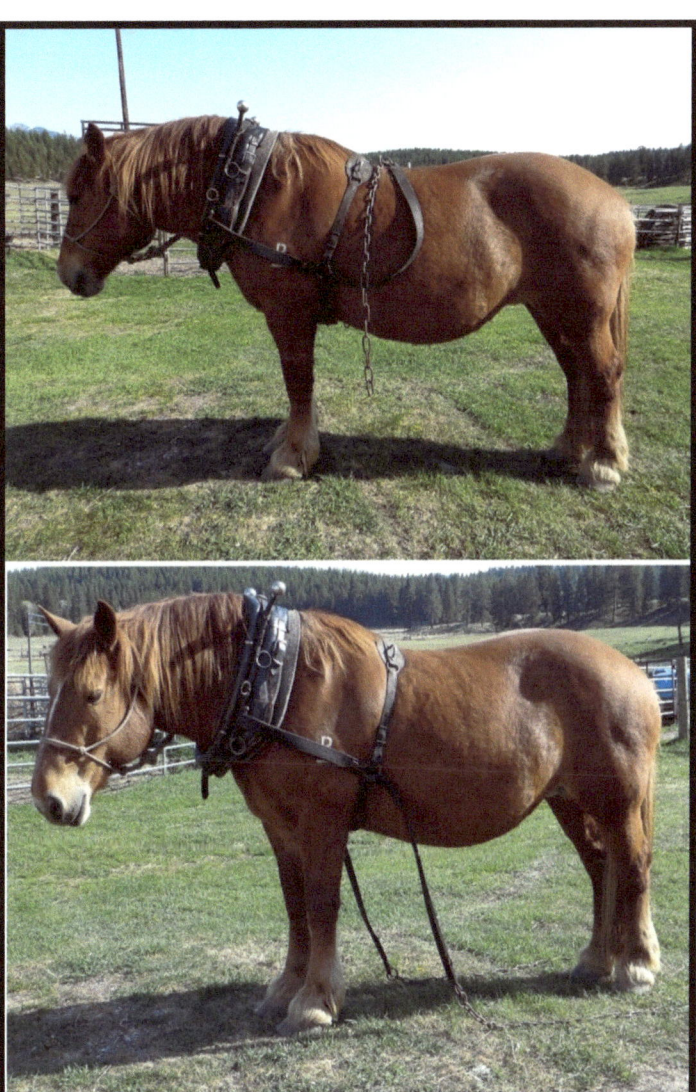

Illustration #6: Half-harness as advocated by Doc's mentors: collar, hames, traces, backpad and belly band. Literally, the front half of the harness. Note how the backpad and belly band admustment maintains the ideal angle of draft.

trace leaves the collar and hame. A lot of people nowadays think that they have to use a D-ring harness to maintain that angle during conditions and situations of work. But I learned from my mentors a long time ago that on a one-piece trace, which is the common type used in western style harness, the backpad/belly band combination will maintain the ideal angle of draft when they are adjusted properly."

Doc concludes, "While these days many people are using more and often heavier harness than they really need for the work they do, it's also important to not go too far. I don't want to encourage people to take off pieces of their harness for no good reason, or if they will need it again real soon. Some people, though, think they can lighten things up or more easily fit a harness by using a breast-collar-style driving harness on their horse or mule and go do work. But the limited surface area of the breast-collar and the way it works on the chest is not intended to handle much of a load. The same thing goes for trying to use a buggy collar when they really should have a collar with larger draft on it.

"There are people who are very successful in all respects with D-ring harness and there are people who are very successful with western harness, as well as all the other varieties in between. What it really comes down to is a personal choice about what works best for someone in their situation. There are a zillion details whichever one you use. Take into account what type of harness is popular in your area and what type of harness people nearby are skilled and knowledgeable about so you can get truly good advice and help when you need it."

The black and white images in this chapter are from America's Rural Yesterday Volumes 1 & 2 *from Mischka Press and are used with permission.*

Variations on Harness

A Percheron team on the Lynnwood Farm in 1937. J.C. Allen photo from *America's Rural Yesterday Volume II: Barn & Farmyard*, published by Mischka Press and used with permission.

When we use draft animals, we have a good idea what harness is because it lets us get our work done. It is interesting to consider, then, the range of definitions that others give to harness:
1. "the gear other than a yoke of a draft animal." (1) This definition in *Merriam-Webster* illustrates how simple harness can sometimes be.
2. "a set of strong leather bands used for fastening around an animal such as a horse so that it can pull a vehicle" (2). This definition from *Macmillan* limits the term to only leather and to only pulling vehicles. Harness can of course be made from synthetic materials, and harness is used to pull logs, harrows and any number of things besides vehicles.
3. "a set of straps and fittings by which a horse or other draft animal is fastened to a cart, plow, etc., and is controlled by its driver." (3) This definition from Google recognizes that in addition to the draft component, a communication component is also part of most harness.

That the definition of harness is not strictly set makes sense because when we work draft animals we're dealing with a very dynamic situation. Each animal is unique in its abilities and temperament, and each teamster is the same. The environment that animal and teamster work in is not only peculiar to them but also changeable. The loads that animal and teamster move can also have their own unique characteristics, so there isn't a single right answer when it comes to how to hitch an animal to a load and get work done safely and efficiently.

Rural Heritage readers generously responded to a request for unusual collar and harness pictures. The responses illustrated that, like other parts of life, human ingenuity and creativity have been applied to getting work done safely and efficiently with animals.

Interestingly, two of the submissions were of collars either partially or entirely made from metal. Sam Moore wrote an authoritative article on metal collars in the June/July 2011 issue of *Rural Heritage* magazine.(4) Sam found several patents that described metal collars, with justifications for the inventions ranging from the need for an adjustable collar to the need to avoid galling the shoulder by avoiding moisture absorption into the collar. One manufacturer offered a one year money-back guarantee. "The makers, to overcome the habits of users of leather collars, have prepared an offer of a year's trial, money back if not satisfied." (5)

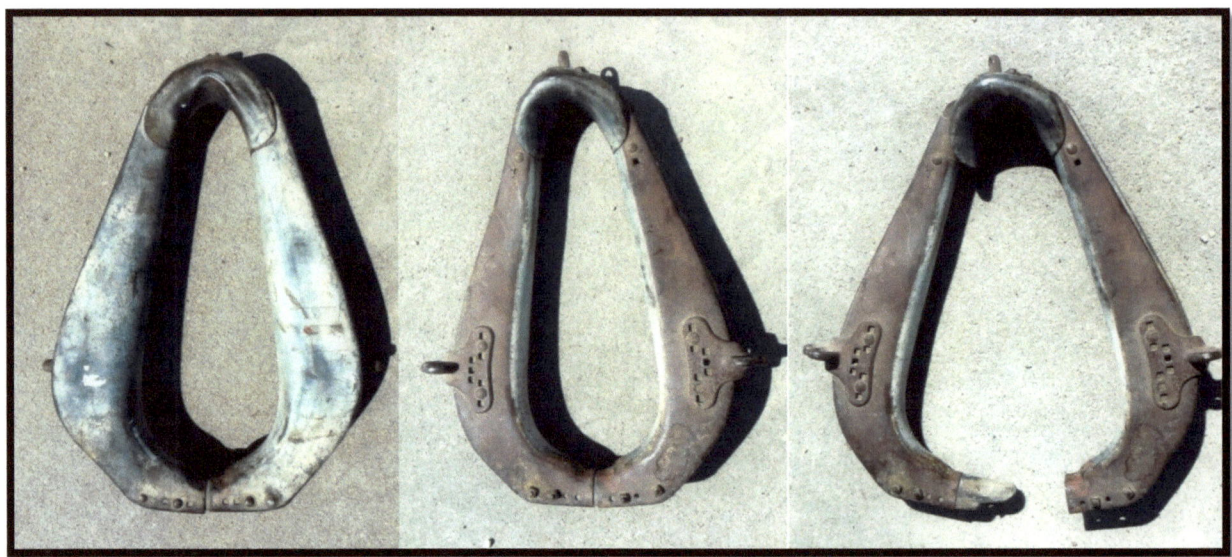

An all-metal collar. Courtesy Gary Rose.

Gary Rose submitted pictures of an all-metal army mule collar, at least that's what he was told it was. "This collar is 100% metal. Have only seen one other; it's in our local [Gordon, Nebraska] museum. Got this one in North Dakota at an auction. No one there knew what it was." Gary generously shared several pictures illustrating its various working parts.

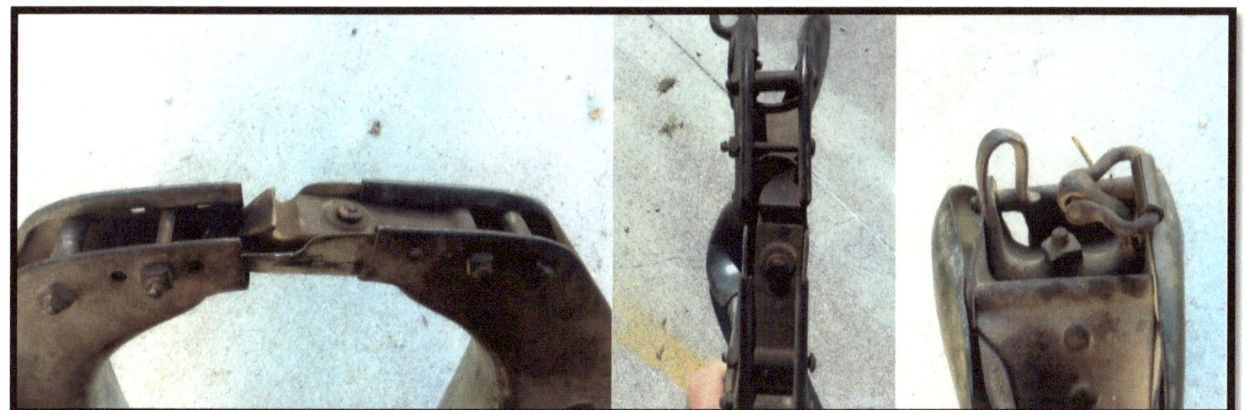

Details of the all-metal collar. Courtesy Gary Rose.

The unusual collar offered by Patty Ryan is less substantial. "Seems to be either a very light collar or some cover for one. Very thin with metal inside it, therefore not flexible. Found it at an auction." Sam Moore's article includes the following from an 1879 patent application: "…formed from thin steel plate of suitable outline by pressing up the same in dies… Provisions were made for the attachment of a leather cover…secured by stitches…or a thin metal cover which…may be riveted in place." (6)

A light collar with metal inside. Courtesy Patty Ryan

A pony-sized harness with both draft and driving characteristics.
Courtesy Michael Miller

Michael Miller sent photos of a harness he purchased at an auction. He found it curious because it seemed to have a combination of draft harness and driving harness features. "The hames are draft style with knobs and all. It is spotted overall. It has mud carriers also and is heavy built like a draft harness. There is no rump ring; it is like driving harness with a slot in the strap from pad to crupper to let the breeching lead up straps to work through from side to side. There are rings in the pad for lines, the check up strap has a hook in the pad for it and there is no strap from pad to collar strap."

Michael then says, "I know this much, it is a slip tug harness, which allows the trace to work up high and down low depending on the terrain." Slip-tug harness also allows the traces and hames to be easily separated from the rest of the harness, which is useful if weight is an issue during harnessing.

No two harness makers, of course, make harness exactly the same way. When someone is able to make their own harness or have it made, it's possible to assemble the features that one wants and leave out those they don't. Especially given that Michael's harness is pony-sized, it's likely that this harness was assembled to meet the particular needs of the person requiring its construction and therefore can't be labeled with any name that might be in general use.

The final pictures were my own submission. The hames are Swedish and the saddle is Norwegian. While they are antique and ornamental now, there is evidence that these were once actually used on equines. The saddle is unusual in appearance compared to most harness saddles used in the United States, but it is similar to the saddle on my modern Norwegian harness. What I find so interesting about these pieces is their decoration. The definitions of harness presented at the opening don't mention aesthetic characteristics at all. Gary Ryan's metal collar seems strictly functional in design. While Michael Miller's harness has spots, and Patty Ryan's collar appears to have some adornment, neither comes close to the colorful and stylistic ornamentation of these Scandinavian pieces.

We are fortunate in this day and age to have access to very good harness that allows us to do safe and efficient work with our draft animals. The harness we have today, of course, is a product that has evolved from many centuries of humans and animals working together. And while it is very good, it isn't perfect. Leather harness for instance gets knocks for being heavy and expensive. Harness from synthetic material gets knocks for chafing and being stiff in cold weather. Harness makers can and do make harness to address these problems, just as the designers of the metal collars were thinking about ways to solve the problems of their day.

Antique Swedish hames and Norwegian harness saddle.
Courtesy Annie Sjoberg

Given that the harness we have today is a product of the past, it's interesting to think about how the harness of the future might differ from the harness of today. What styles, features, or constructs will no longer be in use, just as we left behind all-metal collars? What new understandings, new materials, and new environments will we have that inspire human ingenuity and creativity? Synthetic harness materials have certainly changed what harness looks like in the past forty years.

Perhaps you're like me and have saddle horse friends who are into horse-related bling (bling is "expensive, ostentatious clothing and jewelry, or the wearing of them." (7)) Horse-related bling came to mind when I saw the Scandinavian harness because compared to most harness ornamentation today, such as spots, the highly decorated Scandinavian harness pieces seem ostentatious. Some people like to make functional items visually interesting. Have you heard of 3-D printers? To extrapolate into the future, it seems entirely within the realm of possibility that harness parts could be 3-D printed and highly decorated in times to come, with the possibility that bling will come to the harness world.

As long as there are people interested in working animals in harness, there will be people experimenting with better ways to achieve safety and efficiency. And there will be some people who have an interest in making their harness pleasing to the eye. Thank goodness the definition of harness is broad enough to welcome all to the table!

1) www.merriam-webster.com/dictionary/harness
2) http://www.macmillandictionary.com/us/dictionary/american/harness_1
3) https://www.google.com/?gws_rd=ssl#q=definition+harness
4) Moore, Sam. "Let's Talk Rusty Iron: A Steel Horse Collar?, *Rural Heritage*, Volume 26 Number 3, June/July 2011, p. 86
5) *Harness*, Volume 24, April 1910, p. 36, at https://books.google.com
6) Moore, p. 88.
7) Definition of bling on google.com, 11/2/15.

The author is grateful to Phil Teeter and Annie Sjoberg for sharing their Scandinavian harness pieces with her.

On the Lines

Have you ever been on the lines, working along with your horse (or mule or pony), and something spooked them and it didn't matter how hard you pulled but that horse took off? It's heart-thumping for most of us. What we do about it, of course, speaks volumes about who we are.

Because they are flight creatures, the horse has extraordinarily acute senses and sees things, feels things, hears things, and smells things we humans may be unaware of. The horse therefore, is aware of very subtle stimuli.
– Dr. Robert Miller, veterinarian (1)

It's remarkable, really. When we are working our horses, the sole physical connection we have with them is through our hands down the lines. Our horses can feel the slightest touch of a fly on their flank. They can separate one blade of grass from another when grazing or sort their favorites from a pile of hay. They can tell the weather is about to change without reading the barometer. They obviously have very perceptive senses. And we put their senses to use when we are on the lines.

At the end of the lines there is usually a piece of hardware in the horse's mouth. People have been putting things in horses' mouths for millennia: leather, rope, bone, wood, metal, plastic, rubber. It's remarkable, really, that a flight animal allows us to put such an object in this most sensitive of body cavities. Veterinarian Dr. R.D. Scoggins observes that the equine is the only domestic species that has their mouths regularly used in this fashion (2).

When we are on the lines, we are communicating with our horses. Photo courtesy Cathy Greatorex

Have you ever been on the lines and after just the slightest movement of your hands, your horses do exactly what you want exactly when you want it? What did you communicate down the lines to get this result? More importantly, what did your horses communicate back?

A bit's use as an instrument of control is illusory. If bits were truly effective as instruments of control, then there wouldn't be runaways. Instead, bits must be looked at as instruments of communication. When we are on the lines, we are not controlling our horses, we are communicating with them. We 'speak' down the lines, and they 'speak' back to us with movement (or lack thereof) of certain or several parts of their bodies. It is the quality of our communication on the lines that controls our horses.

Correctly bitting a horse has very little to do with mechanics. It has everything to do with feel, timing and balance. It is much more an art form than a science. In the hands of some individuals, a complex high-port-curb bit is an instrument of communication with all of the delicacy of playing a violin. In another person's hands, a thick hollow-mouthed snaffle may be as dangerous as a surgical scalpel in the hands of a monkey.
– Dr. R. D. Scoggins, veterinarian (3)

Bits apply pressure to sensitive parts of a horse's mouth and head. For a bit to be an instrument of communication, it must apply pressure in a way that the horse understands and is willing to respond to appropriately. Photo courtesy Mary Martin

Bits apply pressure to sensitive parts of a horse's mouth and head. For a bit to be an instrument of communication, it must apply pressure in a way that the horse understands and is willing to respond to appropriately. When we are on the lines, we choose how, when, and how much pressure to apply. When the pressure is applied effectively, it results in our intended communication, and we get our work done. Have you ever had a horse 'pull the bit out of your hands' by grabbing it and pulling the lines away from you? Our horse is communicating back to us that the pressure that we applied wasn't appropriate or understood.

Painless communication leads to more effective control.
– Dr. W. Robert Cook, veterinarian and professor of surgery (4)

The problem with bits is that while they are intended to be used to communicate by applying pressure, improperly used they can inflict pain. For a bit to do its job, for a bit to be an effective instrument of communication, it must not be associated with pain. If we want control when we are on the lines, then we must apply pressure without causing pain.

Resistance to the bit causes rigidity of the neck, which is incompatible with optimum performance.
– Dr. W. Robert Cook, veterinarian and professor of surgery (5)

When horses feel discomfort or pain from the bit, they begin to resist our attempts at communication. And when they resist, our ability to do productive work is adversely affected. When we are on the lines, to do good work, we must use our hands to apply just enough pressure to communicate and not so much pressure that it causes discomfort or pain and leads to less work being done well.

"The driver's hands are not meant to control the horse, but rather to feel the horse's thoughts."
- Anonymous

"As a teacher and clinician," says Doc, "I work with a lot of people who believe or have been told that they just need to find the right bit. The right bit will give them more power and control over their horses to fix the problems they're having. Ninety nine percent of the time, it's us on the back end of the lines connected to the bit where the problem is that needs to be fixed.

"As humans we have little or no inherent understanding about effectively communicating what we want a horse to do, or not do, in a way that makes sense to and works for the horse. Moreover, in view of what we now understand about how horses learn and what motivates them, much of the horsemanship that has been handed down over the centuries is obsolete and not very effective in getting horses to willingly cooperate and comfortably and willingly choose to do as we ask.

"Regretfully, before I learned better, I was a horseman and teamster who too often used harsh cues, excessive or steady pressures, failed to release or released too much, and often miscommunicated on the lines. Because that kind of driving is still very prevalent in spite of the opportunities we now have to learn better ways, it's no wonder so many equines are psychologically anxious, braced, pushing on the bit, physically uncomfortable, and looking for just one more reason to skedaddle when being driven and worked.

"Once an equine experiences stress, anxiety, confusion, frustration, resentment, pain or fear in association with the bit, they never forget it. And they likely will not become as comfortable,

Doc shares, "From my perspective as a lifelong student of the teamster art, I know stress, anxiety, confusion, frustration, resentment, pain or fear in association with the bit isn't necessary. And as a veterinarian I know that for the wellbeing of the horse and the safety of all concerned, it shouldn't be that way. Photo courtesy Cathy Greatorex

confident, relaxed, reliable and safe when driving and working in harness as they could otherwise be. From my perspective as a lifelong student of the teamster art, I know it doesn't have to be that way. And as a veterinarian I know that for the wellbeing of the horse and the safety of all concerned, it shouldn't be that way. The learning opportunities available to us today have the potential to make us the most skilled and sophisticated teamsters the world has ever known. What better gift could we give our horses?"

Have you ever been on the lines, and something spooked your horse, and it didn't matter how hard you pulled on the bit, the horse still took off? What did you do the next time you were on the lines? What did you do to honestly and effectively improve your communication with your horse the next time you were on the lines?

1. Dr. Miller has given Doc Hammill permission to quote him.
2. Scoggins, R. D., DVM. "Bits, Bitting, and Dentistry," February 5, 2003 on the American Association of Equine Practitioners website at http://www.aaep.org/info/horse-health?publication=730
3. Same as #2.
4. Cook, W. Robert, FRCVS., PhD. "Pathophysiology of Bit Control in the Horse," *Journal of Equine Veterinary Science*, 1999 and 2007 at http://www.bitlessbridle.com/pathophysiology.pdf
5. Same as #4.

The Privilege of Harness Care

When we are short of time - and who isn't these days - the thought of hosing down our harness while it's still on our horses and calling it harness care is definitely appealing. This approach to harness care isn't strictly for harness made from synthetic material either. Bernie Samson of Samson Harness Shop, Inc. in Gilbert, Minnesota rightly observes, "Water doesn't hurt good leather harness. If you had to run to the barn every time it threatened to rain, nothing would have ever gotten done when leather harness was the only game in town." Harness care, though, is about a lot more than hosing it off with water.

So far we've discussed a wide variety of topics having to do with harness, including how to choose harness, what different sorts of draft harness there are and how they function, and harness geometry – points, lines and angles of draft. It may seem strange that harness care is a later topic, but in fact harness care becomes easier when we understand how our harness works. Harness care becomes easier when we understand how we use it to get our work done.

We are going to make mistakes; it is inevitable because it's part of human nature. Mistakes can cause injuries. Mistakes can cause safety issues. Good horsemanship is in part about making our mistakes small enough that the injuries or safety issues are small, too.

Good harness care is like good horsemanship. It's about making problems with our harness small enough that injuries or safety issues are small, too. We can make our mistakes small by incorporating routine harness care into our work horse routine. We can make our mistakes small by understanding our harness well enough that we know the difference between mission-critical problems and those for which repair can be delayed. We can make our mistakes small by making repairs as soon as possible after their need is discovered and their urgency understood. We

Good harness care is like good horsemanship. It's about making problems with our harness small enough that injuries or safety issues are small, too.
J.C. Allen photo

can make our mistakes small by remembering the role our harness plays in the relationship we have with our horses.

Harness care products are so numerous as to be mind-numbing. Harness care instructions are almost as numerous and vary in content so much as to be confusing. Fortunately it's likely that we're already taking good care of our harness or we wouldn't be able to get our work done. And like anything worth doing, there's always opportunity to do a better job than we already are.

Steps in Harness Care

Harness care is required regardless of the material that harness is made from. The first three steps of harness care – inspection, cleaning, and repair – are necessary for both synthetic and leather harness. A fourth step, reconditioning, is specifically for leather harness. When appearance of harness is also important, a fifth step, polishing, may be added for either type of harness. Brass hardware, for instance, can be cleaned and polished. Certain types of leather can be polished, too, and some people like to polish their synthetic harness. In all cases, thoughtfulness is required in choice of cleaning, reconditioning, and polishing agents. Just because it's on the market doesn't mean it's the right choice for your situation.

Steps in Harness Care
1. Inspection
2. Cleaning
3. Repair
4. Reconditioning (leather only)
5. Polishing

The inspection step of harness care can range from a brief visual check when the harness is put on or taken off the horse to complete disassembly of the harness with careful and thorough review of each piece for signs of wear. Cleaning can range from removing mud or snow as it accumulates to wiping sweat and dust off with a rag each time the harness comes off the horse to a multi-day process of scrubbing, rinsing, drying and repeating. Repair can range from temporary measures for minor parts of the harness to complete replacement of failed pieces which of course may occur at any time. Reconditioning is necessary for leather harness when it begins to lose its suppleness and depends upon the type of leather used to build the harness.

If someone interested in working horses were to first encounter harness care instructions requiring complete disassembling as often as every week, they could be forgiven for losing interest in working horses because just harness care would take too much time. On the other hand, we know and accept that our cars, trucks, and other machinery require regular routine and minor maintenance, with the occasional big ticket item. Harness care is similar: basic safety checks, occasional cleaning, and periodic "oil change and lube" (for leather harness) keep our harness ready and able to do what we expect it to do, with big investments required occasionally for significant maintenance tasks.

The Coaching Legacy

Bernie Samson suggests that harness care procedures that seem over the top in terms of frequency and thoroughness likely have their roots in coaching. Consider the following from the chapter on harness care in the 1882 book by John Philipson called *Harness: As It Has Been, As It Is, and As It Should Be*:

> *"A careful coachman will pay great attention to his harness room, he will dust it frequently, will polish the wood and brass fittings, and when opportunity offers, will take a pride in pointing out to his friends its good order and neat appearance. He will also be careful to keep everything scrupulously clean, and when brushing or polishing his harness, will select some place where cleanliness is of less importance than in the harness room....*
>
> *"It is not absolutely necessary to clean harness, as is the case with carriages, after each time of using. Should there be no mud, nor very much dust upon the harness, it will be sufficient to brush the oil leather, to dust and wipe the japanned leather, and to rub the buckles and other mountings with a dry rag.*
>
> *"It is however, necessary to wash with a sponge, but without splashing, any parts of the harness which shows signs of sweat from the horse, especially such parts as the insides of the collars, the leather panels of the saddles, the girths, etc. This washing should take place as soon as the horses have been unharnessed and rubbed down; each part being removed in its turn from the hook which it occupied while the horses were receiving the attention of the coachman.*
>
> *"This partial cleansing being terminated, the harness should be placed on trestles provided for the purpose and furnished with hooks and shelves, after being brushed the parts above-mentioned should be rubbed over with a greasy rag dipped in neatsfoot oil."* (1)

Philipson's audience was those for whom appearance as well as safety and function were of paramount importance. Most of us probably find ourselves in environments vastly different than that suggested by Philipson. Yet what ties us to Philipson's words is practicality. He was laying out a practical approach to harness care for his audience, and we too must be practical to ensure the safety and function of our harness and comfort of our horses and the best use of our scarcest resource: our time.

Inspection

The great thing about working with horses is that we've chosen to work at a considered pace rather than a breakneck one. Just as we can only plow a furrow so fast with horses, we can also handle our harness at a measured pace, too, not just moving it from hook to horse without thought but instead pausing to look it over as it comes off the hook, as it is lifted onto the horse, as it is slid into place, all the time evaluating whether it is as ready to do the job at hand as we and our horses are. And when we are done working, reversing the process, not just pulling the harness off and hanging it up but again pausing to look it over to make sure we know what attention it needs to be ready for the next time out.

And after the harness is off the horses, inspecting the horses is part of harness care too. Even just slightly ruffled hair, if it's out of the ordinary, can be an indication that the harness needs to be inspected and adjusted or repaired. From a practical standpoint, taking a few moments as we're harnessing and unharnessing to inspect our horses and our harness often fits more easily into the flow of the work day than adding a separate task to our to-do list.

If we have leather harness, then one of the things we're looking for when inspecting our harness is whether the leather needs to be reconditioned. What are the signs that indicate reconditioning is required? Unlike vehicles that have 'maintenance required' lights, the onus is on us to recognize when our leather harness might be starting to dry out. Dryness, cracking, and loss of suppleness are warning signs. Bernie Samson says that harness leather in good condition should be flexible and supple yet strong at 65° Fahrenheit.

We also need to be on the lookout for signs of rot. "Rotting starts in a leather harness underneath the britchen, between the buckles, and in all those little areas with folds and creases. These are also the highest stress points that tend to give out first, so keep an eye on them." (2) Rot, of course, requires replacement parts, not reconditioning.

For most of us, there are parts of the year when things are slower, when a more dedicated harness inspection is possible. The most thorough inspection is achieved by completely taking the harness apart. Many people are intimidated by this necessary step. Fear sets in; what if we can't get it back together properly? When we understand our harness, though, we have a better understanding of what each part of the harness does and therefore are more likely to know what sort of straps are required where with what sort of connections. Suddenly the harness goes back together easily!

In the meantime, though, here's a helpful hint: "If you need to, make measurements and take notes on how everything came apart so you can put it back together when you're done. Once you've disassembled it and reassembled it a time or two, you'll recognize all the pieces at a glance and won't need the notes." (3) And "A lot of people don't like to take a bridle apart because they're afraid they won't remember how to put it back together. Well here's a trick: take apart one side of the bridle at a time, clean it, then use the other half as a pattern to put it back together. Or keep an illustration handy. In a pinch, call your friendly harness shop." (4) Today's digital cameras and smartphones provide another alternative: take lots of pictures before you take your harness apart to have as reference when it's time to put your harness back together.

Some harness care procedures emphasize complete disassembly weekly while others suggest annually or even less frequently. Each one of us works our horses different amounts in different situations in different weather in different climates, so it is up to us to determine what frequency makes sense. The point of this step, regardless of the type of harness material, is to make sure that every piece has been closely scrutinized, not only the straps, inside and out, but the buckles (including tongues), rivets, and stitching, especially stitching close to hardware. From our understanding of harness, we can then prioritize repair for mission-critical pieces first and then others thereafter.

In the 1997 "Evener" edition of *Rural Heritage* magazine, Mari Lintin made several recommendations about inspecting and prolonging the life of harness:

- "All harness will eventually wear out. If you're in the habit of always buckling and unbuckling from the same side of the horse, parts will wear out quicker. To keep them wearing evenly, occasionally turn straps around where you can…
- "Straps that are always in the same hole—the quarter straps and back straps, for example—accumulate dirt underneath, which causes excessive wear…
- "Your hame straps hold together the front end of your harness; if they go, there goes your whole harness. Replace a hame strap as often as is necessary….
- "The belly band, because it's located where the horse drips sweat onto it all day, is among the first pieces to go. Other parts that get a lot of sweat are the quarter straps and the combination strap, connecting your pole strap to your breast strap." (5)

Routine Cleaning

While for some, cleaning is about aesthetics, the most important purpose for cleaning harness is to remove dirt that can compromise the harness material, leading to damage and failure. Sweat and oils from the horse's coat aren't as much of an issue as dirt is. Dirt, when it works into any type of harness material, can cause it to fray, decay, or break. Of course dirt can also become mixed with sweat and oils and build up, causing comfort issues for the horse and then safety issues as well.

When do you need to clean your harness? And how thoroughly? Again, the answers to these questions are very much dependent on our individual circumstances. Routine inspection and experience will inform the answers. "Wiping your harness down after each [use] will keep dirt and sweat from accumulating, making your horse more comfortable and making the job of thorough cleaning much easier when the time comes. Soon after your harness comes off your horse, wipe it down with a damp sponge or rag, paying particular attention to the 'horse side' of the harness. Don't forget to wipe the inside of the bridle, as many horses sweat around the ears…" (6)

Periodic wiping of leather harness can reduce how often it must be more thoroughly cleaned and reconditioned. Axwood Library suggests: "If you wipe your harness down with Murphy Oil Soap and water every time (or so) that you use it, you will not have to strip and reoil your harness for a nice long time! Mine seems to go for about a year and a half to two years before I have to redo it. If we come in muddy, sweaty or both, my harness is so well preserved, I can hose horse and harness off. A quick wipe down with Murphy Oil Soap and water and it's good as new!" (7) Keeping in mind, of course, that for every person who likes a particular product, there are many who don't!

Stuffing

Each evening after they receive their dinner and before we get ours, our dogs get a piece of rawhide. Like most harness leather, typical rawhide comes from the skin of cattle. Obviously, though, there is a dramatic difference between rawhide and harness leather. Rawhide is stiff and hard at room temperature, where the best harness leather is supple while remaining strong. Harness leather is made through a process involving 'stuffing' the hide with oils to lubricate the internal fibers so that they can move without breaking. Just as our vehicles need lubrication to keep them operating properly, leather harness requires occasional lubrication or reconditioning, too, to ensure that the internal fibers don't dry out, chafe against each other, fray and in time break.

Both rawhide chews and good harness leather come from cow hides; harness leather is 'stuffed' with oils to give it elasticity and life. One harness care step for leather harness is to replenish those oils.

Good quality leather harness, sometimes called well-stuffed or hot-stuffed, is easier to clean than poorer quality leather. If you clean poorer quality leather using the process for hot-stuffed leather, you may end up with a ruined harness. Therefore, if you don't know what sort of harness leather you have, you'll need to test it to find out. Axwood Library suggests the following: "To test the quality of the leather, pick a piece needing [to be] replaced. Clean and prepare it using the [cleaning] method given below and let it dry overnight. After it is completely dry, run it through lukewarm oil (no hotter than 100 degrees). If it absorbs the oil (even after you've dunked it more than once or even let it soak, and it looks and feels good, you've got the good stuff. If it comes out gross, you know where you're at and what you've got." (8)

If you're interested in learning about how harness leather is stuffed and you have internet access, Hermann Oak Leather has a tannery tour video on their website: hermannoakleather.com.

Thorough Cleaning

If a thorough cleaning of your harness is warranted, then some planning is in order. Remember that cleaning is a harness care step independent of harness material. For a thorough cleaning, you will need time to take your harness apart, scrub it and let it dry. If you have leather harness and will be reconditioning it, you'll need at least one additional day.

You will also need space to work, including floor space adequate for taking apart your harness. Some people like a washboard or hooks in the ceiling to support the harness while it's being scrubbed. You'll also need space for hanging the harness while it is drying as well as racks of some sort to support the harness. Extra large sawhorses, hooks in the ceiling, hay racks and pairs of stepladders with 2x4s between them all have been used. The drying space also needs to be out of the sun and preferably room-temperature warm. Too close to a heat source, especially for leather harness, is a problem: "Leather is a porous hide. If you dry it close to a heat source, like a fire or a heater, you'll literally bake the hide. A lot of people make the mistake of drying leather shoes close to the fire. Don't do it with your harness." (9) A source of warm water is also helpful; warm water can help loosen dirt and dirt-impregnated oils.

Regardless of the harness material, a mild soap or detergent is recommended, mixed into lukewarm (or blood warm) water; again, too much heat isn't good for harness. Washing soda is often specified. A sponge and a stiff nylon brush are also important; some people like fingernail brushes. A large amount of newspaper is needed to cover the floor to accept the harness pieces after they have been scrubbed and before they are hung to dry. Murphy's oil soap is sometimes used to remove any residual detergent from leather harness before reconditioning. It leaves an oily residue so may not be appropriate for synthetic harness or for lines/reins. You'll also need numerous cotton rags and at least a five gallon bucket or a hay tub or muck bucket or washtub, something that is large enough to contain your harness pieces. Two can be handy, one to contain the washing soda and water and the second containing just water for rinsing.

Here are harness cleaning instructions from a circa 1920 Farm Encyclopedia that are replicated without much modification in many harness care instructions today: "In cleaning harness, as little water as possible should be used; warm, soft water is best, but hard water may be used if a handful or two of [washing soda] is added to each tubful. Some harness is so dirty that sponging alone will not remove the dirt; in this case it should be soaked for 15 minutes, then scrubbed with soap and a brush, rinsed, wiped with rag or chamois, and hung on a wooden horse to dry…" (10) If your leather is not hot-stuffed, you will not want to immerse your harness in water. Also don't soak any harness pieces such as cruppers or saddles that have padding. Instead, use a rag dipped in the washing water and rung out and then wipe down your harness pieces. You can then dip a rag in diluted Murphy's Oil Soap, ring it out and wipe the residual washing soda off your harness pieces.

Now leave your harness pieces to dry. How dry depends on whether you have leather harness and you need to recondition it.

Repair

Our inspection of our harness will have identified any parts that need repair or replacement. Some additional inspection advice includes:
- "Take the time to check each buckle for soundness, particularly the tongue, which can become bent under stress. Check the buckle holes for signs of stretching. Check all pieces for cracking and loose stitching." (11)
- "Also look for broken loops or keepers, cut straps, cracked leather, bent tongs, broken stitching and worn buckles." (12)

When and how thoroughly you repair your harness will depend on your situation and whether the pieces needing attention are mission-critical. If you've discovered pieces needing repair during a thorough cleaning, then "as soon as they are dry, take them to your favorite saddle maker/repairer and have them fixed. [If you have leather harness,] make sure your repairperson uses hot stuff/vegetable tanned leather when replacing failed harness leather. You don't want to have to replace these pieces again because sufficient quality leather wasn't used." (13) If you have leather harness, getting those pieces repaired before reconditioning the harness will save you from having to set up the reconditioning process twice.

Harness repair is only one of five steps in harness care and like most of them is required for both synthetic and leather harness.
JC Allen photo

In the end, it is up to us to ensure that our harness is safe, functional, and comfortable for our horses. Understanding how our harness works helps us make smart decisions about when and how we repair our harness.

Reconditioning Leather Harness

"Leather will dry out over time, and restoring the fats and oils that were 'stuffed' into the leather during the tanning process will keep it supple and beautiful." (14)

If your inspection indicates that your leather harness needs reconditioning, leave your harness until it is mostly but not completely dry. Mari Lintin says, "The time to put oil to leather is when it's damp dry—not completely dry or totally wet, but in between. You can put your harness in the sun to heat it up and loosen the pores just a little, so it'll absorb the oil better, but don't leave it in the sun for long or it will fry like a piece of bacon." (15) The *Farmers Shop Book* states, "It is not necessary that the harness be thoroughly dry before the oil is applied. As the water is drying out, the oil will draw in." (16)

The choice of oil with which to recondition your leather harness is a personal one. Axwood Library swears by olive oil, and olive oil was also endorsed on the *Rural Heritage* Front Porch. Neatsfoot oil or mixtures containing neatsfoot oil are common; since good harness leather is stuffed with animal-derived fats, it's understandable that neatsfoot oil is commonly available for conditioning harness. Some harness care instructions caution against using neatsfoot oil because it causes damage to stitching. Bernie Samson suggests that applying neatsfoot or any oil to very old traces may lubricate the layers of leather enough that movement between them stresses old stitching and causes it to break; the oil is not the problem; the age of the stitches more likely is. Many on the *Rural Heritage* Front Porch use neatsfoot oil and find it perfect to the task. Leather Honey™ also got good reviews.(17) Again, the choice of conditioning agent is an individual one; what works well or is readily available for one person might not be as good a choice for someone else.

Some instructions suggest dipping harness parts in oil then letting them drain. In 1971, Bernie Samson visited a shuttered harness shop. 'Harness shop,' though, conjures the wrong image. 'Harness maintenance shop' is a more apt descriptor. The shop was located in a large commercial building and had been set up to recondition a large number of leather harness simultaneously. A large vat sat at one end, and a track with hooks ran down one side. Under the track was a trough; harness would be dipped in the warm oil in the tank, then the harness was hung on a hook and moved down the track. The oil would drip off the harness into the trough where the oil was collected and returned to the vat.

Some harness care instructions suggest wiping the conditioner on the leather. A few pieces of the harness, such as saddles, may be awkward to soak and will have to be wiped. Again, lukewarm is helpful because the warmth helps open the pores of the leather to accept the conditioner. Some instructions explicitly warn against wearing gloves because they keep you from making sure the oil isn't too warm and might damage the leather. A warm (but not too warm!) place for the harness to dry is recommended.

The *Old Farm Encyclopedia* says, "Several applications of oil are generally needed, and it will pay to rub it well into the leather with the hands. After the oil has soaked in, sponge the straps with a good grade of castile soap." (18) Axwood Library points out that some pieces of harness may need to be dipped in oil more than once until they quit accepting more oil. Then either use a two-step process of washing soda and Murphy's Oil Soap, or just Murphy's oil soap to remove excess oil. "[Using just Murphy's oil soap may leave the harness] a bit too oily the first time or two I use it, but, I know it has enough oil to be properly preserved and by the time I've wiped it down once or twice, it's about perfect and stays perfect for a long time!" (19)

Mold and Mildew

Mold and mildew are enemies of harness. The *Old Farm Encyclopedia* states, "The presence of mold indicates that moisture is taking the place of the oil, upon which the life of the leather depends." (20)

Mari Lintin warns, "If you throw the harness into the tack room all hot and sweaty and wet, it's going to mildew fast. Even clean harness will mildew, if the air is damp." (21) Bernie Samson cautions that when restoring mildewed harness, keep it away from other harness because the spores travel easily. Do it outside if at all possible, away from other leather.

Visitors to the *Rural Heritage* Front Porch and others point out that air circulation where the harness is stored is crucial to minimizing mold and mildew. A light bulb in the tack room was a common recommendation since it heats the air and causes it to move. Some also use fans. Bernie Samson suggests that sunlight is a good preventive for mildew, as long as the harness doesn't get too hot. One Front Porch visitor said, "I have found that using [my harness] prevents mildew from showing up!" (22) Axwood Library says, "If you prepare harness the way I do, your harness won't mold (though the dirt and sweat on the surface may), no matter how or where you store it, and, if you like the smell of olive oil, it will smell great!"

J.C. Allen Photo

The Privilege of Harness Care

Whether we have a chore horse or whether the farm's existence depends on the work our horses do, we have chosen to work with horses when many of our neighbors have chosen otherwise. We have chosen to work with horses because we want to; we may even have conviction about the subject; and we have skills, hopefully always increasing, that allow us to do the work we do with our horses. Given that horses can choose not to work with us, it is a privilege that so often they work so willingly.

We can see harness care as a time-eater. We can see harness care as a must for safety. We can see harness care as an investment protector. We can see harness care as a necessary evil. Or we can see it as something more. Harness care is an integral part of this rewarding work we do with horses. In a day and age when we have alternatives to working horses, harness care is one way that we express our belief in the rightness of the work. Harness care is one way that we demonstrate our appreciation for the work our horses do. In the end, just as working our horses is a privilege, harness care is a privilege, too, even if sometimes we have to remind ourselves of that!

The black and white photos in this chapter are from America's Rural Yesterday, Volume II: Barn and Farmyard, *published by Mischka Press and used with permission.*

1. Morrissey, Jenifer. ""Neither Carrot Nor Stick," *Rural Heritage*, February/March 2011, p. 109-110.
2. Philipson, John. *Harness: As It Has Been, As It Is, and As It Should Be.* London, Edward Stanford, 1882, p. 83
3. Lintin, Mari. "Treat Your Harness with TLC," http://ruralheritage.com/tack_room/tlc.htm
4. http://axwoodlibrary.com/cleaning-harness/
5. Same as #2.
6. Same as #2.
7. http://www.carriagedriving.net/index.php?m=a&a=19
8. Same as #3
9. Same as #3.
10. Same as #2
11. http://www.shadygrovehaflinger.com/harness.html
12. same as #6
13. http://www.freedmanharness.com/cleaninginstuctions.htm
14. Same as #3.
15. Same as #6.
16. Same as #2.
17. Roehl, Louis M. *Farmers Shop Book*, Bruce Publishing Co., New York, 1950, pages 314-315. Courtesy Bernie Samson.
18. "What Kind of Oil to use on Tack," at http://ruralheritage.com/messageboard/frontporch/18100.htm
19. Same as #10.
20. Same as #3.
21. Same as #10.
22. Same as #2.
23. Brabant owner in SC at http://ruralheritage.com/messageboard/frontporch/18104.htm

Parting Thoughts

Each of us works our equines at our own place and at our own pace. We have different equines than anyone else, our own work to do, and our own approach to using our equines to do that work. Because our working situation with our equines is uniquely our own, we have a unique perspective on what it takes to be a teamster and to get our work done. Harness is just one part of the picture; nonetheless it bears heavily on the safety and efficiency with which we get our work done. After reading this book about harness, hopefully our understanding of harness is more thorough and we have a greater appreciation for the role harness plays in doing safely and efficiently the work that needs to be done.

In his Preface, Doc divides teamsters into two groups. Group A rarely, if ever, experiences close calls, mishaps, runaways, wrecks or injuries. Group B, on the other hand, occasionally has those types of experiences, where sometimes people and horses or mules get hurt. The teamsters in Group A always have good reasons for the way they do things, and good reasons for not doing them some other way. The wisdom of the many teamsters in Group A is included in this book. In Doc's Preface, he extends an invitation to readers to join Group A. We hope this book has given you encouragement in that regard.

*   *   *   *

My husband was watching a TV show one year before the Superbowl that was a contest between various Superbowl ads from the past. In the end, the first place commercial featured the Budweiser Clydesdales, and second place also featured these draft horses. Isn't it something that horses were featured in the top ads? Not artificial monsters, not high tech special effects, not human beings doing violent things, but flesh-and-blood horses? And isn't it something that it was draft horses?

Around the same time, I read an article about a young man who was drawn to the world of working horses by the Budweiser Clydesdales. His was a different sort of endorsement of this hitch; bringing these words from the late Steve Bowers to mind:

In this world that has been highly polluted in many ways with the machines of men, one sparkling glimmer of hope is the person who has useful work for horses, and knows how to train for that work with uncommon skill… (1)

I think one of the things that people appreciate about the Budweiser ads and about watching draft horses in general is that they inspire hope: that there are ways to get things done that are more harmonious than the norm. And in these times, inspiring hope about the future is definitely a good thing. We as draft horse teamsters, above other types of horsemen and women, have an uncommon opportunity when with our horses. By putting them to useful work, and doing it well, we make the future look brighter for any and all that may be watching. And maybe we can attract more people to working with equines, too!

*   *   *   *

There's surely more to say about harness than appears in the previous pages. For instance one day I hope to collect Doc's thoughts on collar fit all in one place; fortunately many of his thoughts are already included here. Hames are another topic we could address. And Doc teaches students in his workshops about a number of harness improvements that he's devised and tested that could be addressed. Just touching on these topics will likely spur Doc and friends to share wisdom on other subjects about using harness safely, functionally, and comfortably, in short using harness wisely and well.

We sincerely appreciate your interest in learning to use harness wisely and well. We know you'll then contribute positively to the long tradition of the teamster's art.

1) Bowers, Steve. *A Teamster's View: More and Different*, Bowers Farm, Fort Collins, Colorado, 2001, p. 200.

Doc Hammill Horsemanship

Doc and Cathy help you to Truly Understand and Gently Influence Equines by teaching you:

- Deeper UNDERSTANDING of HORSES' Minds
- Better EQUINE COMMUNICATION
- Stronger RELATIONSHIP BUILDING Skills
- Improved and refined GROUND WORK & DRIVING Techniques

These are Teachable, Learnable skills.
We Love teaching them...you will love learning them.
We Offer a variety of proven learning opportunities to fit Your learning style and budget with:

- Hands on total immersion *Driving, Working, Training Horses to Drive Workshops*
- Doc's Instructional DVDs
- Home Study- with individualized coaching from Doc
- Books
- Articles

Doc Hammill Horsemanship

provides you with incredible learning experiences from which you will gain a deeper understanding of the horse's mind. Using Doc's proven approach, you'll learn to establish a relationship with your horse based on trust, respect and you as the gentle leader. This all important relationship will lead to training outcomes and safety you have only imagined.

www.DocHammill.com

Doc: (406) 250-8252
Cathy:(406)890-3083
Email: workshops@dochammill.com

DVDs by Doc Hammill
available at dochammill.com

Fundamentals Video #1

An introduction to the fundamentals of driving and working horses in harness. Topics include: Getting Started, Lines And Line Board, Exercises with Lines, Line Chair, Commands, Catching and Haltering, Collars and Pads, Grooming, Hames, Introduction To Bits, Harness Up, Exercises With Cones, Team Lines Introduction, Hitching The Team, Driving Over The Tongue, Removing Harness, Communicating With Horses. DVD / 2 hours

Fundamentals Video #2

A continuation of the introduction to the fundamentals of driving and working horses in harness. Topics include: Fitting Collars, Grooming, Properly Adjusted Harness, Adjusting Britchen, Harnessing Tips, Hitching the Single Horse, Bits, Introduction to Mowing, Securing Neck Yoke, Dump Rake, Adjusting Team Lines, Intro To Skidding Logs, Butt Rope and Jockey Stick. DVD / 2 hours.

Fundamentals 3 and 4

Driving and Working Horses in Harness: Fundamentals 3 and 4 continues Doc's coverage of the basics of working with horses in harness. 2 DVDs / 4 hours

Topics covered in Fundamentals 3: Harness: Pull/Holdback, Hame Strap vs. Fastener, Hooking Up Single Lines, Hooking Up Team Lines, Preflight Check, Attaching Doubletrees, Lines: Control & Finesse, Horsedrawn Grader, Knots Review, Horse Follows Too Close, Footcare: Ready For Farrier

Fundamentals 4 topics include: Coming When Called, Bridles and Check Reins, Breast & Pole Strap Options, Using The Buckback Rope, Reshaping Collars, Point Of Draft, Intro To Working In The Woods, Bungee Tie, Managing Collar Sores, Lines Hooked Up Wrong, Footcare: Trimming Feet

Gentle Training 1: The Round Pen

Doc uses a Clydesdale colt to carefully explain and demonstrate round pen techniques throughout three complete training sessions captured in real time.
3 DVDs / 6 hours

Gentle Training 2: Daily Opportunities

Daily interaction can and should be more than just feeding and care giving. These moments provide powerful opportunities for you to become your horse's most important and valued companion, leader, and trainer. In essence -- training all the time. In this DVD, Doc will help you to work cooperatively and safely with your horses or mules.
DVD / 1 ¾ hours

Preventing Wrecks:
Essential Advice Regarding Harness, Equipment, Knowledge, and Skill

Learn how to prevent common wrecks with horses in harness from a respected master horseman. This DVD presents essential advice regarding harness, equipment, knowledge, and skill.

"One of the things I've learned over time is that the truly great teamsters rarely -- if ever -- have upset horses, close calls, mishaps or wrecks, while the less meticulous horsemen often do. The master horsemen follow a set of safety rules and pay incredible attention to detail, which keeps them and their horses safe." –Doc

DVD / 1 ½ hours

Teaching Horses to Drive: A Ten Step Method

Doc uses a mule, a saddle horse and draft horses to take you through his ten step method for gently training horses to drive.
2 DVDs / 3 ½ hours

The Horses Can Do It!

Move over dump trucks and other diesel powered equipment -- here come the horses: Barney, Misty, Dillon, Tom, and Ginger. They're ready for work. Watch the horses plow, make hay. and haul logs and firewood, and MORE!

The Horses Can Do It! captures the exciting sights and sounds of horses at work, intermixed with music. Doc also answers questions like "Do horses sleep?", and "What do horses eat?" It's sure to have everyone saying, "AGAIN!" Great for ages 2-8 and children of ALL ages.
DVD / ½ hour

Books by Jenifer Morrissey

All books by the author are available at willowtrailfarm.com and amazon.com

THE PARTNERED PONY: WHAT'S POSSIBLE, PRACTICAL, AND POWERFUL WITH SMALL EQUINES
ISBN #: 978-0692580240

When it comes to equines – horses, ponies, donkeys, mules - different people think of the word 'partner' in different ways. For some it is the beginning step in a path of horsemanship. For me, it is not a step. Rather it is a way of being with equines that anyone can adopt at any level of training.

So what is a Partnered Pony? It's a pony whose human wants a shared life with their small equine. It's endless what partnering with a pony can look like: work, play, shows, chores, training, feeding, tack/harness, commuting, celebration, recreation, competition, riding, driving, packing, draft work. Every pony-person-partnership will have their own list unique to them. The stories in this book illustrate many of these dimensions.

Of course, partnering with ponies isn't new or modern. Most pony breeds were created or evolved specifically to provide all-around assistance to their human keepers. Ultimately, my aim in sharing all of these stories is to encourage partnering with ponies because there is so much that is possible, because they are practical, and it can be profound. It's my hope that others will discover what I have: that one lifetime isn't enough.

FELL PONIES: OBSERVATIONS ON THE BREED, THE BREED STANDARD AND BREEDING
ISBN #: 978-0-615-91086-4

The Fell Pony is one of Britain's native mountain and moorland breeds, hailing from the border region between England and Scotland. The breed has long been stewarded by a community of individual breeders. This form of stewardship is in contrast to a centralized breeding program or strict rules on breeding. It can therefore be more difficult to get a sense of the breed. To begin to understand the breed, then, one needs to ask questions.

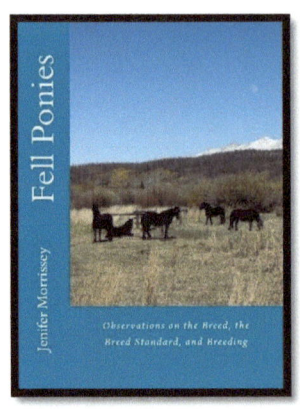

This book is a collection of answers to questions that the author has posed since her stewardship of the Fell Pony began. Every day she encounters some new bit of information that either answers a question, prompts a new one, or refines an answer she previously obtained. It is her hope that providing these answers in the form of observations will encourage more questions to be asked and fresh answers to be discovered. The Fell Pony breed can only be strengthened by such inquiries.

A HUMBLING EXPERIENCE: MY FIRST FEW YEARS WITH FELL PONIES
ISBN #: 978-1-439-21753-5

Considered one of the mountain and moorland breeds of British Ponies, Fell Ponies are classified as rare even in their home country. Fell Ponies numbered less than 40 in North America when the author bought her first mare, and there are now about 350 on the continent. The book chronicles the author's first seven years learning about and experiencing the breed. Through more than forty stories and over one hundred full color photographs, Morrissey touches on breed history and conservation, natural horsemanship, sustainable agriculture, and draft power. Morrissey's first humbling experience was the birth of her first foal, a filly. The book concludes with a second humbling experience, the birth of that filly's first foal. Stunning photography from the mountains of Colorado and the fells of Cumbria portray the many ponies that have crossed the author's path so far. Morrissey served for several years on the governing council of the Fell Pony Society of North America.

MY NAME IS MADIE
ISBN #: 978-0-578-13161-0
My Name is Madie tells the story of a remarkable Fell Pony filly. Written for pre-teens, the book captivates adults.
- Just read this book and I recommend it highly. It is a lovely story told so well. Looking forward to the next Jenifer. – Kathleen Charters
- I love the book and got an extra one to give to an 11 year old. Thanks for beautiful pictures and stories. – Becky Capeloto

WHAT AN HONOR: A DOZEN YEARS WITH FELL PONIES
ISBN #: 0692308555
This book begins where the author's first book about Fell Ponies, A Humbling Experience, left off. The first honor that her imported Fell Pony mare Beauty gave her was a daughter. The book ends with an honor bestowed by Beauty's English breeder. In between are over one hundred stories and even more color photographs about these rare British ponies living high in the Colorado Rockies.

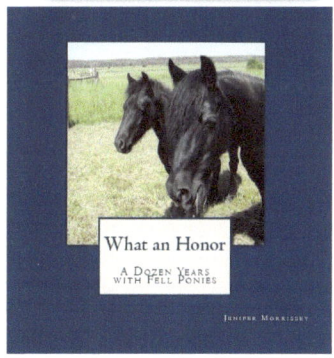

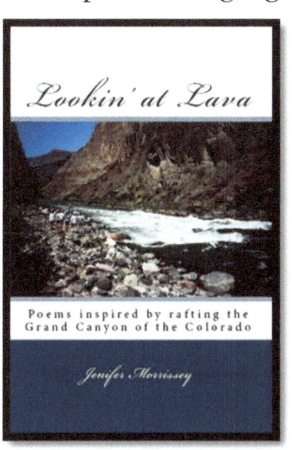

LOOKIN' AT LAVA: POEMS INSPIRED BY RAFTING THE GRAND CANYON OF THE COLORADO
From "An Adventure Was In Store:"
These poems began pouring from me
As the adventure drew to a close.
They seemed better able to capture
The experience than just simple prose.

www.ingramcontent.com/pod-product-compliance
Lightning Source LLC
Chambersburg PA
CBHW041117300426
44112CB00002B/15